INTERNATIONAL ENCYCLOPAEDIA OF ISLAM

Vol.-9

Science and Islam

INTERNATIONAL ENCYCLOPAEDIA OF ISLAM

Vol.-9

Science and Islam

Editor

A.H. Qasmi

ISHA BOOKS
DELHI-110 033

International Encyclopaedia of Islam
(*Religion*)

ISBN: 81-8205-320-X (Set)

ISBN: 81-8205-329-3

Published in 2006 in India by
Isha Books, D-43, Prithviraj Road,
Adarsh Nagar, Delhi-110 033

Printed at : Rajdhani Printers, Delhi.

Contents

Preface

Man is a social creature. It is the society where he learns how to live in this vast cosmos. Apart from society, people are divided into different castes, cultures and creeds. All these factors go in developing a man's personality. Of all the factors, mentioned above, religion is most important.

There exist about more than two thousand religions in the world today. A religion is regarded as a sacred institution, which governs a man's life here and hereafter and teaches him how to lead a happy and prosperous life.

What's unique to Islam is its endowment to humanity from the divine creator or the Almighty. It is not a set of principles and dogmas scribed by a scholar or thinker. It was sent on the earth circa fifteen hundred years ago, but its principles and preachings hold good even today. Besides showing humanity a straight way to the eternal success, it also has a say in various other walks of human life, such as economy, politics, human rights, social relations, judiciary, marriage and so on and so forth.

Another distinguished feature of Islam is that apart from being the latest religion, it is also the last one. That is to say, whatever is there in Islam, it is valid upto to the doomsday. Now, there will not come any other religion till the Day of Judgement. Therefore, it is the most powerful and as well as the most human-nature-friendly.

Given the present global scenario, there was being felt a dire need to bring out such a mini-encyclopaedia of Islam which may cater to the maximum needs of man in the least possible sheet of paper.

The present series is an humble attempt in the same direction. It comprises ten volumes which cover all the major disciplines of human life like, Prayer, marriage, justice, human rights, social justice and so on.

We are sure that the endeavour would prove to be a capsule of treasure of knowledge about Islam, prepared perfectly. Nevertheless, considering the adage 'to err is human', we would be obliged if the readers suggest some improvements for further editions.

Editor

1

Story of Success

A map of the physical features of Western Asia and North-East Africa shows two important river valleys, one of the Tigris and Euphrates, the other of the Nile, and between them high ground, broken rather abruptly by the Red Sea. These conditions are due to geological changes with which we are not at present directly concerned: we start from a point when the two great river valleys already existed, with a good deal of barren hghland between. Those two valleys were the homes of two primitive civilizations, which was the earlier is still not decided.

In both cases the rivers concerned overflowed and flooded the surrounding country regularly every year, and the particular river-valley culture which grew up there was based on the artificial control of these regular inundations, draining the swamps and directing the water so as to fertilize the fields. It is commonly assumed that in primitive society land was held in common, each member of the tribe entitled to his share, but not to permanent ownership of any particular piece. Whether this is universally true is disputed, probably it does apply so long as tribes are nomadic. But in the river-valley culture of Mesopotamia and Egypt the productivity of each field depended a great deal on human labour, irrigating and draining the land, so that private ownership developed at a fairly early date and population became stationary.

The people of the barren highlands between the river valleys remained nomads, not recognizing the rights of private property and in all respects at a much more primitive stage of social evolution than the settled inhabitants of the valleys. The life of those nomads was hard and bare, it generally was, and still is, on the border of starvation ; there always was a temptation for those nomads to raid the fertile and productive settlements, and when their numbers became too great to be able to make a living out of the meagre resources of the desert highlands, they tended to overflow into the valleys. Thus all through ancient history the kingdoms of Assyria, Babylonia, and Egypt found their nomadic neighbours a perpetual nuisance, and it was always necessary to provide for the protection of the frontiers, those frontiers being the precise level at which it ceased to be practicable to raise the water from the rivers to irrigate and fertilize the land. Whenever military power so far decreased as to make the guardianship of the frontiers insufficient to protect the settled country from Arab raiders, then Arabs came down to raid the country, then to settle in the rich and productive territory and reap the benefits of a cultivation at others' expense, usually subjugating and sometimes enslaving the unwarlike population already settled there.

Historical Background

Such a raiding and settlement took place towards the end of the seventh century A.D., when the raiding Arabs were united in a religious fraternity based on the religion taught by the Prophet Muhammad (PBUH). It does not seem that Muhammad himself had any project of foreign conquest, but such conquest followed because the people of the area invaded were exhausted by prolonged warfare, distracted by internal divisions, and disaffected by harsh government, though some of that harshness was the inevitable result of war conditions. The success of their expeditions seems to have surprised the Arabs and encouraged them to undertake the permanent occupation of the countries they had conquered. They had not the least desire to cultivate the soil or settle down to agricultural work, their idea was to establish a military occupation and live on the fruits of the toil of the native inhabitants. In this they were, no doubt, influenced by the precedent of the Arabs stationed along the Persian and Roman frontiers, On both those frontiers it had been found impossible to dislodge the Arab tribes and both countries tried the same solution, permitting the tribesmen to settle there and paying them a subsidy on condition that they guarded the frontier against any other Arabs who tried to invade the Persian or Roman territories.

The Arabs already settled and paid were greatly envied by the hungry nomads of the desert, their existence seemed an ideal one, and when they conquered the eastern provinces of the Roman Empire and the kingdom of Persia they counted on living a similar kind of life, occupied in hunting and occasional warfare and supported by the tribute paid them by the conquered population. Nor were the conquered people unwilling to toil and pay tribute, as they were to be disarmed and freed from the hated military service which was the task they most disliked.

It is a debated point whether Muhammad intended his religion to be a universal one, or for the Arabs alone. Quran 34, 27, says, " We have sent thee to mankind at large, to announce and threaten." But the context shows that this refers to the Prophet warning men of the approaching end of the world and is itself one of the signs that the end is near, and is thus interpreted by tradition (Bukhari, Sahih, i, 93, 43, d. i: Muslim, Sahih, i, 53, 55). It is necessary for all Arabs to believe in Muhammad if they are to escape hell (Muslim, i, 54), but it is not stated to be necessary for non-Arabs to believe, though those who join gods to God, that is to say, are polytheists, are doomed to hell in any case. As regards the non-Arab world, the Quran seems to contemplate conquest rather than conversion (Qur., ix, 19-23). One passage in the Quran says, " and one day We will summon up in every people a witness against them from themselves : and We will bring thee (Muhammad) up as a witness against them : for to thee We have sent down the book which makes all things clear, a guidance and a mercy, and glad tidings to those who reconcile themselves with God " (Qur., 18, 91). In another place the Quran says, " thus We have made you a central people that ye may be witnesses in regard to mankind, and that the Apostle (Muhammad) may be a witness in regard to you" (Qur., 2, 137). But these passages fall far short of a definite missionary command to go forth and preach Islam to all the nations of the earth.

In the later years of his ministry Muhammad preached his religion to all the Arabs and endeavoured to unite the tribes in one confederacy. " Fight until there is no more civil discord and no worship save that of God" (Qur., 2, 189) : " fight against those who oppose you, but do not attack first " (Qur., 2, 186), "kill and expel them" (Qur., 2, 187): "when the sacred month is over slay the polytheists, but spare the pagan Arabs who are in league with you" (Qur., 9, 1-4), but these commands were preparatory to the reduction and unification of Arabia. They find their best explanation in Muhammad's own conduct, for he strove hard to draw all the Arabs into his fold, though tolerating those who were" people of the book", i.e. Christians or Jews. His attitude was endorsed by the policy of the early Caliphs, men who had been his intimate companions and trained by him, men who knew his outlook as no others could, and they for some time insisted on all converts to the religion of Islam also becoming members of an Arab tribe. Much weight must be attached to the expressed reluctance of the older Muslims to spread wider into the outside world lest the multitude of strangers brought in as converts might outnumber the native Arabs, by their influence changing the character of their religion and mode of life, apprehensions which subsequent events showed were justified.

Origin of Writing: The traditional and legendary biography of Muhammad attributed to Ibn Ishaq and known to us in an edition expurgated by Ibn Hisham represents him as sending letters to foreign monarchs, the King of Persia, the Roman Emperor, and others, inviting them to become Muslims, but that biography was composed in its earliest form about a century after Muhammad and contains a great deal which cannot be regarded as historical.

There can be no question that Muhammad intended to include all the Arabs in the brotherhood of Islam. Those Arabs were the inhabitants of Arabia, not quite the artificial Arabia marked on the atlas, but all the desert highlands of Western Asia, spreading up into a tongue in Syria. In that northern area, between the two great monarchies of Parthia-Persia and Rome were the two groups of border tribes subsidized by the monarchies and to some extent settled and civilized. Muhammad was very anxious to draw these border tribes into his fraternity. The Arabs along the Persian frontier had some grievances against Persia and joined the Muslims, but threw off their allegiance as soon as Muhammad passed away.

In order to gain the Arabs of the Syrian (Roman) frontier Muhammad sent an envoy to invite them to embrace Islam, but that envoy was killed at Basra, a crime against the Arab tradition of the sacred character of an ambassador. So an army was sent under Zaid to avenge this. But the border Arabs being in Roman employ obtained the help of Roman legionaries and defeated the Arabs. For some time no further action could be taken as the Arabs were busily engaged elsewhere, but in 632 an army was assembled and preparations were made to invade Syria. But Muhammad died whilst the expedition was waiting to set out. Then Abu Bakr was appointed caliph or " successor " and ordered the army to set out. After forty days it returned laden with booty, so there was no difficulty in raising new forces. In 634 these forces invaded Syria, where they met small resistance, and that only from an ill-trained local militia. No one as yet supposed that the Arabs were venturing on more than an ordinary raid, nor do the Arabs themselves seem to have thought that they had undertaken more than that.

Certainly these Arabs were not fanatics who tried to force their religion on the conquered : they preferred them to remain toilers as before and themselves to live on the produce of their labour. Such was the system laid down in the "Constitution of Umar", an apocryphal production of later date, but indicating in general outline what was the earlier Arab policy. The picture sometimes given of a host of fanatical Arabs rushing forward with a sword in one hand, a Quran in the other, and forcing people to turn Muslims or be killed is very far from the fact. The cynical Arab is not inclined to be a fanatic. There have been plenty of fanatical Muslims, but they were not Arabs but converts of other races who were converted to Islam at a later date. The Arabs did not force the people they conquered to embrace their religion, they left the conquered population to follow their own religion, laws, customs, and use their own languages. They were to be tribute producing and the Arab ideal was to live at ease on the product of their labour.

In Syria, which was of primary importance because in 661 the Khalifa with his court and government settled in Damascus where they remained for more than eighty years, the Arabs found themselves rulers of an area which had been a Roman province subject to the fully developed Roman law and with a highly organised administration. This they took over as it was. Any Roman official who wished to remain under Roman rule were given every facility to remove to some part which still remained Roman. Many did so remove, but many others were content to live under Arab rule, and of these numbers rose to high office and dignity in the Muslim state. For the first twenty years or more the records continued to be kept in Greek, and the civil service was almost exclusively Christian. There already were a number of Arab tribes settled along the border, they had been subsidized by the Byzantine government as defenders of the frontier, and these were Christians. As old established settlers they had become wealthy and considered themselves socially superior to the Muslim invaders, poor hungry nomads of the desert, and had no hesitation in asserting themselves, the Muslim Arabs admitting their claims to aristocratic status.

Some of the ruling dynasty married women of these Christian tribes, and that was rather resented by the Muslims. Under the Caliph Abd al-Malik (685-705) there was a good deal of jealousy because the Christians had a monopoly of all the posts in the civil administration, and the Caliph tried to employ Arabs in their place. But the change was not successful, the Arabs did not understand the details of business and the Christian officials had to be restored. This is easy to understand because the oriental practice is, not to draw up accounts so that an outside auditor can understand and check them, but to keep them in such a way that nobody but the established officials can possibly understand them : it is done deliberately so that the established officials may keep the business in their own hands and secure a permanent monopoly.

The most that Abd al-Malik could do was to get the records kept in Arabic instead of Greek, and to use Arabic on the coinage. Bishop Arculf of Gaul made a tour of the Holy Land in about 700 A.D. and speaks with much appreciation of the hospitable way he was received by the Muslim rulers, the freedom with which he was allowed to travel about, and the generally friendly attitude of the Arabs and their rulers. Until the days of the Crusades, Syria and Egypt were practically Christian lands under the rule of the Muslim Arabs, their rule mainly confined to the collection of taxes, and that they did very thoroughly.

In the earlier period of the Umayyad Caliphate at Damascus there was even a fashionable tendency to deride Islamic ways and customs. This is well illustrated by the poetry of Abu Malik Ghiyath ibn Salt ibn Tariqa al-Akhtal, who was born at Hira about 640 and died about 710. He belonged to the Taghlib clan of the Jusham ibn Bakr tribe and lived and died a Monophysite Christian. His poems refer to St. Sergius, the Holy'Cross, to monks, and he uses Christian oaths, though there are very few direct references to Christianity in his Diwan. He refused to change his religion (Diwan, p. 154), and derided those whom he described as becoming Muslims by pressure of hunger rather than by conviction (ibid., 315). He composed poems in honour of Yazid, the son of the Caliph Muawiyyah, 'his brother Abdullah, and others of the royal family. He was formally recognized as poet laureate by Abd al-Malik, whom he celebrated as well as his relations and derided their enemies, a real courtier.

In his poems there appears evidence of the survival of ancient pagan Arab usages in the days of the Umayyads, and some striking instances of the tolerant attitude of that dynasty. Many of his verses contain biting sarcasms on Islam, and such passages have prevented many Muslims from full appreciation of his poetic merits, but in his times he and his rival Jarir were the leading poets of the Arabs. He particularly expresses his contempt for all those who abandoned their ancestral religion, Christian or pagan, to conform with that of the reigning monarch.

The most admired passage in his works is his panegyric of the Umayyads (Diwan, 98-112). In spite of his contemptuous attitude towards Islam this poet was patronized by the Caliph Abd al-Malik, though not greatly favoured by his successor Walid I. He probably died before the end of Walid's reign, though Ibn Abd Rabbi prolongs his life to the reign of Umar II. Probably his death should be dated about 710 A.D.

A loose tone about religion prevailed at the Umayyad court, which did not find favour with the stricter Muslims, and it was one of the causes of the hostile atmosphere and Umayyad feeling which grew in intensity until it led to the downfall of the dynasty. The old tribal rivalries of pre-Muslim days still influenced the Arabs, and there was a deep-rooted antagonism between the worldly tone of Damascus, and the cities of Mecca and Medina, and the more orthodox attitude of those who regarded themselves as Muslims in the first place, and Arabs only in a secondary place. The only exception to this among the Umayyad Caliphs was Walid I (705-715), who was a really religious man and put the interests of Islam before political or racial considerations. At the other extreme Yazid I (680-683) is still cursed by the orthodox as an enemy of religion. It was an army sent by him which engaged in the battle of Karbala (10th October, 680), and was responsible for the tragic death of al-Hussain, the surviving son of Ali the Prophet's son-in-law. And it was an army sent by him which besieged the holy city of Mecca and (accidentally) burned the sanctuary of the Kaaba (November, 683).

Damascus, the official capital of Syria, was a partly Greek city, not so thoroughly Hellenized as Antioch. It was the seat of Christian Bishops who ranked next after the patriarchs of Antioch in the ecclesiastical hierarcny of Syria : it possessed a school which, though not equal to those of Alexandria and Antioch, yet had attained considerable eminence by the time of the Arab conquest, and retained its good repute after that event. Amongst its alumni were the theologian Sophronius, who became Bishop of Jerusalem (634-38), and Andrew of Crete (circ. 650-720), who studied there after the Arab conquest, became a monk in Jerusalem, and finally Bishop of Crete. The Arabic historians say that at the time of the conquest the financial agent of the Roman government in the city was Sergius (Sarjun) who was responsible for making terms with the invaders, on which account Eutychius calls him a traitor. But the citizens, deserted by the government, had no choice in the matter and it is probable that everyone supposed that the Arab attack was no more than a raid on a large scale and that after plundering the town the Arabs would go back again to the desert.

The governor of such a city normally was a financial agent whose duty it was to raise the imperial taxes and commonly bore the honorary title of Patricius which had been granted to all superior officials by Constantine. He had been appointed by the Emperor Heraclius, but like many other officials continued in office after the Arab conquest under Muawiyyah, when he was governor of the province, and remained when Muawiyyah became Caliph. Finally he acted as minister of finance for the whole Islamic state and paymaster-in-chief of the Arab army. Yet he remained a Christian, and long after becoming minister of finance built a Christian church. His son was treasurer under Abd al-Malik, and his grandson was chief minister under some of the later Caliphs. The office and title of Wazir had not yet come into existence.

It is said that the second member of this family purchased a slave named Cosmas, a monk who had been captured by the Arabs during a raid on Italy, and employed him as tutor to his son John. When Cosmas had taught him all that he could he begged permission to retire to a monastery, and on obtaining leave he went to the Laura of St. Sahas, near Jerusalem. The author of this John's biography was John of Jerusalem who lived in the tenth century, a good while after the events he records, and like many hagiographers of the time used freely matter which would now be regarded as legendary, but the main lines of John's life seem to be reliable. It appears that this John was the son of Sergius, afterwards known as St. John of Damascus, son of an important official in the Arab state, was himself attached to the court and acted as " chief adviser " to the Caliph, probably Hisham (724-743). After serving the Caliph for some years John asked leave to resign, and followed his tutor to the Laura of St. Sabas where, after a period of rigorous discipline, he was ordained to the priesthood some time before 735. He died before 743. To him is due the earliest treatise on the controversy between Christianity and Islam, the "*Disputatio Christiani et Saraceni*" which is printed in Migne's Patrologia Graeca, xcvi, 1335-1363.

This work shows that there was great freedom of religious discussion in eighth-century Damascus, and that Christians were permitted to criticize the established religion very freely. The text says, " When the Saracen says. . . . You reply. . . ." John gives proof of a good knowledge of the Quran and familiarity with Muslim ritual and doctrine. The identification of St. John of Damascus with the son of Sarjun ibn Mansur was first made by William of Tripoli.

Theodorus Abucara (d. 826) was St. John's pupil, and he also left works on the controversy with Islam. Obviously there was unrestrained intercourse between the two religions and no reluctance was felt about discussing religious differences quite freely. It may reasonably be supposed that such intercourse introduced the Muslims of Damascus to a general knowledge of Christian theology and philosophy, and within the next following generations ideas and problems suggested by Greek philosophy appear affecting Muslim thought.

A parallel infiltration of Greek thought took place in jurisprudence so that the earliest speculations of the Muslim jurists are tinctured by theories gathered from the Roman law which itself contains elements gathered from Stoic philosophy, and thus Greek philosophical teaching was passed on to the Arabs through a legal medium. Roman law at the time of the Arab conquest circulated in the eastern provinces in Greek, and slightly modified by local conditions, but it contained the Stoic principles which the lawyers of Rome had drawn from Greek sources. Prominent among these philosophical-legal theories was the doctrine that man has an innate sense of what is just and right, of what the Stoics called the Law of Nature. This was also assumed by the early Muslim jurists who appealed to "opinion" to supplement and even to supplant the written law when cases arose for which no provision had been made. Here, however, it is to be noted that the earlier indications of this Stoic doctrine appear, not in Syria where the Roman law was established, but in Iraq, and especially at Basra.

That the Arabs were first brought into contact with Roman law in Syria and Egypt is certain. They had conquered those provinces and found there a complicated system of land tenure, contractual law, and commercial legislation dealing with things of which the simple nomads of the desert had no previous knowledge. Much of this they adopted, indeed such adoption was inevitable, and it henceforth was incorporated in Muslim law. It is true that there are some branches of law which had already been incorporated in Jewish law, and those may have come through a Jewish medium to the Arabs, but it is more probable that most of the law dealing with land tenure, contract, usufruct, inheritance, and certain other matters came direct from the customary law already prevalent in Syria and Egypt when the Arabs conquered those lands, and that established law which they found there was the Roman law.

In the parallel case of theology it may be noted,

(1) One of the earliest theological problems faced by the Muslims was that of the eternity of the Quran. The older doctrine was that it was eternal, co-eternal with God. Then the problem arose, if this were so, then God is not the one source and creator of all things, for there must have been an uncreated Quran, like a second god, side by side with the One. This was hotly debated. The sect of the Mutazilites held that the Quran was created by God and, as the author must precede the work produced, the Quran must be less eternal than God. The orthodox maintained that the Quran is co-eternal

with God, though the words in which it is expressed, like the paper on which it is written, may be created and so not eternal with God. Ultimately the orthodox opinion prevailed and the Mutazilites became extinct, for those who now call themselves by that name in India are modernists of recent date, in no way connected with the old Mutazilites. The point is that in the discussions between the Mutazilites and those who adhered to the orthodox theory very much the same arguments are used as were employed in the Arjan controversy in the Christian Church, much of this repeated in the writings of St. John of Damascus. In Christian theology the term " Word " was used as a mystical name for Christ, as it was used by St. John in the fourth gospel, whilst the Muslims used the same term to denote the written word in the Quran, but in general the arguments are the same. It is difficult to avoid the conclusion that the problem involved was suggested to the Muslims by Christian theology, the teaching of St. John of Damascus, or some other.

(2) Another early problem concerned the freedom of the will. If God is almighty, then everything is overruled and directed by him. Therefore man has no freedom. But Greek ethics assumes that man is responsible only when he has free choice, and the Quran gives commands and prohibitions in such a way as to imply that man has such a choice. The Mutazilites argued that as God is just, he will only punish men when they have been free to choose and have chosen wrong. From this and the preceding point the Mutazilites called themselves " the People of Unity and Justice ", of unity because admitting only One Creator, One Source, and so asserting that the Quran is created, and of justice as defending the freedom of the will as necessary for man's responsibility.

(3) A third problem concerns the qualities of God. God as the sole source of all that is must be a unity, not compounded : so God has no qualities or accidents, he is himself essence. The only attributes that can be predicated of God are negative, that he is eternal or having no beginning or end, that he is infinite as having no limitations, and so on. This, however, seems to be contrary to the Quran which does apply qualitative adjectives to God. The orthodox opinion is that these attributes given in the Quran may be applied to God because they are so applied, but they do not convey the same meaning as they would if applied to men, nor do we know what they imply. This was already taught by Plotinus and other neo-Platonists, and it would seem that the problem and its solution was borrowed by the Arabs from them.

At first sight it seems that these traces of Greek influence on Arab thought most likely connect with Syria where Arabs and Christians had very free intercourse ; but the first traces of that influence appear in Mesopotamia towards the middle of the eighth century. Greek influence may have been applied at more than one point, or may have spread from one area to another. It must be admitted that we have very little evidence of philosophical or theological speculation in Syria under the Umayyad dynasty, the dynasty which began with Muawiyyah: such matters seem to have made little appeal to Arab interest at that period. The beginnings of speculative thought in philosophy and theology and of interest in scientific research arose in Mesopotamia, and more especially in Basra, to a less degree in Kufa. These two cities were in the area where were the ancient cities of Hira and Jundi-Shapur, and it is quite possible that a general influence due to intercourse between Muslims and Christians had been engendered before the direct transmission of Greek science from Jundi-Shapur to the Muslim community had commenced.

After their first outspread and contact with the Roman and Persian armies, the Arabs set themselves to learn the methods of warfare used by the Romans, realizing that something different was now required from the rapid raids and retreats which had sufficed for desert warfare. The Byzantine writer, the Emperor Leo Tacticus, describes the Arabs as imitating the order and discipline of the Roman army in all details. And that was natural, for the most influential Arabs under the Umayyads were those of the Syrian border who had been trained as auxiliary Roman forces. At the same time it must be admitted that the Persians also had already endeavoured to copy Roman military methods. One of the new forms of warfare was the use of engineering for besieging fortified cities and for constructing fortifications for their own defence. For this latter purpose they imitated the rectangular fortified camp characteristic of Roman military methods. In each conquered area they planted such camp cities, often on ill-chosen sites. In Palestine the chief such camp city was Jabia, in Egypt it was Fustat, in Ifriqiya, Qairawan. But none of these were of so great importance as the two camp cities in Iraq— Basra founded by Utba ibn Azwan in 635 or 637, and Kufa founded by Saad bin Waqqas a little later. These played a very leading part in the history of Islam.

When the Umayyads seemed to be secularized and indifferent to religion, and their laxity spread, as it did, to Medina and Mecca, many of the stricter Muslims were greatly discouraged and removed from those places such as Medina and went out to one or other of the Iraqian camp cities, which thereby became the homes of orthodoxy and incidentally of resistance to a Caliphate commonly regarded as disloyal to religion.

The intellectual life and interests of Basra and Kufa were directed by religion and centered in Quran study and theological sciences more or less connected with the Quran. At first these sciences were chiefly those concerned with the Quran text and that especially meant grammar and lexicography, but later on opened out so as to include jurisprudence, tradition, and philosophy, all to a great extent directed and tinctured by ideas gained from Greek studies. Greek authorities were not used or read, but there are clear indications that their substance had filtered through and at Basra and Kufa impinged on Arabic culture far more than was the case in Damascus. It must not be overlooked that Hira, the great Nestorian stronghold, was not far from Basra and a good deal of its population drifted to the camp city.

Grammatical and literary studies began at Basra with Abu-al-Aswad ad-Duali, the friend and confidant of the Prophet's son-in-law, Ali. It naturally happened that many of the people of Iraq who had learned Arabic only late in life when they were converted to Islam committed many solecisms in reading the text of the Quran, and these errors distressed Ali. So he appealed to ad-Duali to draw up some rules for the guidance of those who were not well used to the use of the only language permitted for prayer and reading the revealed word. But ad-Duali was prevented from carrying out this command by Ali's murder on 21st January, 661, and he was reluctant to take any steps to assist the governor Ziyad ibn Abihi whom he regarded with disapproval because he, after serving Ali, had transferred his services to the Umayyad usurper Muawiyyah.

Though Ziyad renewed Ali's request ad-Duali held back and did nothing. Then one day he heard a reader mispronounce two vowels in the text of Qur., 9, 3, so as to pervert the sense from " God is free from (the covenant of) the idolaters, and His Apostle (also is free) " into " God is free from (the covenant of) the idolaters and (from the covenant of) His Apostle ", and this misrepresentation of the inspired word so shocked him that he forthwith began to devise methods to prevent similar errors. For this purpose he introduced vowel points into the hitherto unpointed Arabic text and began giving instruction in the grammar and vocabulary of the Arabic language. Incidentally in doing this he seems to have been to some extent influenced by Aristotle's logic, not by any of the Greek grammarians.

From Abu-al-Aswad ad-Duali came a regular succession of grammatical students and teachers in Basra. Nearly a century later similar grammatical lectures were commenced at Kufa by Abu Muslim Muadh ibn Muslim al-Harra (d. 723 or 727), who at one time was tutor to the sons of the Caliph Abd al-Malik. These two centres developed rival schools which agreed in theory, but differed in practice. As yet the works of the ancient poets, valuable in illustrating and explaining the older usages of the language, were not collected in written Diwans, but transmitted by word of mouth, often altered and interpolated in their transmission. Aware of this the Basra school carefully criticized the poetry heard and rejected that which did not fit in with accepted standards, whilst the Kufans accepted all that was heard and are said to have used a good deal of forged material. At first sight it seems that the Basri method was better, but against that it must be noted that by that method the examples were made to fit the rules drawn up, whilst the Kufi grammarians had to adapt their rules to meet the spoken use, which is sounder.

The line of oral transmission of the two schools formed a grammatical pedigree which led down to the great Basri grammarian Abu-al-Hasan (or Bishr) Amr ibn Uthman al-Harithi, commonly known as Sibawaih (d. between 783 and 816) who, it must be noted, was not an Arab himself but a Persian and compiled his grammar under the early Abbasids.

At Basra arose the first indications of Mutazilite thought, with evidence of the solvent effect of Greek philosophical speculation on Arab theology, and in Iraq round about Basra were the first traces of juristic theory showing evident traces of Roman law and the philosophical theories adopted by Roman lawyers. Obviously the results of Greek influence began to appear, not in Syria where the ruling Muslims were in such close contact with Christian theology and its philosophical speculation, but in Basra, though we have no direct evidence of intercourse with Greek and Christian elements there. Damascus and its court were given over to sports and politics, and theological speculation could not have sunk very deep. Basra, on the other hand, kept alive a scholarly tradition and must have been impressed by Greek teaching, possibly through Hira, more probably through Jundi-Shapur, and so shows the first traces of Arab Hellenization.

Glorious Era : Muawiyyah had assumed the Caliphate at Jerusalem in 661, but at once removed to Damascus, where he had already spent several years as Governor of Syria. At his accession began the rule of what is known as the Umayyad dynasty, which ruled Islam until 749. That dynasty suffered a break in 684 when it passed from one family to another, but the new family, descended from Marwan, was a branch of the Umayyad clan, so the monarchy remained in Umayyad hands, and that was the case until 744, when a second Marwan, not of Umayyad blood, assumed power by military force. The court and administration were settled at Damascus until 724 when the Caliph Hisham removed to a country residence, and after that the Caliphs went to Damascus only to be installed, and then retired to reside elsewhere, but the administration remained at the Syrian capital until the accession of Marwan II in 744. The court necessarily accompanied the Caliph, but in 744 not only the court but also the administration were removed to Harran, which thus became the capital, and Damascus sank to the level of a provincial town, a change greatly resented by the Arabs of Syria.

Under the Umayyad dynasty the Caliphate was a purely Arab state. Its intellectual output consisted entirely of poetry, largely of the old desert type, some of it so far modified as to reflect the tone of the courts of Hira and of the B. Ghassan, all in the spirit of the Jahiliya or " times of ignorance " before the coming of Islam. Its poets praised their patrons, derided their rivals and enemies, pictured the perils of the desert life, or sang the echoes of ancient tribal wars. The culture and science of the Greek world found no place in their compositions and apparently meant nothing to them.

Under Marwan II the Syrian army was disaffected, the Kharijites of Iraq revolted and entrenched themselves in Mosul. Marwan was unable to march against them, his hold on Syria was too insecure and he had to send an army down into Arabia where there was another Kharijite revolt.

His more serious trouble, however, threatened from Khurasan in East Persia. The Persians were dissatisfied : they felt that the Arab conquest of Persia had been due to a series of accidents, to domestic revolution which undermined their military organization and to the rash conduct of their youthful king. They longed for an opportunity to try issue again with those whom they regarded as half-civilized nomads. In such conditions it was inevitable for conspiracies to flourish, indeed the whole Umayyad period shows the community of Islam seething with dissatisfaction and ready for revolt, partly on racial grounds, resentment at the way in which the Arabs domineered over them even after they had embraced Islam, partly on religious grounds, regarding the Umayyads as lax in religious observance. Amongst the Persians were many adherents of the house of Ali, and these regarded all the Caliphs, except Ali himself, as usurpers. They recognized the leadership only of those descended from Ali.

The extremer Alids even preferred Ali to Muhammad himself. All these Shiites, as they were called, were divided amongst themselves into many sects, but all agreed in disapproving the Arabs. At length a revolutionary outbreak took form, its centre in Khurasan, but its propaganda spread by secret agents who circulated everywhere through the world of Islam, except in Spain where Muslims had their own troubles.

The identity of the person who was to be set upon the throne after Marwan was deposed was kept secret until the revolution had reacned a successful end, then it was disclosed that the one selected as Caliph was Abu-al-Abbas of the Hashimite clan of the Quraish tribe, the same tribe as that to which the Umayyads belonged. The throne merely passed from one Arab family to another.

Abu-al-Abbas was invested with the caliphate in the great mosque of Kufa on 28th November, 749, and made it his first task to exterminate the surviving Umayyads and their adherents, and this he did so drastically as to earn for himself the surname of al-Safah "the butcher". Of the deposed dynasty only one young man escaped and, after incredible dangers and hardships, reached distant Spain where he became head of an independent state, and later on his descendants assumed the title of Caliph in opposition to the dynasty of Abu-al-Abbas. There are stories of other Umayyads who found refuge in the remoter parts of Africa, but these seem, to have been adherents of the dynasty, not themselves of Umayyad stock.

The downfall of the Umayyads was a definite turning-point in the history of Islam. The Abbasid Caliphs were no less Arab than the Umayyads, but they had gained their throne largely by Persian help. Their chief ministers were Persians more often than Arabs. The heirs of several of the earlier Abbasid Caliphs were educated in Persian surroundings and had Persian blood as the result of intermarriages. Persian ideas and Persian interests rivalled, in many cases displaced, Arab ideas and interests, and so to a certain extent Islam became Persianized. For all that the caliphate and its subject must still be classed as Arab : they were commanded by a ruling dynasty which was Arab, they used the Arabic language, professed an Arab religion, and held in unbroken continuity from the desert men who had conquered the near East.

At first the Abbasid Caliphs lived at al-Anbar on the

Euphrates. They had no desire to go to Syria where prevailing feeling was strongly pro-Umayyad. But the second ruler of the Abbasid line, Abu-al-Abbas brother al-Mansur was determined to found a new capital. After considering various sites he at length decided to build at Baghdad, a town of considerable antiquity which had been known in Babylonian times as Bag-Da-Du, a name of unknown origin. By a play upon words later Persian writers gave this name a fanciful Persian derivation and made it mean "the Garden of God ".

In making this choice he was guided by the advice of his minister, the Persian Khalid ibn Barmak, and having resolved on building he called in the services of two astrologers to lay out the foundations and select a propitious hour for setting the first stone in position. The astrologers chosen for that purpose were an-Nawbakht, who was a Persian, and Mashallah ibn Athari, a Persian Jew, of Marw.

Guided by these astrologers al-Mansur laid the first stone of his new capital towards the end of the year 762, and three years later the building was sufficiently advanced for occupation to commence. Many of the inhabitants came from the neighbouring camp cities of Basra and Kufa, both hotbeds of sedition and always restless and fanatical. The presence of these new citizens helps to explain why from the outset Baghdad showed a turbulent and troublesome atmosphere. One suburb of the city known as Karkh, which had already existed as a Persian village, was given over to Persians.

Al-Mansur desired to make his capital a city whose fame should radiate through all Islam, and for this purpose he invited to it a number of distinguished scholars, Quran readers and preachers, grammarians and traditionalists from the two neighbouring camp cities which had already become recognized centres of Muslim scholarship, as yet restricted to Quranic and theological studies. Such men of learning were then beginning to form a respected middle class which later rose by court favour to high offices in the State, but was entirely distinct from the older aristocracy of the Arab tribal chieftains of noble pedigree who had dominated Islam under the Umayyads. The learned men of Kufa and Basra, many already famous, formed a kind of academic aristocracy which tended to act as a check on the arrogant pretensions of the hereditary nobility who had proved a source of danger in the court of Damascus and were still disaffected towards the Abbasid dynasty which they regarded as semi-Persian. Unfortunately al-Mansur suffered from the unprincely vice of avarice, and the rewards he offered were so moderate and were paid so grudgingly that he earned the nickname Abdud-Dawaniq " father of sixpences".

In 765 al-Mansur was taken seriously ill with some gastric disorder and was advised to send for the Nestorian physician Jirjis ibn Bukhtyishu, head of the academy and hospital at Jundi-Shapur. This was the first contact of the court at Baghdad with the family of Bukhtyishu which afterwards played an important part in the cultural education of the Arabs. Nothing is known of the Bukhtyishu who was the father of this Jirjis, but as the name occurs several times in the course of the history of Baghdad it is convenient to classify him as Bukhtyishu I.

Of all the East Persians who had helped the Abbasid revolution and afterwards came west to share the prosperity of the new dynasty, the most distinguished belonged to the wealthy and well-born family of the Barmakids, originally of Balkh in Bactria, but afterwards settled at Marw. This family was descended from the Barmaks or hereditary abbots of the Buddhist monastery of Nawbahar in Balkh, but had conformed to the Mazdean religion some time probably not long before the Muslim conquest, and then embraced Islam. Khalid ibn Barmak, the head of the family, was minister of finance under as-Saffah, and was made governor of Mesopotamia by al-Mansur. His son Yahya, at one time governor of Armenia, was entrusted by al-Mahdi with the education of his son who afterwards became Caliph as Harun ar-Rashid, and he appointed Yahya Wazir of the whole empire and entrusted him with unlimited power. In this office Yahya showed himself a wise and just administrator, and under his guidance the empire prospered. Of Yahya's three sons Fazl was governor of Khurasan, then of Egypt, and Jafar succeeded Yahya as Wazir. But the family, after being the first in wealth, power, and honour in Islam, fell from its high estate in 803 for reasons which were a mystery to contemporaries and never have been adequately explained. Yahya died in prison in 806, Jafar in 909. Other sons seem to have been set at liberty after Yahya's death. At the accession of al-Amin in 808 all surviving members of the Barmakid family were set free and had property and honours restored to them.

The Barmakids were keenly interested in Greek science, which was then the subject of much attention at Marw, and brought with them this taste, finding a kindred spirit already existing in the Nestorian academy of Jundi-Shapur.

Jirjis ibn Bukhtyishu, who had come from Jundi-Shapur to attend al-Mansur, remained in Baghdad as court physician until advancing years caused him to ask to be released and he retired full of honours to Jundi-Shapur where he died in 769. In 785 al-Hadi, mindful of Jirjis' excellent services, invited his son Bukhtyishu II, who had succeeded his father as head of the academy and hospital to go to Baghdad, but at court he had to face such determined opposition from Abu Quraish the Queen's physician that for the sake of peace he was sent back to Jundi-Shapur. Under Harun ar-Rashid he was again summoned to court to treat the Caliph for severe headaches, and later his son Jibbrail was brought to court and remained there until his death in 828-29. Whilst he was there the influence of the Barmakid Wazir was making itself felt and efforts were being made to introduce to the Arabs the revived scientific learning derived from Greek sources, which was already spreading amongst the Syriac-speaking Christians. The Barmakid Yahya was an enthusiastic supporter of this revival of science with which he had been in touch in Marw, and was warmly supported by the Nestorian scholars of Jundi-Shapur.

Harun ar-Rashid became Caliph in 786. He had been educated in Persia and under Persian influence at the hands of Yahya the Barmakid and throughout his reign showed strongly pro-Persian sympathies. He took great interest in science and literature, far beyond any of his predecessors, and the Hellenistic movement in Islam matured under his auspices. His reign was afterwards looked back upon as a golden age, but the caliphate had already begun to show signs of decay : in 800 he consented to the practical independence of the Aglabid governor of Qairawan in Libya, the beginning of a process of devolution which finally brought about the disintegration of the empire. Neither he nor any other of the Abbasid Caliphs were able to extend their rule over Andalus, which had been a province under the Umayyads.

Influenced by his Barmakid minister Harun gave active support to the scholars who studied and translated Greek scientific works, sending out agents to purchase Greek manuscripts in the Roman Empire, a generous policy which brought a good deal of important material to Baghdad, and this was supplemented by similar generosity on the part of private persons who spent freely on manuscripts and translators. A good deal of the material thus obtained was medical and so appealed to the physicians of Jundi-Shapur, and this was rendered into Syriac as had been the case in former times, but before long Arabic versions made their appearance, at first translated from the Syriac, later directly from the Greek originals. The works of Aristotle were familiar in Syriac translations, and with them were commentaries and summaries, some composed in Syriac, others translated from the Greek. But at first the Aristotelian material was confined to the logical treatises. It was not until some time after the death of Harun ar-Rashid that a serious and direct examination of Aristotelian philosophy was undertaken by Arab scholars. Derived through Syriac versions and commentaries the teaching of Aristotle was strongly tinctured with neo-Platonism, and that type of thought continued to colour Arabic philosophy to quite later times.

There seems reason to suppose that some of the earliest direct translations from the Greek was concerned with astronomy and mathematics. At an early date the *Sindhind,* an Indian treatise on astronomy and connected mathematics, based on Alexandrian teaching, was translated into Arabic, perhaps by means of a Persian version. It is said that the translators into Arabic were Ibrahim al-Fazari and Yaqub ibn Tariq. Of the former of these Masudi says, " I will also cite the astronomer Ibrahim al-Fazari, author of the celebrated poem on the stars, astrology, and the study of the skies" (Masudi, Muruj, viii, 290), and then goes on to name him as one of al-Mansur's personal friends. The celebrated poem on the stars is not extant. He is said also to have been the first Arab to make an astrolabe. The son of this Ibrahim was Muhammad (d. between 769 and 806), who is sometimes mentioned as having been the translator.

The date of a translation which is ascribed sometimes to the father, sometimes to the son, must be regarded as uncertain. Yaqub ibn Tariq was a distinguished mathematician who is said to have been the author of a treatise on the sphere and another on the karaja or arc of 225 , following the tradition of Archimedes who divided the circle into 96 degrees, and also to have drawn up astronomical tables. That the Sindhind was translated so early as al-Mansur is doubtful, but obviously the translation was well known to Abdullah Muhammad ibn Musa al-Khwarizmi, who made it the basis of his astronomical tables, but his work came some fifty years later, and the tables are now lost, but are cited and incorporated in later work by Maslama al-Majriti. When tables are only known to us by being cited or incorporated in later work, we can never be sure how they have been touched up or improved, and how much remains of the original.

In order to understand and use the *Sindhind* it was found necessary to make translations of the Almajest of Ptolemy and Euclid's Elements, and these seem to have been translated directly from the Greek and to have been the earliest translation thus made. It is stated that it was made from a Syriac version, and this is not disproved by the absence of any such version surviving : Syriac literature is not rich in mathematical works. In favour of an early rendering from the Greek we have only the presumption that reference must have been made to the original to get an accurate rendering of the technical terms, a matter of the utmost importance in mathematical work. The Arabic versions were several times revised and corrected by comparison with the Greek text, so the earliest may have been made before Harun ar-Rashid, or in the early part of his reign. There is a tradition that the translations of Euclid and the Almajest were made at the suggestion of Jafar the Barmakid, which would put them before 803, when the Barmakids fell into disgrace. If the observatory at Jundi-Shapur was in use before the time of an-Nahawandi (813-833), of which we cannot be certain, no doubt the necessary equipment in mathematics was available there and would be in Syriac. It is of course quite possible that the necessary mathematics were obtained from Indian works, not from Euclid or Ptolemy. The " Sons of Musa " had an observatory in Baghdad, but that would be after the time of Harun ar-Rashid.

Not much can be learned from the two astrologers who assisted al-Mansur in laying the foundations of Baghdad, though both of these are said to have produced mathematical, astronomical, or astrological works. One of these, an-Nawbakht (d. 776-7), is described as a convert from the Zoroastrian religion and a favourite of al-Mansur. He is said to have been the author of a work on judicial astrology and to have compiled astronomical tables, but of these works nothing survives. His son Abu Sahl al-Fadl an-Nawbakht (d. circ. 815) was Harun ar-Rashid's librarian and made translations from the Persian. The other astrologer, Mashallah, is said to have been a Jew of Marw whose name had originally been Misha, short for Manasseh (Fehrist, i, 273). Several of his works survive in Hebrew or Latin translations. Amongst these was a popular work on astronomy, not astrology.

It seems fairly certain that medical material came through a Syriac medium, direct translation from the Greek coming later. This may have been the case also with astronomical and mathematical material, but extant Syriac translations seem to be contemporaneous with the Arabic versions, not earlier, most indeed the work of Hunain ibn Ishaq or his school. It may be that mathematics and astronomy came through Indian authorities, not translations from the Greek but based upon Greek teaching, and translation from Greek into Syriac and Arabic came later when efforts were made to check and correct the available material. Certainly the earliest Arab mathematicians, such as al-Khwarizmi, knew a great deal which does not appear in the Greek authors and much of which (but not all) can be traced to Indian workers. There are gaps in the chain of transmission which it is not easy to fill up.

Knowledge Transferred : Baghdad was founded in 762. Harun ar-Rashid became Caliph in 786 and in his reign Baghdad became the centre of a movement which aimed at translating Greek scientific material into Arabic. In the twenty-four years intervening between the foundation of the city and the accession of Harun ar-Rashid influences must have been at work to prompt this undertaking. Of such influences two were obvious, one radiating from Marw far away in Khurasan in the east, the other from Jundi-Shapur near at hand. Marw in Khurasan was indeed distant, but it had a great deal to do with early Baghdad.

The Abbasids had been set upon the throne by a rebellion which had its source in Khurasan and which drew its chief support from that province.

The Marw family of the Barmakids supplied the all-powerful ministers who guided and to a great extent controlled the Abbasid government. Many Persians, especially those of Khurasan, had flocked west to share in the triumph of the revolution and claim their share in its spoils. At the Abbasid court Persian influence very much thrust the Arab element into the background. The Persians were not modest about this : the Arabs had been arrogant, now the Persians repaid them with greater arrogance, deriding the Arabs as semi-barbarous-nomads of the desert, parvenus without a history behind them, devoid of culture. This anti-Arab demonstration, open and plainly expressed, went by the name of the Shuubiya, an organized, virulent, and outspoken expression of anti-Arab feeling.

A typical figure of the times was Abu Muhammad ibn al-Muqaffa, a Persian who entered the service of Isa ibn Ali, uncle of the first two Abbasid Caliphs, and became a convert to Islam, though many regarded his conversion as insincere. He translated from Pahlawi or Old Persian the book known as *Kalila wa-Dimna*, itself a translation of a Buddhist work brought from India by the Christian periodeutes Budh who had been sent to India to procure drugs, and with the drugs brought back this book and the game of chess. Ibn al-Muqaffa' produced a translation which is regarded as a model of classical Arabic, and as such is still studied in schools. He also made a translation of the Persian *Khudai-nama*, a biographical history of the Persian kings, calling his Arabic version Siyar muluk al-Ajam. This work no longer exists, but it formed the basis of Firdausi's *Shah-nama* and many long extracts are given in Ibn Qutaiba's *Uyun al-akhbar*. In Arabic he composed a treatise " on obedience due to kings " (al-durr-ul-yatim fi taat a-mulk, printed Cairo, 1893 and 1326, 1331 a.h.).

He also wrote several short treatises on "*Adab*", etiquette, duties of civil servants, and good manners, a favourite subject in Old Persian literature. Living in Basra and feeling secure in the protection of noble patrons he permitted himself many impertinences towards Sufyan ibn Muawiyyah al-Muhallibi, the city governor, jeering at him as " Ibn al-mughialina " (son of the lascivious female), all of which Sufyan endured in silence. After the rebellion of 'Abdullah against his nephew al-Mansur the Caliph agreed to pardon his uncle and Ibn al-Muqaffa' was directed to draw up a formal letter of pardon for the Caliph to sign. In this letter he inserted " if at any time the Commander of the Faithful act perfidiously towards his uncle Abdullah ibn Ali, his wives shall be divorced from him, his horses confiscated to the service of God, his slaves set free, and Muslims absolved from allegiance to him". Al-Mansur read this draft and asked who had composed it. On hearing that it was drawn up by Ibn al-Muqaffa' he said nothing, but sent a letter to Sufyan telling him that he might deal with the secretary as he saw fit. Various accounts are given of the way in which the governor gratified his resentment towards Ibn al-Muqaffa' by putting him to death, all of them extremely cruel. This took place in 757-8 (Ibn Khallihan, i, 432-3).

The cradle of the Shuubiya was Khurasan and its capital Marw. Harun ar-Rashid himself was educated at Marw and had strongly pro-Persian leanings. The astronomical records kept under the Sasanid kings of Persia were continued under the Arabs and were continued in Persian, not in Arabic, until much later. From Marw came some of the earliest translators of astronomical works, and it would seem that Khurasan was the channel through which astronomical and mathematical material came to Baghdad, for which very probably the Barmakid ministers, natives of Marw, were the agents. There was, it is true, an observatory at Jundi-Shapur, but we know little of its activity before the time of Ahmad an-Nahawandi (813-833), who made observations there some years after

Harun's death. Some of the astronomical and mathematical material seems to have been obtained from India, derived from a Greek source in the first place, but probably it was transmitted to the Arabs through a Persian medium, though the actual Persian works whereby it was transmitted are no longer extant.

Jundi-Shapur was near Baghdad and under the Abbasid Caliphs distinguished physicians were summoned thence to court. Successful in their professional work they remained in Baghdad as court physicians and became men of wealth and influence. Their success inspired other physicians to follow them and they, with scholars from Marw, formed a group under court patronage which became something very like an academy, a society of scholars rather than a teaching body. The men of Jundi-Shapur were accustomed to study Greek science in Syriac translations : gradually these Syriac versions were supplemented by Arabic ones, and finally the Arabic versions replaced them.

There is a legend that the Sindhind, the Hindu revised form of Brahmagupta's *Siddhanta*, was translated into Arabic as early as the reign of al-Mansur. It was an early translation, though probably not so early as that. But it proved useless as the Arabs could not understand it. It is related that Jafar the Barmakid perceived the reason of this to be that the Arabs lacked the preliminary knowledge of geometry and astronomy necessary to follow it, and at his advice Harun ar-Rashid ordered a translation to be made of Euclid's Elements and Claudius Ptolemy's megale (synaxis)? To this title the Arabs added the article al- and changed the *megale* into *megiste*, deliberately, it would appear, for Yaqubi writing in 891 explained that "the meaning of *al-majisti* is ' the greatest book' " (Yaqubim, ed. Houtsma, Leiden, 1883). Thus, the work appears in Arabic as *Kitab al-Majisti*, which in medieval Latin became *magasiti*, presumably an attempted vocalizing of the unpointed *majesty*. It does not appear that the translations of Euclid and Ptolemy were made until after the reign of Harun ar-Rashid, so the story that they were suggested by Jafar ibn Barmak is dubious.

The translator of the *al-Majisti* is said to have been al-Hajjaj ibn Yusuf ibn Matar al-Hasib, who finished it about 827, which was well after the fall of the Barmakids and after the death of Harun ar-Rashid. The same translator is said to have made an Arabic version of Euclid's Elements, not including Book X which was later (about 910) translated with Pappus' commentary by Said ad-Dimishqi. The translation of Euclid by al-Hajjaj with the commentary of an-Naziri (d. circ. 923), who also wrote a commentary on the al-Majisti, was published by T. O. Besthorn and J. L. Heiberg, Euclidis elementa ex interpretatione al Hadschdschadschii cum commentario an Naziri arab. et lot., ed. notisque . . . Copenhagen, 1893. The earliest commentary on Euclid seems to have been that of al-Abbas al-Jawhari (d. circ. 833). Another tradition represents the translation of the *al-Majisti* was made by Saki ibn Rabban at-Tabari, a native of Marw and a Jew as his name ibn Rabban " the rabbi's son " denotes. Marw, one of the centres of Greek scholarship, had many Jewish neighbours who formed a colony of their own as was the Jewish custom, for they preferred to live in communities where the Jewish law could be observed.

On the road between Marw and Balkh lay the city of Maymana which was at one time called al-yahudiya "the Jewish (city)", but that name was changed to Maymana "the auspicious" at the request of its inhabitants who disliked the association with Jewry. This Sahl is described as having gone to Baghdad in the days of Harun ar-Rashid and having made the translation for him. He was a distinguished scholar and teacher of Marw who was known there as Barbun "the surpassing". Some account of him is given by his son Ali ibn Sahl ibn Rabban at-Tabari (d. 850) in his great medical work *Firdaus al-Hikhma* "the Paradise of Wisdom " (ed. I. Siddiqi, Berlin, 1928). Yet another tradition represents the translation of al-Majisti as made by Sahl and revised by al-Hajjaj. This early version of the work was subsequently revised by Hunain ibn Ishaq (below), later by Thabit ibn Qurra (below), then by Muhammad ibn Jabir ibn Sinan al-Battani (d. 929). Al-Hajjaj's translation of Euclid was revised by Qusta ibn Luqa about 912-13.

The earliest information which the Arabs obtained about Aristotle from Syriac sources was confined to his logical works which had been translated and retranslated into Syriac, and on which several commentaries were accessible. The corpus of Aristotelian logic included the Categories, the Hermeneutics, the Prior Analytics, the Posterior Analytics, the Topics, the Sophistica, the Rhetoric, and the Politics, these last two works classed with the logical treatises by the Arabs. To these was added by Yuhana (or Yahya) *ibn Batriq* about 815 another work, unfortunately a spurious one, the *Sirr al-asrar* or "secret of secrets", which was accepted as Aristotelian. It is a work of miscellaneous contents, including physiognomy and dietetics.

Not long afterwards, about 835, a Christian of Emessa named Abd al-Masih ibn Abdullah Waima al-Himsi translated another apocryphal work, the so-called *Theology of Aristotle*, really an abridged paraphrase of Plotinus, Enneads, iv – vi (cf. Fr. Dieterici, Die sogennante Theologie des Aristoteles, Leipzig, 1882).

About the same time lived Abu Yahya al-Batriq (d. between 798 and 806), who made an Arabic translation of an astrological work, the Tetrabiblos of Ptolemy. A commentary on this was written by Umar ibn al-Farrukhan (d. circ. 815), and a paraphrase by Muhammad ibn Jabir ibn Sinan al-Battani (d. 929).

Jibbrail I, the son of the otherwise unknown Bukhtyishu' I of Jundi-Shapur had attended al-Mansur, then retired to his own city and there finished his life. His son Bukhtyishu' II for a time acted as court physician to al-Hadi, but had to go back to Jundi-Shapur because of the opposition raised by the Queen's physician. He returned to the court of Baghdad under Harun ar-Rashid and attended both the Caliph and his minister Jafar the Barmakid. Before his death in 801 this Bukhtyishu' recommended his son Jibbrail II to the Caliph, and he in due course became court physician. There is no evidence that the first two members of this family did anything to promote Greek science amongst the Arabs, but the second Jibbrail did, and as he acted in conjunction with Jafar ibn Barmak it is obvious that he held an influential position in Baghdad even before his appointment as court physician. Bukhtyishu' died in 801 and then Jibbrail became the caliph's physician, after Harun's death in 808 continuing to serve his son al-Amin.

But this led to his imprisonment when al-Mamuni became master of Baghdad and all those who had been supporters of his brother al-Amin fell into disgrace. He was set free in 817 to attend the Wazir Hasan ibn Sahl and lived without other disturbance until 829. He, no less than Jafar ibn Barmak, was a patron and encourager of the work of translation from the Greek, a great admirer of Greek medical science, but was not himself responsible for any translation. He was the author of a *Kunnash* or medical compendium in Syriac in which he drew freely from Galen Hippocrates and Paul of Aegina; this manual was long in use amongst Syriac-speaking practitioners and did a good deal to familiarize them with Greek medical teaching. The work is now lost, but some knowledge of it can be obtained from the tenth century Syriac lexicon of Bar Bahoul, who uses it to illustrate technical medical terms (*Bar Bahoul*, edited by R. Duval, Paris 1888-1898).

It was largely at his suggestion that Harun ar-Rashid sent into the Roman Empire to obtain manuscripts and commissioned translations from the Greek. He and other contemporary patrons not only provided for Arabic translations but also encouraged the preparation of improved Syriac versions, for it is worth noting that a new and better series of translations into Syriac was being made at the same time that translation into Arabic was commenced. Translation into Syriac went on as long as the Jundi-Shapur academy was in existence.

The general conclusion is that the work of translation of scientific material began under Harun ar-Rashid with the encouragement of the Wazir Jafar ibn Barmak, and that this at first was especially concerned with mathematical and astronomical works, several of them translated by scholars from Jafar's own city of Marw. The translation of medical works perhaps began a little later, and was associated with Jibbrail II. But there seem to have been some other translators not connected with the semi-official group gathered at court. Medical works came through Syriac versions in the first place and so did at least some of the astronomical and mathematical material, but in this latter direct reference to the Greek originals seems to have taken place earlier. This is as might be expected, for it was in mathematics that absolute accuracy in terminology was most important.

Arabic lacked the technical terms used by Greek scientists. Sometimes the Greek terms were simply transliterated, but very often those terms show that they have passed through an Aramaic (Syriac) medium on their way, and this is more obvious in medical works than in mathematical and astronomical. As has been noted, the desire of more accurate scientific knowledge led to the preparation of more careful translations or the revision of existing versions, but it also resulted in the compilation of commentaries as well as original treatises based on the Greek authorities with citations illustrated and explained by original work. The encouragement of science became fashionable under Harun and many of the leading courtiers became patrons and spent freely on their scientific protege's. Not all of these may have been inspired by a pure love of science. When it became a fashion at court it is likely enough that many ambitious of advertising themselves found this a means of doing so. Outside court circles the scientific movement made small appeal. The Arabs generally took little interest in it: their learned men still spent their time in the study of Quran, jurisprudence, and grammar. So far, until the end of the reign of Harun ar-Rashid, no real work was done in the Aristotelian philosophy, Aristotle was treated only as an authority on logic.

Harun ar-Rashid died in 808, leaving the empire to his two sons al-Amin and al-Mamun, the former taking the western half with his capital at Baghdad, the other the eastern half with Marw as his capital. This naturally did not work and civil war between the two brothers followed inevitably. Al-Mamun's army, led by abler generals, obtained the upper hand, until in 812 under the leadership of Tahir it besieged Baghdad. This siege involved terrible sufferings and al-Amin was compelled to lay heavy requisitions on the citizens. At this the merchants entered into correspondence with Tahir. Discovering that he was betrayed al-Amin tried to escape and was on his way to make his submission to Tahir when he was found and murdered by some Persian freelancers. These tragic events form the subject of an epic poem by al-Khuzaimi, a type of poem rare in Arabic.

At the death of al-Amin the whole empire fell into the hands of al-Mamun, but he preferred to remain at Marw and sent Hasan ibn Sahl to Baghdad as his deputy. Hasan's rule lasted six years, a period of tyranny and disorder gradually merging into anarchy, of which al-Mamun was kept in complete ignorance. At last the city revolted and elected Mansur ibn Mahdi governor until such time as al-Mamun could take over control in person. There was another reason why Baghdad was dissatisfied in addition to the tyrannical misrule of Hasan. Al-Mamun had invited the Shiite claimant to the throne, Ali ar-Rida, to Marw, received him with exceptional honour, and promised to make him his heir. This caused great offence at Baghdad which had no desire to be under Shiite rule.

At length the Caliph was made aware of the critical state of affairs and warned that unless he went to Baghdad and took matters in hand for himself the caliphate would pass out of his hands. Thus warned he set out for Baghdad in 819, first disposing of Ali ar-Rida by poison. With him he took an extensive and extravagant court, as well as an army and also a select company of scientists, for he himself was deeply interested in scientific studies. At Baghdad he was welcomed with great rejoicings. He was a man of handsome presence, a thing which counts for much in oriental princes, generous, even lavish to extravagance in his expenditure and generally regarded as prudent, determined, of sound judgment, and clemency. According to the historians he was endowed with every grace and favour of an ideal prince. Educated in Marw in a neo-Hellenistic atmosphere, he applied philosophical principles to Muslim doctrines : no doubt others did the same, some of them men of exemplary piety, but they were careful to preserve external decorum by treating matters of religion with respect. Not so in case of al-Mamun. He had a taste for discussing religious problems and this he did with considerable freedom, so that one of his courtiers once addressed him in jest as " Prince of Unbelievers ", a jest which was allowed to pass but its maker was never forgiven. Pro-Persian and anti-Arab, son of a Persian mother and married to a Persian wife, he had little in common with the narrow fanaticism of the typical Baghdadite.

Unfortunately he was so far convinced of the Tightness of the Mutazilite views that he was determined to force them upon his subjects, selecting as a test point the question whether the Quran was, or was not, created. In 837. He published a decree penalizing any who did not agree that it was created and so not co-eternal with God. This decree was deeply resented as an innovation, for Islam has never recognized the Caliph as a religious teacher. The doctrines of religion are defined, not by the State, but by those who are learned in theology. As the penal was not successful, al-Mamun reissued it in stricter terms with many peevish complaints about the non-observance of his commands, and established a *mihna* or inquisition before which any person could be brought and examined as to his opinions, suffering punishment if they differed from the officially authorized rationalism. Under this law there were some martyrs and many suffered imprisonment and other punishments, amongst them Ahmad ibn Hanbal, a revered and greatly honoured traditionalist and jurist. All those who suffered were regarded as saints.

Ten years after his arrival in Baghdad al-Mamun attempted to repeat the experiment of the Greek geometer Eratosthenes and measure the earth's arc. To do this he assembled a number of scientists in the plain of Sinjar in Mesopotamia, west of Mosul. The leading scientists thus gathered were Abu-Taiyab Sanad ibn Ali (d. after 860), who afterwards directed the erection of the observatory in Baghdad, Yahya ibn Abi Mansur al-Maimuni, a freed man of al-Mamun's family, al-Abbas ibn Said al-Jawhari (d. after 833), and Ali ibn Isa al-Astur-labi. He divided these scientists into two parties which moved apart until they saw a change of one degree in the elevation of the pole. The distance travelled was then measured, and it was found that one party had travelled 57 miles, the other 58 miles, each mile reckoned as 4,000 " black cubits ", a measure of length specially devised for this experiment. In 832 the experiment was repeated at Qasian, near Damascus.

When Jibbrail left Jundi-Shapur for Baghdad he was succeeded as head of the academy and hospital there by Abu Zakriya Yahya ibn Masawaih (d. 857), a Nestorian who was the son of a druggist and had received his training as a pupil of Isa b. Nun, who became Nestorian patriarch in 823. At that time medicine was in such great repute that it was regarded as the foremost form of scientific education and consequently it is common to find that Nestorian and Mono-physite clergy in Asia often had a medical training rather than one in *litterae humaniores*. But Ibn Masawaih left Jundi-Shapur and went to Baghdad at Jibbrail's suggestion, and was introduced at court as a skilful physician and one learned in Greek medicine. He was the author of a treatise on ophthalmology entitled *Daghal al-ayn* "the disease of the eye", and also a collection of medical aphorisms *An-nawadir at-tibiyya,* which he dedicated to his pupil Hunain ibn Ishaq. This work attained great popularity and was translated into Latin, but wrongly ascribed to St. John Damascene.

In later times Ibn Masawaih's treatise on the eye was so greatly esteemed that it was selected as one of the set books for the examination established by the Caliph al-Qahir (932-34) for the licence to practise medicine, an examination at first under the direction of Sinan ibn Thabit. There is also an "Instruction for the examination of oculists" which is ascribed to him, but it is simply a cram book based on the *Daghal al-ayn* probably a later compilation made for the use of examination candidates.

The *Daghal al-ayn* "is the earliest treatise on ophthalmology, the Greek, Syriac, and other special textbooks being lost. It is written in bad Arabic, with many Greek, Syriac, and Persian technical terms, a rather confusing compilation without system, and doubtless intermixed with later interpolations. One complete MS. is extant in Taimur Pasha's library (Cairo), another in Leningrad " (M. Meyerhof, *The Book of the Ten Treatises,* Cairo, 1928, ix-x). Analysis and extracts of this work in German by M. Meyerhof and C. Preufer, Die Augenheilkun.de des Juhanna ibn Masawaih, in Der Islam, vi, 1915, pp. 217-56.

The most celebrated of all translators of Greek scientific works into Arabic was Hunain ibn Ishaq al-Abadi (d. 873 or 877). The outline of his life and work are well known from his autobiography written in the form of letters to Ali ibn Yahya in 875. (Text from two manuscripts in the Aya Sofia Mosque at Stambul, ed. with translation by G. Bergestrasser, Leipzig, 1925.) He was a native of Hira, the son of a Christian (Nestorian) druggist.

In later life he learned Arabic, so presumably he did not belong to the ruling class of Hira which was Arabic-speaking, and this is endorsed by his name Abadi, which shows that he belonged to the subject people of Hira. As a young man he attended the lectures of Ibn Masawaih (above) at Jundi-Shapur, and so far carried the approval of his teacher that he was made his dispenser. But later he annoyed Ibn Masawaih by asking too many questions in class, and at last his teacher lost patience and said : "What have the people of Hira to do with medicine? – go and change money in the streets," and drove him out weeping (Ibn al-Qifti, 174). Expelled from the academy Hunain went away to "the land of the Greeks " and there obtained a sound knowledge of the Greek language and familiarity with textual criticism, such as had been developed in Alexandria. In due course he returned and settled for a time at Basra where he studied Arabic under Khalid ibn Ahmad then, some time before 826, proceeded to Baghdad where he obtained the patronage of Jibbrail and for him prepared translations of some of Galen's works.

Harun ar-Rashid died in 808 and al-Mamun succeeded in 813, after the brief and stormy reign of al-Amin, so that Hunain's activities belong to a period later than Harun ar-Rashid. The excellence of his translations, far surpassing any previous work of the sort, greatly impressed Jibbrail who then introduced him to the three "Sons of Musa", wealthy patrons of learning. Their father, Musa ibn Shakir, after a life spent in the lucrative profession of a brigand in Khurasan, had reformed and been pardoned, then settled down to spend his declining years in cultured leisure. He entrusted his sons to the Caliph al-Mamun, who appointed Ishaq ibn Ibrahim, and later Yahya .ibn Abi Mansur to be their teachers, and from those preceptors they received a training in mathematics. They were not so much interested in medicine, but patronized Hunain chiefly because of his excellence as a translator. Of these "Sons of Musa" the eldest Muhammad rose to high office under the Caliph al-Motadid (892-932), and distinguished himself in astronomy and geometry, a second son Ahmad excelled in mechanics, and the third son Hasan became a celebrity in geometry.

They had a house in Baghdad near the Bab at-Taq, the gate at the eastern end of the main bridge over the Tigris, opening into the great market street of East Baghdad, and there they built an observatory where they made observations during the years 850-870. To them we owe a treatise on plane and spherical geometry, a collection of geometrical problems and a manual of geometry which was translated into Latin by Gerhard of Cremona (d. 1187) as " Liber Trium Fratrum de geometria " (ed. M. Curtze in Nova Acta d. Kais. Leap. Carol, deustscen Akad. Naturforscher, xlix, 109-167), which long held its own as an introduction to geometry. They were generous patrons of scientific research and according to Ibn Abi Usaibia spent at one time an average of 500 dinars (say £200) a month on their scientific proteges.

The " Sons of Musa " introduced Hunain to the Caliph al-Mamun some time before Jibbrails death in 828-29, and apparently at Jibbrail's suggestion the Caliph founded an academy which he called the "House of Wisdom" (Dar ul-hikhma) as an institution where the preparation of translations from Greek scientists would be made and circulated amongst the Arabs, placing Hunain in charge. From that time forwards the work of translation went on steadily, and before long Arab students found themselves equipped with the greater part of the works of Galen, Hippocrates, Ptolemy, Euclid, Aristotle, and various other Greek authorities.

The work of translation was twofold, versions were made in Arabic and also in Syriac, these were later to replace the defective translations already in use. Ibn Masawaih, the teacher who had expelled Hunain from Jundi-Shapur, was reconciled to him and became his warm supporter. Hunain had many other friends and clients, mostly physicians of Jundi-Shapur and those who had removed to Baghdad and used the Arabic language, like Salmawaih ibn Bunan an alumnus of' Jundi-Shapur who became court physician to al-Mutasim in 832. All these were better translations than had been known in the past and were made from good Greek manuscripts, many of them procured by agents of the Caliph who were sent into the Roman Empire and empowered to spend considerable sums on the purchase of the best codices.

Altogether Hunain translated into Syriac twenty books of Galen, two for Bukhtyishu' Jibbrail's son, two for Salmawaih ibn Bunan, one for Jibbrail, and one for Ibn Masawaih, and also revised the sixteen translations made by Sergius of Rashayn. He translated fourteen treatises into Arabic, three for Muhammad, one for Ahmad, sons of Musa. He and his assistants produced versions both in Syriac and Arabic, though no doubt some of his staff excelled in one language rather than the other. Most of the translators of the next generation received their training from Hunain or his pupils, so that he stands out as the leading translator of the better type, though some of his versions were afterwards revised by later writers.

The complete curriculum, of the medical school of Alexandria was thus made available for Arab students. This included a select series of the treatises of Galen which was :

> 1. De seeds. 2. Ars medica. 3. De pulsibus ad tirones. 4. Ad Glauconem de medendi method. 5. De ossibus ad tirones. 6. De musculorum dissectione. 7. De nervorum dissectione. 8. De venarum arteriumque dissectione. 9. De elementis secundum Hippocratem. 10. De temperamentis. 11. De facultatibus naturalibus. 12. De causis et symptomatibus. 13. De locis affectis. 14. De pulsibus (four treatises). 15. De typis (febrium). 16. De crisibus. 17. De diebus decretoriis. 18. Methodus medendi.

The range and method' of Hunain's work is known to us from his autobiography, the *Risalat Hunain ibn Ishaq*, letters written to Ali ibn Yahya in 865, of which the text with translation has been published from two manuscripts in the Aya Sofia Mosque at Stambul, by G. Bergestrasser, Leipzig, 1925, a work which has been analysed by Dr. Meyerhof in Isis, viii (1926), 685-724.

Al-Mamun's reign came to an end in 833 and he was succeeded by his son al-Mutasim (833-842), who found it difficult to control the populace of Baghdad and formed a guard of Turkish slave-soldiers. But this body-guard, holding a privileged position, soon became insubordinate and many complaints were made about their conduct. At last al-Mutasim in 836 removed himself and his court to Samana, and there the Caliphs reigned until 892. These disorders affected scholarship adversely and the "House of Wisdom" fell into decay which was not checked during the brief reign of Wathiq (842-47).

As Wathiq's son was too young to occupy the throne his brother Mutawakkil (847-861) was invested with the caliphate. His accession made a great change. The previous Caliphs had been tolerant in religion, al-Mamun was generally regarded as a free-thinker. But Mutawakkil was of the strictest orthodoxy and fanatical in his orthodoxy, possibly afraid of the disaffected attitude of the Syrian Christians. He was of sadistic temperament, mischievous and capriciously cruel. Though not himself a scholar like al-Mamun, he was a patron of science and scholarship and reopened the Dar al-Hikhma, granting it fresh endowments. The best work of translation was done during his reign, as the training of the staff and experience were bearing fruit.

Mutawakkil's personal relations with Hunain were chequered. It is related that the Caliph told him to prepare poison for his enemies and, on Hunain's refusal to do so, cast him into prison. Not long afterwards he was released and Mutawakkil explained that he had only desired to test his loyalty to the traditional standards of medical practice. Then a Nestorian physician named Israil ibn Zakriya at-Taifuri, or else his friend Bukhtyishu', denounced him as a heretic, that is a heretic from the Nestorian standard, for Hunain had never conformed to Islam.

The Nestorian Church, like other tolerated religious communities, was self-governing in its private affairs and could punish heretics and other offenders, though the Caliph quite gratuitously comes into the story. It is said that Mutawakkil ordered Hunain to spit on a picture of the Holy Theotokos and on his refusal handed him over to the Nestorian Catholicos Theodosius who imprisoned and scourged him.

The implication seems to be that the Caliph invited him to repudiate Christianity, and when he refused to do so handed him over to the Nestorian Catholicos for punishment. Just possibly this vague and confused story contains an echo of the iconoclastic controversy which at that time was disturbing the Eastern Church. Mutawakkil further confiscated Hunain's property, including his library, a loss which he felt sorely. After four months he was set free because of a remarkable cure following his treatment of a court dignitary, and his goods and library were restored. The whole matter sounds very much like an intrigue amongst the court physicians, as on his release the other court physicians had to pay him 10,000 dirhams compensation.

After his release he lived another twenty years, which he employed in making translations and correcting those made by others. In 861 Mutawakkil was murdered by his Turkish guards at his son's instigation. Hunain enjoyed the favour of that son Montasir (861-62), and of his successors Mostain (862-66), Motazz (866-69), Muhtadi (869-70), and Mutamid (870-92), and was engaged in making a translation of Galen's De constitutione artis medicae at the time of his death, which took place in 873 according to the Fehrist, or in 877 according to Ibn Abi Usaibia, who is often inaccurate in his chronology. According to I.A.U., Hunain was the author of more than a hundred original works, but only a few of these are extant. Hunain, the greatest of the translators, must be reckoned to the credit of Jundi-Shapur, although his fuller and more accurate knowledge was gained by his studies in the " land of the Greeks ", for those travels and studies were prompted and directed by what he had learned at Jundi-Shapur under Ibn Masawaih.

Although Mutawakkil was bigoted, fanatical, and sadistic, he was a generous patron of scientific research and is generally reckoned as having re-endowed the " House of Wisdom ", which probably means that it was reopened after the disturbed period which followed al-Mamun's death and its endowments restored to it. The best work of this academy was done under Mutawakkil, for by that time experience told and Hunain was surrounded by well-trained pupils.

Amongst those who worked with Hunain must be noted his son Ishaq, who died in November, 919 or 911, and his nephew Hubaysh ibn al-Hasan, who was at work in the days of Mutawakkil. He translated Greek texts of Hippocrates and the botanical work of Dioscorides which became the basis of the Arab pharmacopoeia (infra). It is noteworthy that most of the names of planys in Arabic show that they have passed through an Aramaic (Syriac) medium (cf. Loew, Aramaische Pflanzennamen, 1881).

Another noteworthy pupil was Isa ibn Yahya ibn Ibrahim who was a translator of Greek medical works into Arabic. Almost all the leading scientists of the succeeding generation were pupils of Hunain.

Although Hubaysh is given as the translator of *Dioscorides*, the current Arabic version is more commonly ascribed to Hunain's pupil Staphanos ibn Basilos, who translated the work into Syriac, and this Syriac version was then translated into Arabic by Hunain himself (or Hubaysh) for Muhammad, one of the "Sons of Musa". But another independent version of *Dioscorides* was afterwards made in Spain (cf. below).

About 908 the Christian priest Yusuf al-Kkuri al-Qass translated Archimedes' (lost) work on triangles from a Syriac version, and this was afterwards revised by Thabit ibn Qurra.

He also made an Arabic translation of Galen's *De simplicibus temperamentis et facultatibus,* which was afterwards revised by Hunain ibn Ishaq.

About the same time lived Qusta ibn Luqa al-Balbakki (3. 912-13), a Syrian Christian who translated *Hypsicles,* afterwards revised by al-Kindi, Theodosius' *Sphaerica,* which was afterwards revised by Thabit ibn Qurra, Heron's *Mechanics,* Autolycus, Theophrastus' *Meteora,* Galen's catalogue of his books, John Philoponus on the Physics of Aristotle and several other works, and also revised the existing translation of Euclid.

Abu Bishr Malta ibn Yunus al-Qannai (d. 940) was responsible for a translation of the Poetica of Aristotle.

Medical and logical works were translated also by the Monophysite Abu Zakriya Yahya ibn Adi al-Mantiqi "the logician" (d. 974), amongst them the Prolegomena of Ammonius, an introduction to Porphyry's Isagoge.

To these may be added the late translator Al-Hunain ibn Ibrahim ibn al-Hasan ibn Khurshid at-Tabari an-Natili (d. 990) also the Monophysite Abu Ali Isa ibn Ishaq ibn Zera (d. 16th April, 1008), who prepared versions of medical and philosophical works. With these the series of translators in Asia comes to an end. After this the work changes to commentary and exposition, occasionaly revising earlier translations,

A final phase of translation appears in Andalus, the Muslim occupied Spain. There the fugitive Umayyad prince Abdur Rahman had established an independent kingdom in 755. The eighth prince of that Undalusian state Abdur Rahman III in 929 adopted the title Caliph and so from 929 to 978 there were Caliphs of Cordova, usually with strained relations with the Abbasids in the east, but friendly with the Emperor of Byzantium who was their enemy. In 949 the Byzantine Emperor Constantine VII sent an embassy to Cordova and amongst the presents he sent to Abdur Rahman was a copy of *Dioscorides* in Greek with painted pictures of the many plants described in the text. This book attracted much attention, but no one in Cordova could read Greek, so the Caliph in thanking the Emperor begged him to send someone who could translate and explain the work.

In 951 the Emperor sent a monk named Nicolas, who was able to speak Arabic, and he not only made translations of *Dioscorides* and other Greek works, but began teaching the Greek language, his lectures arousing great enthusiasm and being attended by many court officials, including Hasdai ibn Shaprut, the Jewish Wazir. Translations of *Dioscorides* already existed, that of Hunain ibn Ishaq from the Syriac version of his pupil Stephenos ibn Basilos, and the version made by an-Natali for the Prince Abu Ali as-Sanjuri. But Nicolas made an improved translation in which pains were taken to identify the plants described, thus laying the foundation of a serious study of botany which very quickly bore fruit in the work of Abu Daud Sulaiman ibn Juljul (circ. 1000), physician to Abdur Rahman's successor Hisham II, who wrote a supplement to Dioscorides describing a number of plants found in Spain, a land peculiarly rich and varied in its flora, but not known to the Greek author. Although there was a very productive cultural harvest in Andalus and the reign of Abdur Rahman III was the golden age of Undalusian culture, there does not appear to have been any further output of translations from the Greek there. The Undalusian version of Dioscorides as made by Nicolas exists in a Bodleian manuscript. Apparently the older version prepared by Hunain ibn Ishaq or an-Natali was quite unknown in Spain.

Thabit ibn Qurra is prominent amongst those who revised and corrected Arabic translations of mathematical and astronomical works, and introduces a new source of pro-Greek interest. He was a native of the town of Harran, the ancient Charrae, where men adhered steadfastly to their ancient paganism, although the deities worshipped there bore names borrowed from the Greek pantheon. It was in the midst of Syriac Christian culture, between Edessa and Rashayn, situated on the Bellas, a minor tributary of the Upper Euphrates. It was famous for the purity of the Aramaic spoken there, and this was sometimes attributed to its comparative freedom from Jewish or Christian influences, though in fact there was a Christian bishop and presumably there was a Christian congregation there. It seems to have been in touch with the renaissance of Greek learning which affected both the Nestorian and Monophysite churches and its thought was strongly tinctured with neo-Platonism.

Our knowledge of the ancient religion of Harran is chiefly gleaned from the observations of ad-Dimishqi, who died in a.d. 1327, long after the city had passed into obscurity and who could only have had traditional information about its religion. His information is summarized in Chwolson's Die Ssabier under Ssabismus, ii, 280-411. From that we learn that the Harranians had five great temples dedicated respectively to the First Cause, the First Reason, the Ruler of the World, Form, and Soul. There were seven other temples dedicated to the seven planets. It was an anomaly for a pagan city to enjoy religious freedom under Muslim rule and noninterference was not due to the city being obscure as it was the capital of the province of Diyar Mudar and under the last Umayyad Caliph Marwan II it was the residence of the court and government administration. The Fehrist relates a story that al-Mamun towards the end of his reign passed by Harran on a military expedition, and he and his officers were astonished at the strange and uncouth appearance of the townsmen. He asked who they were, and was shocked to learn that they were pagans. This implies that Harran was unknown to Muslims generally and a remote isolated district, which is not true.

Al-Mamun ordered the people to adopt one of the recognized religions, Islam, Judaism, Christianity, or Mazdeanism, before he came back that way. He never did come back, but the people were alarmed at his threats and many of them conformed to Islam or Christianity : Mazdeanism seems to have ceased to make converts by then ; but others adhered to their paganism and sought a way to escape the Caliph's anger. A certain lawyer offered to show them a possible way of doing so for a consideration, and when they had paid him his fee he advised them to claim to be Sabaeans (Sabia), as those are mentioned in the Quran as one of the "peoples of the Book" (Qur., 2, 59; 22, 17; 5, 73), and no one knew who the Sabaeans were. The story is obviously apocryphal : the Harranites could not have been so little known in the days of al-Mamun as his father Harun ar-Rashid had already put pressure on them as heretics and their city had been the seat of government under Marwan II. The story is an attempt to explain how the Harranites came to be called Sabaeans, a name which we now recognize as not belonging to them.

The real Sabaeans were a people of South Arabia, with whom Harran had no concern. But the Mandaeans of the Lower Euphrates, the Haemerobaptists of the Christian fathers and the rabbinical writers who earned the title of "baptists" from their frequent and punctilious ablutions, were in Aramaic called Sabain from the root SB' "ummerse". Those Mandaeans were Gnostics who inclined to astrological beliefs, possibly actual star-worshippers. The people of Harran were not Gnostics, but they had temples dedicated to the planets, which gave some colour to the confusion between them and the Mandaeans. Harranite neo-Platonism might possibly be confused with Gnostic beliefs. It is characteristic that the Harranites claimed that their religion had come to them from Hermes. It is an interesting instance, though not a unique one, of the way in which the Muslim law was sometimes evaded.

Thabit ibn Qurra (d. 901) " was originally a money-changer in the market of Harran, and when he turned to philosophy he made wonderful progress and became expert in three languages, Greek, Syriac, and Arabic. ... In Arabic he composed about 150 works on logic, mathematics, astronomy, and medicine, and in Syriac he wrote another fifteen books " (Bar

Hebraeus, Chron., x, 176). About 872 he was excommunicated by the High Priest of Harran, unfortunately we know nothing about the ecclesiastical discipline of Harran— and sent to Kafartutha, near Dara, but he remained staunch to his religion. "Our fathers," he said, " by the help of God stood firm and spoke boldly, so this favoured town never was polluted by the error of Nazareth (Christianity), and we are their heirs and transmitters of paganism in these days : fortunate is he who bears his burden in hope strengthened by paganism (ibid.). He maintained that it was the pagans who first cultivated the land, founded cities, made ports, and discovered science (ibid.)." After wanderings in various lands he met Muhammad, one of the " Sons of Musa", who recognized his scholarship and took him to Baghdad where he did most of his work.

He made translations of Apollonius, Archimedes, Euclid, Ptolemy, and Theodosius, or revised existing translations. He also composed several works on astronomy and mathematics. It has been supposed that he was responsible for the extremely mechanical form in which Ptolemy's cosmography was presented to the Arabs, but that hardly seems justified. In mathematics he introduced the theory of "amicable numbers", a Chinese idea. Such numbers are those in which one is the sum of the factors in the other. Thus, if $p = 3.2^n - I$, $q = 3.^{2n-1} - I$, and $r = 9.2^{2n-1} - I$, assuming that n is a whole number, then $a = 2^n pq$, and $b = 2^n r$ are amicable numbers. Suppose $n = 2$, then $p = 3.2^n - i - II$: $q = 3.2^{n-1} - I = 5$: $r = 9.2^{2n-1} - I = 71$: so the amicable numbers are $a = 320$, $b = 284$. Nothing very much results from this investigation, but it was continued by Maslama al-Majriti and a few other Arab mathematicians.

Thabit had a son Abu Said who became physician to the Caliph al-Qahir. He also was a pagan, but the Caliph tried to convert him to Islam and fell into the habit of using the most bloodthirsty threats to force him to do whatever he wanted, until the unhappy physician fled to Khurasan and remained there until al-Qahir was dead. Then he returned to Baghdad and lived there until his own death in 943. Thabit had many pupils, one of whom a Christian named Isa ibn Asd translated into Arabic various works which Thabit had composed in Syriac.

About 932-34 the city of Harran was destroyed either by the Alids, as Hamawi says, or by Egyptian invaders as Dimishqi asserts. The contemporary historian, John of Antioch, describes this destruction.

In 975 Abu Ishaq ibn Hilal, secretary to the Caliphs Muti' and Tay', obtained a decree granting religious toleration to the Sabaeans of Harran, of whom there were many in Baghdad—some were still there in the eleventh century—one of whom the most distinguished were the mathematician Abu Jafar al-Khazin, a convert to Islam, and Ibn al-Wahshiya, author of a work known as "the Nabataean Agriculture" (*Kitab al-falaha an-nabatiya*), which pretended to be a translation from ancient Babylonian. This work was finished in 904 : it is a collection of popular beliefs, superstitions, and legends. It gives no real botanical information but simply aims at proving that the ancient Babylonian civilization existed ages before the rise of the Arabs whose culture was a comparatively recent and inferior one. In fact it is an example of the strong anti-Arab animus characteristic of the early Abbasid period. However, the work had no influence on the development of intellectual culture amongst the Muslim Arabs.

Knowledge Transformed

Reverse Process : The widespread and rapid translation of Greek philosophical and scientific works into Arabic following the Muslim conquests of the seventh and eighth centuries had barely passed its peak before the next great wave of transmission began. Around the twelfth century, teams of scholars began the translation into Latin of the considerable and enhanced treasury of Muslim science, that is, science in Arabic. Much of this work was done in Spain, the principal cultural crossroads joining medieval Islam and Europe. This enterprise, for the first time making Greco-Arabic knowledge available to scholars and scientists in Western Europe, accelerated considerably after the Christian reconquest of Spain had embraced Barcelona, Toledo, and Seville.

The translators included Jews and Christians from Spain and other parts of Europe, as well as Muslims. This multiracial, international fellowship remained hard at work until Jews and Muslims were expelled from Spain in the late fifteenth century. Mozarab (Christians living under Muslim rule as if they were Arabs), Mudejar (Arabs remaining in Spain after the Reconquest), and Moriscos (Muslims who, outwardly at least, converted to Christianity) also played a part in the undertaking, which produced what was in effect a twelfth-century pre-Renaissance renaissance that provided the libraries of Europe's monasteries and other intellectual centers with a flood of classical knowledge never before available in the West and now enriched with Muslim contributions.

Among these translators, the most famous by far were an Italian, Gerard of Cremona, a Scot working in Sicily, Michael Scotus, and a Carthaginian, Constantine the African. They, their contemporaries, and their successors provided translations of the major Greek scientists, from Euclid and Hippocrates to Ptolemy, Galen, and others, as revised and annotated by such Muslim thinkers as Al-Razi, Al-Battani, Ibn Sina, and Al-Khwarizmi. Gerard was especially prolific, turning out more than one hundred translated texts.

The range embraced by the translators was comprehensive, including medicine, the natural world, meteorology, geology, mathematics, and physics. With this Muslim-enriched legacy, Europe's scholars were inspired to revolutionize their view of the world around them, as well as to redefine current intellectual, technological, and social goals. Medicine and the physical sciences received particular attention, as they had in the first flood of translation, reflecting renewed emphasis on practical needs. Aristotle's scientific texts were fully translated before some of his more abstract philosophical works.

The work of translation on such a scale involved many frustrations, hazards, and deficiencies. The Arabic language presented medieval translators (whose facility with the original Greek was generally minimal) with a truly difficult obstacle course, filled with alien linguistic devices, as well as terms that defied translation and thus had to be simply transliterated. Identification and selection of works to be translated often presented difficulties, since many Arabic manuscripts represented not only the work of different translators but even of different authors not always clearly identified. Sometimes it was hard to distinguish between what was original Greek content and what was subsequent commentary by someone other than the original author. Moreover, since many translators found Arabic easier to handle than classical Greek, a considerable number of original Greek works were given less priority or overlooked entirely.

Despite the difficulties of translation and the sometimes erratic selection of works to be translated, the great majority of important ancient texts were available to European readers of Latin by the fourteenth century. Soon, came the means of disseminating such a wealth on an unprecedented scale: In 1445, Johann Gutenberg printed his first book from movable type. Invigorated with a new, humanistic spirit and armed as never before with a classical heritage, the Western establishment, focusing on concerns closer to home, soon abandoned much of its interest in Islam and forgot the significant Muslim contribution to its culture. At the end of the Middle Ages the modern, and far from trusting, relationship between the West and Islam was beginning to take shape.

The cultural influence of Islamic civilization on the Christian West affected everything from architecture to zoological research. The influence of Muslim sciences was perhaps less apparent than that of Muslim arts. However, few, if any, of the scientific disciplines that began to be transformed in the West during the late medieval and early Renaissance centuries could have developed as they did without the clarification, renovation, and enhancement that had been achieved by Muslim scientists.

By the seventeenth century, when Ottoman Turkey gave up conquest and began losing control of some of its territory, Europe was on the offensive, militarily, economically, and culturally. New technological instruments and techniques had been developed or imported: papermaking, printing, and gunpowder had begun to change the way whole populations lived, battled, perished, learned, and survived. New social and cultural forces were shaping a civilization that could only become progressively more alien to an Islamic one increasingly less dynamic in character, form, and purpose. The growth of a prosperous and influential merchant class; the Italian Renaissance with its secular, neo-classical, anti-clerical interests; the fierce Reformation that split the Christian Church—most of these developments could only be perceived by Muslims as threatening.

Furthermore, by the nineteenth century, when Islamic lands had begun to fall under colonial control by European powers, devout Muslims could only perceive as a particular menace the Western secularism generated by increasingly humanistic ways of thought focused far more on humans on earth than on God in heaven. The remnants of the Muslim empire, losing unity, strength, and supremacy, settled mostly into a defensive and restrictive political and cultural rigidity. Islam as a culture was closing its doors and its mind to the dangerous world taking shape just beyond its shrinking borders. Many decades would pass before much new and significant knowledge could be imported into Islamic society from outside, let alone generated within it.

The growing dominance of Europe ultimately brought about cracks in the Muslim wall. Ignoring traditional warnings about imitating foreigners, Ottoman leaders adopted some practical Western developments that had clearly promoted the growth of European power, innovations such as new military and naval weapons and strategies and the establishment of a postal system that could help to disseminate necessary knowledge about what was afoot in the world beyond Ottoman borders.

The Ottomans also promoted book publication on an unprecedented scale. Moreover, Muslims began going abroad as never before to scout the new world and its ways, and increasing numbers of Western visitors were admitted to Muslim territories. However, the cautionary wisdom that prevailed in Islam for generations urged Muslims not to get too close to Westerners but to learn what they could about them. As the world proceeded into the modern age some understanding developed between Muslims and infidels; this was to increase at times, decrease at others, but the gains to both sides accrued slowly.

Natural History : Natural History comprises the study of every thing in this universe. It begins with the arrival of Hadrat Adam (peace be upon him) in this world. As mentioned in the Holy Quran, he was taught the names and the properties of all the things. The ancient Greek and Roman natural historians included both the animate and the inanimate objects in their study. It is however, commonly used for the study of minerals, plants and animals. The term Natural History in this sense goes back to Aristotle (384-322 BC) who established it on firm scientific footing.

The celebrated Roman natural historian Pliny (23-79 AD) dealt with varied subjects such as: astronomy, chemistry, geology, mineralogy, botany, zoology, anthropology, etc., in his classical work Historia Naturalis. During the early Muslim period, most of the scholars had varied and diverse interests. The works on Natural History are scattered in books on literature, philosophy, cosmology, theology, history, geography, agriculture and medicine. Upto the eighteenth century AD the biology and geology were combined under the term Natural History. The term biology was introduced by a German naturalist Treviranus (1776-1837) in his work entitled, Biologic, Oder philosophic der lebenden Nature (Biology and philosophy of living nature) published in 1802-1806. By 1880, however, Natural History had budded off geology, botany and zoology as independent sciences (Sedgwick & Tyler, 1917).

The study of Natural History in Islam aims at seeing the wisdom of the almighty Allah manifest in his creations. When a Muslim looks at the phenomena of nature, he is struck by the wonderful harmony and perfection in the spectrum of all creations ranging from inanimate to animate. This leads him to the flawless plan of the Creator. Every Muslim is invited to study what is in the heavens and on the earth in the following verse of the Holy Quran .

Say : Observe all that is in the heavens and on the earth.

The Holy Prophet of Islam (peace and blessings of Allah be upon him) laid down the principle for research in his proverbial saying :

> "By studying nature, a Muslim intends to have the cognizance of the Creator contrary to the present western thinking, he does not differentiate between the study of science and that of the religion. He rather thinks that there is no demarcation between what is religious and what is not. Islam is a perfect way of life and does not allow any such division It guides its followers in all the spheres of life. It is perfect unity. So the study of Natural History, for a Muslim, is harmonious rather than conflicting with his religious values. "In Islamic civilization, Natural History has always played a central role as the integrating and all-embracing matrix within which particular descriptive sciences of nature have been cultivated, from

mineralogy to zoology. It has sought to integrate particular forms of knowledge of the natural order into universal principles of a metaphysical and cosmological nature and it has sought to study nature not only with respect to other physical and biological forms and vis-a-vis man's relation to these forms but most of all as the 'signs' or 'portents' (ayat) of Allah to be contemplated rather than simply analyzed" (Nasr, 1976).

The study of Natural History for the cognizance of Allah was taken from the Muslims by the early natural historians of the West such as John Ray (1659-1705) and Carolus Linnaeus (1707-1778). Cam (1959) remarks on the Linnaean systems.

"These (characters) were those that had greatest degree of affinity, and to put them together in this way was to follow out the plan of the Creator Himself. Taxonomy could thus be regarded as a highly religious duty".

This tradition is perceptible upto the first half of the 19th century AD. Regarding this trend, Barber (1980) remarks:

"The first purpose of the study of Nature, therefore, is to teach us that God exists. The second is to illustrate God's attributes. For just as in admiring a well-made watch, we inevitably admire the skill of the watch-maker who made it, so, in admiring the various beauties and perfections of Nature, we are inevitably led to think of the beauty and perfection of God Who designed them. This, in brief, is natural theology. Its key concept is Design. Nothing happens by chance (or by natural selection), everything by Design. The more we learn to understand and appreciate Design in nature, the more closely we approach a knowledge of God."

The human knowledge can be divided into two categories—revealed and acquired. The source of revealed knowledge is Wahl or revelation from Almighty Allah; whereas the sources of the acquired knowledge are observation and experimentation. The revealed knowledge is passed on to the mankind by Allah through his Prophets (peace be upon them).

Since the only revelation preserved in original is the Holy Quran, it is the sole source of the revealed knowledge. This knowledge, however, is supplemented by the sayings of the Prophet Muhammad (peace and blessings of Allah be upon him), as he would not speak but with the consent of Allah. Hence this knowledge is the absolute truth. The acquired knowledge, on the other hand, is the relative truth. There is always a room for improvement in this kind of knowledge. A new discovery or a new circumstance may change the entire face of the relative truth. Whereas the absolute truth is true for all times.

To make this point clear, I shall discuss a few examples from the recent branches of Natural History: the Systematics, the Biogeography, and the Evolution.

One of the preoccupations in the systematics (including taxonomy) is the naming of the plants and animals and their classification. The names of the familiar plants and animals are known even to the most primitive tribes. Such names were known to the ancient people as well. Some sort of grouping was also known to them For instance, the familiar animals were grouped into the fishes, the reptiles, the birds, the mammals, the worms, the insects, the snails, etc. Another sort of grouping was based on their habitats the land animals, the flying animals, the aquatic animals, etc.

However, it was the Swedish naturalist Linnaeus (1707-1778) who devised the scientific method of naming and grouping the plants and animals. This system is accepted, with some modifications, even today. When this system was proposed by

Linnaeus, it was not welcomed from all the quarters. It was even criticized by Button (1707-1788) and some other prominent naturalists of his time. One such example is discussed at some length by Cain (1963). However, the Linnaean system was so well-framed and so carefully improved by later authors, that it was ultimately accepted all over the world. But in the recent years even the utility of this remarkable system has been questioned by Cam (1959) and others.

The second example is from the domain of geology and biogeography. There were two main rival hypothesis about the nature and extent of the land-masses and the ocean-basins: the hypothesis of the continental drift, and the hypothesis of the permanence of the land-masses and ocean-basins. In the first half of the present century, the hypothesis of the permanence was favoured by most of the biogeographers, geographers and the geologists. But in the late sixties, new discoveries in the geological field furnished new evidences in the favour of the continental drift. As a result, two of the major opponents of the continental drift (i.e. P J. Darlington and G. S. Myers) were converted into its favour.

The study of the evolutionary processes is a favourite topic in Natural History. Several concepts explaining the organic evolution were proposed in the past. Of these, two theories proposed by Lamarck and Darwin became very popular. The second theory, originally proposed jointly by Charles Darwin and A. R. Wallace in 1858, was elaborated by Darwin (1859) in his book entitled "The origin of species" by means of Natural Selection. This theory found so many supporters that the theory of Lamarck was almost universally rejected. The theory of Natural Selection was greatly modified in the light of the recent developments in the population genetics and related fields. This theory became so dear to the most of the biologists all over the world that they embraced it as if it were a matter of belief with them. But recently this theory has been challenged by some well-known authorities. For example, Rosen (1978) after laying down his objections on this theory concludes:

> "When 'natural selection' is stripped from our technical vocabulary and irrelevant argument ceases in consequence, I am confident that evolutionary theory will still afford geneticists, embryologists, and systematists endless happy hours of useful contention and strife".

From the above discussion it becomes clear that the conclusions based on our present knowledge may not be true tomorrow It is only the revealed knowledge that remains true for all times. There is no need for submitting our ideas based on the absolute truth to the ideas based on the relative truth. Because the latter is bound to change along with the progress of the human experience through the passage of time.

This does not mean that the Muslims should not accept the new ideas and discoveries. A great emphasis has been laid on the acquisition of knowledge from all sources by the Holy Prophet (peace and blessings of Allah be upon him) in his various sayings. Thus we must study Natural History and other sciences but without affecting our faith based on the Holy Quran and Sunnah.

The Naturalists : A naturalist is one who studies Natural History. Natural History in its widest sense comprises the study of Nature which is best explained by the following verse from the Holy Quran:

> Say: Observe all that is in the Heavens and on the Earth.

It is however, commonly used to denote collectively the sciences of biology and geology. In a restricted sense, it is used for the various branches of field zoology: Systematics, Ecology and Zoogeography. In this article, I have restricted myself to the senior Muslim Naturalists of the South Asian Subcontinent, who have made significant contributions in these fields during the 14th century Hijri.

The Fourteenth century Hijri dawned when most of the Muslim world was occupied by the Europeans and the conditions for the scientific progress were extremely unfavourable for the Muslims. The works on Natural History and other sciences were carried out mainly by the non-Muslims. However, Muslim Naturalists initiated contributing in these fields in the 2nd quarter of the 14th century. After Independence, the conditions have become favourable and a lot of work has been done in various institutions in the South Asian Subcontinent.

2

Cultivation and Growth

The Saracen Empire was dotted all over with Colleges, and in the heyday of Muslim power, Spain alone boasted of 70 libraries. Colleges were also established in Mongolia, Tartary, Persia, Mesopotamia, Syria, Egypt, North Africa, Morocco and Fez. Great was the patronage that learning received at this time. To give an adequate statement of the results of this imposing scientific movement would far transcend the limits of these pages. The ancient sciences were gradually extended and new ones brought into existence.

At various centres of the Empire observatories were established under al-Mamun, and by exchanging observations Islam succeeded in revising the astronomical tables of Ptolemy, and in ascertaining, with greater precision, the obliquity of the ecliptic and the orbits of the sun, the moon and the planets. In a most ingenious manner Al-Beruni, who is considered the most profound and original savant and mathematician that Islam produced in the realm of natural science, determined the magnitude of the earth's circumference. He brought out in 1030 A.D. an account of the whole science of astronomy called Al-Qanun at-Masudi fin Nojum. He has discussed scientifically the then controversial theory of earth's rotation on its axis and made accurate determination of latitudes and longitudes.

Two of the oldest Muslim astronomers Al-Farghani and Al-Battani were the preceptors of Europe and under the name of Al-fragani and Albategnius enjoyed high and widespread reknown. Abu Abdullah Muhammad ibn Jabir al-Battani, undoubtedly the greatest astronomer of his time, made his observations and studies in al-Raqqah from 877 to 918. His contributions were original. According to Prof. Hitti, "He made several emendations to Ptolemy and rectified the calculations for the orbits of the moon and certain planets. He proved the possibility of annular eclipses of the sun and determined with greater accuracy the obliquity of the seasons and the true and mean orbit of ecliptic, the length of the tropical year and the seasons and the true and mean orbit of the sun".

Al-Battani wrote a large treatise and compiled astronomical tables. His greatest claim to fame is undoubtedly that, if he did not discover, he at least popularised the first notions of trigonometrical ratios as we use them today. Ptolemy used chords, for the calculation of which he had only one main theorem, a very clumsy one. Al-Battani substituted the sine for the chord. He used tangent and cotangent and he was acquainted with two or three fundamental relations in trigonometry. Joseph Hell has rightly remarked that "In the domain of trigonometry the theory of sine, cosine and tangent is an heirloom of the Arabs. The brilliant epochs of Peurbach, of Regiomontanus, of Copernicus, cannot be recalled without reminding us of the fundamental and preparatory labours of the Arab Mathematician."

Writing about the great advance made by the Muslims in the domain of mathematics, Joseph Hell comments thus: "taking over the elements of mathematics from Euclid, the decimal system from the Indians in the ninth century, they soon made substantial progress. The adoption of the sign 'Zero' (Arabic Sifr) was a step of the highest importance, leading up to the so called arithmetic of positions. With the help of the Arab system of numbers, elementary methods of calculation were perfected; the doctrines of the properties of, and the relations between, the equal and the unequal and prime numbers, square and cubes, was elaborated; algebra was enriched by the solution of the third and fourth degrees, with the help of geometry and so on. About the year 820 A.D. the Mathematician, Al-Khawarizimi, wrote a textbook of algebra in examples, and this elementary treatise-translated into Latin-was used by Western scholars down to the sixteenth century."

Besides an important treatise on astronomy, Al-Khawarizimi also wrote a book on astronomical tables and another on algebra. The first was translated into Latin by Adelard of Bath, the two others by Gerard of Cremona, the treatise on astronomy and that on arithmetic are known only from these Latin translations. His book was used until the sixteenth century as the principal mathematical text book of European universities and served to introduce into Europe the science of Algebra, and with it the name. His work was also responsible for the introduction into the West of the Arabic numerals, called Algorisms" after him.

The Muslim contributions in the field of Chemistry and Physics are also of far reaching importance. Joseph Hell has paid genuine tributes: "The oldest chemists, as a body, were alchemists. This notwithstanding, in their writings we find items of chemical knowledge which cannot be shown to have existed anterior to their times. They knew alum, salt petre, salammonia alkali prepared from tartar and salt petre; and among them we first notice the knowledge of mineral acids. The increase in the number of artificially prepared substance; the perfection of methods handed down from the Greeks; and application of these methods to most diverse materials are the striking achievements of the Arabs in the domain of chemistry. If, in this direction, they advanced considerably beyond the Greeks, it was due to the fact that in the place of hazy, mystical speculations they introduced objective experiments into the study of nature."

The father of Arabic alchemy was Jabir ibn-Hayyan, who flourished in Kufa about 776 A.D. He acted on the assumption that base metals such as tin, lead, iron and copper could be transmuted into gold or silver by means of a mysterious substance. He emphasised the importance of experimentation and made a distinctive advance in theory and practice of chemistry. He described scientifically the two important chemical operations of calcination and reduction. He improved on the methods of evaporation, sublimation, melting and crystallisation.

The later physicians succeeded in displacing the works of Galen and Hippocrates for several centuries and substituting their own at the universities. Of this class of original writers the oldest is Muhammad ibn Zakriya al-Razi (865-925). According to Prof. E. G. Browne, "Al-Razi was the greatest and most original of all the Muslim physicians, and one of the most prolific as an author." His erudition was all embracing and his scientific output remarkable, amounting to more than 200 works, half of which are medical. He also wrote a monumental work Kitabul-Mansuri in ten volumes of which a Lattin translation appeared in Milan in the eighties of the fifteenth century. Parts of it have been recently rendered into German and French. One of the most celebrated of his monographs, is that on "Smallpox and Measles" (al-judari-wal-Hrisbah). It was first translated into Latin in 1565 and later into several European languages, including English and went into forty editions between 1498-1866. According to Prof. P K. Hitti, author of History of the Arabs, this treatise served to establish Al-Razi's reputation as one of the keenest original thinkers and greatest clinicians not only of Islam but of the Middle Ages. The most important medical work of Al-Razi was Al-Hawi (the Comprehensive book), an encyclopaedia in the annals of medical information.

It was translated into Latin under the auspices of Charles I of Anjou by the Sicilian Jewish physician, Faraj ibn Salim

(Tamagni) in 1279 and was repeatedly printed from 1488 onwards. These works of Raze exercised a remarkable influence on European medicine.

The most outstanding and illustrious personality in the domain of medical science after Al-Razi is that of lion Sina, universally known to the West as Avicenna (980-1037) and called by the Arabs Al-Sheikh-al-Rais. Among his scientific works the leading two are Kitab-al-Shifa (Book of Healing) and Al-Qanun fit Tibb (the Canons of Medicine). This book is the culmination and masterpiece of Arabic systematisation. This medical encyclopaedia deals with general medicines, simple drugs, diseases affecting all parts of the body from the head to foot, specially pathology and Pharmacopoeia. The Qanun was published in Arabic in Rome in 1593. It was translated into Latin by Gerard of Cremona in the twelfth century. It became the textbook for medical education in the schools of Europe. The demand for it may be gleaned from the fact that in the last thirty years of the fifteenth century it was issued sixteen times, fifteen editions being in Latin and one in Hebrew, and that it was reissued more than twenty times during the sixteenth century. In 1930 Cameron Gruner partly translated this book into English, called A Treatise on the Canons of Medicine of Avicenna. From the twelfth to the seventeenth centuries the Qanun served as the chief guide to medical science in the West. Dr. William Osier, author of the Evolution of Modern Science, has rightly remarked. "The Qanun has remained a medical Bible for a longer period than any other work."

Optics was developed to its highest degree by Ibn-al-Haitham (Alhazan) of Basra (965 A.D.). His main work is "On Optics", the original Arabic is lost, but the book survives in Latin. He opposes the theory of Euclid and Ptolemy that the eye sends out visual rays to the object of vision. He discusses the propagation of light and colours, optic illusions and reflections. Alhazan examines also the refraction of light rays through transparent medium (air, water). In detailing his experiments with spherical segments (glass vessels filled with water), he comes very near to the theoretical discovery of magnifying lenses which was made practically in Italy three centuries later, whilst more than six centuries were to pass before the law of sines was established by Snell and Descartes. Roger Bacon (thirteenth century) and all medieval Western writers on optics notably the Pole Witelo or Vitellio—base their optical works largely on Alhazan's Opticae Thesaurus. His work also influenced Leonardo da Vinci and Johann Kepler.

In the field of geography too, the Muslims made a great headway. During Caliph Al-Mamun (813-833) the government appointed a Committee under Muhammad ibn Musa al-Khawarizmi to make a survey of the globe. Seventy great minds worked to explore the field and ultimately they were able to produce the first map of the globe in 830 A.D. This activity of the Arabs heralded the dawn of a new adventure in the rough seas. Guided by this scientific data, Columbus was inspired to hazard out in the seas five centuries later, believing that the earth was a globe, and not a flat saucer. Thus in search of Indian condiments, Columbus, who had been taught this knowledge of geography by one Arab, found the American continent. When Vasco de Gama, after his circumnavigation of the African continent in 1498 A.D. had reached Malindi on the east coast of Africa, it was an Arab pilot, Ahmad ibn Majid, who showed him the way to India. According to Portuguese sources this pilot was in possession of a very good sea map and of other maritime instruments. The same pilot is also known as the writer of a sailing manual for the Indian Ocean, the Red Sea, the Persian Gulf, the South China Sea and the East Indian Archipelago."

Bertrand Russell in the History of Western Philosophy remarks that Umar Khayyam the only man known to him who was both a poet and a mathematician, reformed the Calendar in 1079 A. D.

Robert Briffault in his book, the Making of Humanity, had honestly expressed the indebtedness of Europe to the Arabs: "It was under the influence of the Arabs and the Moorish revival of culture and not in the 15th century, that a real renaissance took place. Spain, not Italy, was the cradle of the rebirth of Europe. After steadily sinking lower and lower into barbarism, it had reached the darkest depths of ignorance and degradation when cities of the Saracenic world. Baghdad, Cairo, Cordova and Toledo, were growing centres of civilization and intellectual activity. It was there that the new life arose which was to grow into a new phase of human evolution. From the time when the influence of their culture made itself felt, began the stirring of a new life.

"It was under their successors at the Oxford School (that is, successors to the Muslims of Spain) that Roger Bacon learned Arabic and Arabic Sciences. Neither Roger Bacon nor his later namesake has any title to be credited with having introduced the experimental method. Roger Bacon was no more than one of the apostles of Muslim Science and Method to Christian Europe; and he never worried of declaring that knowledge of Arabic and Arabic Science was for his contemporaries the only way to true knowledge. Discussions as to who was the originator of the experimental method .... are part of the colossal misrepresentation of the origins of European civilization. The experimental method of Arabs was by Bacon's time widespread and eagerly cultivated throughout Europe.

> "Science is the most momentous contribution of Arab civilization to the modern world; but its fruits were slow in ripening. Not until long after Moorish culture had sunk back into darkness did the giant which it had given birth to rise in is might. It was not science only which brought Europe back to life. Other and manifold influence from the civilization of Islam communicated its first glow to European life.

"For although there is not a single aspect of European growth in which the decisive influence of Islamic culture is not traceable nowhere is it so clear and momentous as in the .genesis of that power which constitutes the permanent distinctive force of the modern world, and the supreme source of its victory, natural science and the scientific spirit.

"The debt of our science to that of the Arabs does not consist in startling discoveries or revolutionary theories, science owes a great deal more to Arab culture, it owes its existence. The Astronomy and Mathematics of the Greeks were a foreign importation never thoroughly acclimatised in Greek culture. The Greeks systematised, generalised and theorised, but the patient ways of investigation, the accumulation of positive knowledge, the minute method of science, detailed and prolonged observations and experimental enquiry were altogether alien to the Greek temperament. Only in Hellenistic Alexandria was any approach to scientific work conducted in the ancient classical world. What we call science arose in Europe as a result of a new spirit of enquiry, of new methods of experiment, observation, measurement of the development of Mathematics, in a form unknown to the Greeks. That spirit and those methods were introduced into the European world by the Arabs.

It is highly probable that but for the Arabs, modern European civilization would never have arisen at all; it is absolutely certain that but for them, it would not have assumed that character which has enabled it to transcend all previous phases of evolution.

By the tenth century the intellectual superiority of the Arabs was recognised in Europe. The first Christian to take up the torch of learning was Gerbert (Pope Sylvester 11, d. 1003 A.D.). He introduced Arab astronomy and mathematics, and Arabic numerals in place of the clumsy Roman ones. He was followed by many, especially Constantinus Africanus in the eleventh century, and Bishop Raymond (Raimundo) in the twelfth century. As early as the eleventh century Toledo became a centre for the transmission of Arabic culture and science to Europe. Raymond (d. 1163 or 1164) established a regular school of translation at Toledo. A number of translators flourished there.

Among the scholars, who flocked to it from all over Europe, were Gerard of Cremona (d. 1187 A.D.). John of Seville, Under the supervision of Archdeacon Domenico Gundisalvi, and with the cooperation of the Hebrew Johannes ben David, the school of the Archbishop of Toledo rendered into Latin a large number of Arabic works on science and philosophy. Gerard, who was the Hunain ibn Ishaq of Toledo, translated into Latin more than seventy Arabic books on different subjects. Among his translations were the surgical part of Al- Tasrif of Al-Zanarawi, the Kitab al-Mansuri of Al-Razi and the Qanun of Ibn Sina, Banu Musa's works, Al-Beruni's commentary on Khawarizmi the tables of Jabir b. Aflah and Zarqawi. John of Seville under the patronage of Raymond translated several works of Avicenna, Qusta Ibn Luqa and Al-Farghani. Gundisalvi translated the Kitab al-Nafs (Anima), the Kitab al-Shifa (Sufficientia) of Ibn Sina, Al-Kullyat (Colliget) of Ibn Rushd's commentary on it. There were many other translators at Toledo who had neither command over the languages nor sufficient knowledge of the subject matter. They translated word for word and, where they failed to understand, Latinised the Arabic words.

The Italian Plato of Tivoli, Michael Scotus, Robert of Chester and Hermanns Allemanus (Teutonicus) were other famous translators of the thirteenth century. They flourished at Tarrangona, Leon, Segovia, Pamplona and other northern cities of Spain. Thus Spanish Arabic learning permeated through all Europe. It passed from the portals of Toledo through Provence and the Alpine passes into Lorrains, Germany, Central Europe and England. Constantine travelled for 30 years in Muslim lands and on his return he taught Arabian medical sciences at Salerno and translated Arabic works into Latin. Adelard of Bath was the first of a long series of Arabic scholars of England who travelled extensively in search of Arabic books. He visited Syria, Sicily and Spain.

On his return to England he translated several works on mathematics and astronomy. Among the most important works he translated was the astronomical tables of Al-Majriti (126 A.D.). Several European Orientalists like Mirabilis, after making the tour of the Muslim countries, were so much impressed that on their return home encouraged their students to leave the European schools for those of the Arabs and this yielded beneficial results. The valuable works of the Arab astronomers and scientists were widely studied in Europe and became basis of modern astronomy and science. Most of the star names in European languages are derived from Arabic origin such as Acrab (Aqrab-Scorpion) and Phurked (farqad-calf). In the mathematical vocabulary there are other examples of Arab influence. Algebra, Cenit (zenith), Nadir (nadii – the point opposite to the zenith), and Cipher are borrowed from Arabic words. Elixir (Ar. al-aksir-a kind of medicine). Alcohol (Ar. alkohol- highly rectified spirit of wine), Antimonlo (Ar. antimun, Eng. antimony), Alcanfor (Ar. Kafur, camphor), are examples of medical terms of Arabic origin commonly used in European languages.

> "Not till the education of Europe passed from the monasteries to the universities, not till Muslim science and classical forethought and industrial independence broke the sceptre of the church, did the intellectual revival of Europe begin."

The Achievements

At the present time when Physics, in its theories of Relativity, Quantum and Atom, is achieving startling advancements in the intellectual life of human race, the Muslims cannot allow themselves to remain indifferent to and ignorant of the ever-new discoveries in this field.

The theory of Relativity may be described as a new and peculiar theory of the nature and interconnection of 'space' and 'time'. The principal points of this theory are as follows:

1. Space and time have no existence apart from the rods and clocks with which they are measured.
2. The events whose relations constitute the spatio temporal order of nature are identical with the sense data of individual fields of experience. Einstein insists that they are not to be conceived as terminal effects of an external world, but rather they are to be conceived as overlapping and interpenetrating. In place of a world of extra-individual causes, stresses Montague, "we are to substitute a system of inter individual laws as the norm or standard for measuring and comparing our experiences. We are to adopt a relativistic form of epistemological monism rather than epistemological dualism of traditional science"
3. Space and time do not vary independently as Newton believed. They are as dependent upon each other as upon the experiences by which they are measured. When events are observed to happen they have no meaning apart from where they are observed to happen. Two events are intrinsically simultaneous only when they occur at the same place.
4. Time is the fourth dimension of our world whose other three dimensions are those of space. The four dimensional world of space time is hyperbolic. As regards the dimension of time, when free of gravitational or other forces, it is parabolic.
5. Einstein's "light" is the most wonderful thing in the world. Its velocity is a definite, finite quantity. Though

> finite, yet it behaves in one respect like zero and in another, like infinity. The movement of light in space combined with its movement in time causes it, as it were, to stand still. In short, light is for Einstein, the only absolute in a world where all else is relative.

Einstein's theory is based partly on an assumption and partly on facts. But according to the Michelson-Morley experiment, there is reason for doubting the assumption that the velocity of light is independent of the velocity of its source. In the same way Lorenz and Fitzgerald are not in agreement with the assumption of Einstein, enunciated above. Even it is true, it is apparently paradoxical. Any finite velocity previously imagined will give unequal results when unequal velocities are added to it. The velocity of light is like an infinite quantity in that any other velocity added to or subtracted from it leaves it unchanged.

The rest of the theory consists of the supplementary assumption which must be made in order to keep the primary assumption from conflicting with facts of observation. These assumptions, as we have seen, include the belief that not only measuring rods but clocks also change their units as they change their velocities, and that the velocities which cause these changes are not absolute with reference to a fixed ether, but relative to anything whatever. We must not belittle these assumptions by interpreting them merely as a new set of metrical conventions. They are partly methods to give subjective rates and partly (alleged) physical facts.

We need not indulge ourselves into the criticism of the theory, except stating the fact that there are situations in which the Einsteinian assumptions of the theory appear to contradict.

> "This puzzle, it may be noted, is touched upon by Eddington, though not so far as I have discovered, by Weyl, Eddington solves it rather lamely, as it seems to me by forbidding his traveller to Arcturus ever to

> return to earth and debate as to who really did the travelling, on the ground that the awkward situation thus created would be asymmetrical. But one would suppose that two people each of whom was younger than the other would suffer from an excess of symmetry rather than from a lack of it."

Under modern researches, we cannot suppose that light is made up of corpuscles emitted by bodies as they move, for light is, in all respects, is like a wave. What really counts in the motion of anything is not its change of position in a supposed absolute space, nor is it merely relative change of distance from any and every other object. From the Quranic Sura, Al-Asr which forms the universe of this paper it is clear that motion, in its space time dimensions, is the relation of the moving body to its own past and the relation of what moves to the source from which the motion originated. The meaning of the Sura may be conveyed by two terms "auto absolutism" and " intra- relativism." We have to take note of the fact that what counts in acceleration is neither the change with reference to an absolute space nor the change with reference to bodies outside the system and unconnected with it. The Quran says:

> "Glory be to Him Who created pairs of all things, of what the earth grows, and of their kind and of what they know not!

And a sign to them is the night: We draw forth from it the day, then lot they are in darkness;

And the sun moves on to its destination. That is the ordinance of the Mighty, the Knower.

And the moon. We have ordained for it stages till it becomes again as an old dry palm-branch.

Neither is it for the sun to overtake the moon, nor can the night outstrip the day. And everyone of them floats on in an orbit.

And a sign to them is that We bear their offspring in the laden ship.

And We have created for them the life thereof, whereon they ride.

And if We please, We may drown them, then there is no succour for them, nor can they be rescued.

The Verses clearly indicate that what does count in acceleration is the change of parts of a system with reference to one another, and this infra-relative change is at the same time auto-absolute that is, a register of the difference between the past and the present states of the system as a whole when the planets.- the sun and the moon were accelerated with uniform velocities they registered, in their motions, the differentiation of man's present state from his past.

Thus, the basic concepts of physical sciences are mass, space and time. The other conceptions are derived by combination of these notions. The philosophy had been under the influence of these sciences from the very inception, ultimately resolving their differences at the end of 19th century. Social sciences came under the influence of the physical sciences in the beginning of the 20th century. Thus the velocity of moving body is expressed by dividing the space, through which the body moves, by the time during which it moves; and the velocity of the body at any instant can be expressed by the limit approached by the fraction as 's' and 't' approach zero. Acceleration is the rate at which a velocity is changing. Force is the product of mass and the acceleration. Momentum can be expressed as the product of mass and velocity. Energy can be expressed as one-half of the product of mass and square of the velocity.

According to Prof. Karl Pearson, while these conceptions are sufficient for the ordinary purposes of mechanics, we could form concepts of higher orders of acceleration which would conform to the same laws of geometrical representation and combination as apply to simple acceleration as to velocities. The rate at which an acceleration was changing or tending to change would be the first of the higher orders of acceleration, and the rate at which this rate itself was changing or tending to change would be the second of the higher orders of acceleration. Each of these successive orders of acceleration is derived from the preceding order by dividing the time factor and taking the limiting value which he resulting fraction approaches as the numerator and denominator approach zero. This process is known as differentiation and the series of higher orders of acceleration which result from the process constitute what are called the higher derivatives of space with regard to time. Inasmuch as force is defined as the product of mass and simple acceleration to which mass is subject, we use the term "super-force" to denote the product of a mass factor and any higher order of acceleration which it may embody or to which it may be subject.

There are two kinds of apprehensions that are neither conception nor sense perception. I can apprehend an object with specific sensory qualities but not continuous with me in space or time. This is imaging. For example, I can call up the visual image of the front door of my house, or the auditory image of the tune of Yankee Doodle. Images of this sort are for some faint and schematic, and for others detailed and vivid. People differ a great deal in this respect, but whether the images are faint or vivid, they are not located or dated with reference to the person imaging them. They are like objects in a picture or events in a novel.

The other kind of apprehension that is neither conception nor sense perception is something which has no name. I am going to call it "a non-sensory perception." It is the opposit of imaging for imaging had the sensory content of a perceived object but lacked the consciousness of a space-time bridge connecting it with the perceived, and non-sensory perception has the, bridge but lacks the sensory content. I am immediately or directly aware of the space beyond the surface of an opaque wall, and of the time that is before and after the sense filled patch of duration that is termed my "specious present." I do not perceive what fills this trans sensory time and space. But I have a perceptual assurance of the space and time being there whether filled or empty. I think that it was this characteristic of space and time as experienced by us that made Kant call them neither concepts nor sense data but "a priori perception". For reasons which I cannot go into here, I feel that they guarantee their own authenticity or validity and that they are concrete and singular or individual rather than abstract and universal. All spaces and times are parts of one spare and one time.

Let us now turn from these old questions of the relation of space and time to the subjects that know them and to the objects that fill them, consider the newer question of the relation of space and time to each other.

What are their similarities, and what are their differences? Are they sufficiently similar to be fruitfully combined into a single four dimensional continuum of space-time or time-space containing and contained in and concrete realities? Are they co-dimensional attributes distinguishable in thought but as inseparable in existence as the length and breadth of a solid are inseparable from its thickness?

The independent or quasi -independent variable properties, shared in common by all elements of an assemblage, constitute its dimensions. Thus, the points of our space are a three dimensional assemblage because it is necessary and sufficient to define each of them in terms of these independently variable distance relations to someone of them chosen as is origin.

Now, the objects that occupy space or fill it with sensory content of some kind are differentiated from one another, irrespective of their content, in terms of the position or distance and direction of their points from a point chosen as origin. Thus, I can say that the middle point of a given object is distant from the middle point of the floor of this room one foot northward, two feet westward, and three feet upward. An object whose points were defined in this manner would be unambiguously placed in space; but in order to differentiate it from another similar object occupying the same points tomorrow or yesterday, it would be necessary to add a fourth independent variable, that of time. Then the object would not only be placed but also dated. Now, it is obvious that this fourth or temporal dimension is very similar to the dimensions of space, but it is also obvious that it possesses very puzzling points of difference. Let us try to formulate first the similarities, and then the differences, between time and a spatial dimensions;

1. The series of dates or instants is continuous and infinite like the series of one-dimensional point on a line.
2. Intervals of time are like internals of space in that they are measured in terms of specific sensory content and in relation to some point or instant chosen as origin.
3. Spatial objects have position or locus in virtue of the relation of their points to some other points chosen as origin, and in addition to their position, they have size and shape, in virtue of the relation of their points to one another. Their size is determined by the distances between their extreme of bounding points and their shape by the directional relation of the internal distances to one another. The size of a body is, then an extrinsic property depending on its relations to other bodies or to units of distance chosen independently of the body itself. The shape is an intrinsic property, because the directional relations of a body's internal distances are constant, regardless of what the units of distance may be or how it may change. A strictly one-dimensional object would have only size because there would be no

plurality of directions to be related. With reference to the time dimension, durations are like spatial lines in that quantitatively they differ only in size, that is, in being longer or shorter.

If the foregoing similarities of time to one dimensional space were the whole story, then indeed, time would long ago have been recognized to be not only a fourth variable, differentiating sensory objects from one another, and vaguely analogous to a spatial dimension, but quite definitely and simply as the fourth dimension of space.

It is because of the differences, either seeming or real, between the series of instants in time and the series of points on a line that we have had to wait until recently for the conception of four-dimensional continuum.

It is to be inferred from the Sura al-Asr that the dimensions are something more than mere independent variables. Not only is each of them a continuum in itself, but each is continuum with others. The Quran repudiates the traditional standpoint, which indicates that no such continuous passage from the time dimension to the other dimensions of space-time can be found. Apparently time is not so homogeneously and continuously different from a direction in space as is the latter from a direction perpendicular to it.

What the Quran has stated the scientists have now arrived at something like the four-dimensional continuum of space time. It was made known by Minkowski in the address Raum and Zeit. The world, as Minkowski calls it, consists of lines or histories whose intersections constitute episodes that as absolute and objective and which are separated from one another by spatiotemporal intervals also absolute and objective.

The aspect of reality which is not included in the four dimensional universe of world tracks is referred to by the Quran in its Sura al-Asr as the flow of the time. Time thus not only extends into the past and future but according to the Quran, it flows at uniform rate and in an irreversible direction:

> "And every nation has a term; so when its term comes, they cannot remain behind the least while, nor can they precede (it). (7 : 34).
>
> "He it is Who created you from clay, then He decreed a term. And there is a term named with Him; still you doubt". (6 : 2).

The verses above indicate that the movement or march of things through time differs in a peculiar way from all other movements - it differs in being universal and uniform. The now and then of time have many resemblances to the here and there of space. But there are two great differences. When a thing goes from here to there, the other things in the universe do not move with it, but when a thing goes from now to then, from today into tomorrow, everything else goes also and must go along with it. Nothing can go faster or slower in time than anything else. In short, time is a space differing from what we call "space" not in itself, but in the fact that all things move, and move together, in it, whereas in ordinary space things can move or not, and in different and opposite directions. Ordinary movements, are thus localized and differentiated from their environment. They are relative and therefore observable; but movement in time is universal and absolute, and therefore not noticed for what it is but ascribed confusedly to the flowing of time itself.

It is because of this march through time of the universe as a whole, with all things abreast, that there can be no such thing as an enclosure of empty time, though there might be of empty space. A true spatial vacuum may or may not be physically possible, but a temporal vacuum within existence is not even imaginable. In short, no matter what number of spatial dimensions a world might possess, so long as it moved as a whole in some further dimension, that motion, provided it was cumulative and therefore irreversible, would be felt as time. Outside the sphere is the future; inside the sphere is the past; on the growing, swelling surface is the present, which is the spatial plane of possible action and reaction of all material existence.

Now, the space of our actual world contains numerous material particles which interrupt its continuity and homogeneity. How shall we make the pure ether, which pervades the smooth surface of our soap-bubble universe, conform to the granular rigours of atomic existence? It is true that as long as nothing hinders the normal rate, the being will regard himself as moving in empty space. From the Sura al-Asr, we infer the following facts :

1. The striking, similarities and the striking contrasts between space and time, are harmonized and explained by the three dimensional system as the surface of a four dimensional hypersphere; and this hypersphere is to be conceived as possessing a uniform cumulative movement of expansion. We participate in it as the flow of passage of time.
2. Some, at least, of the material systems that move on the surface of three-dimensional space are pervaded by secondary systems composed of forms of potential energy which are created whenever motion is changed into stress. These systems extend down into the past below the three-dimensional surface of space. They are thick in the direction of the fourth dimension, but their thickness appears to us as the duration evidenced in the spacious present and in memory. They have all the characteristics of minds, and they are minds, initiated by means of the body, but not dependent on the body for their continuance.

The Quran interrelates the physical and psychical into one entity. Materialism, according to the Verses 7 : 23 to 25, will lead man to an idealism in which matter is not derived but transfigured. We must remember that there is a Mighty Energy that creates and pervades the expanding hypersphere of our four- dimensional universe. As the systems of energy that pervade our brains are in themselves our very souls, so too, that cosmic energy may be in itself a soul, akin to and in touch with our own.

From the Sura ar-Rahman, generally, and more particularly from its verse 29 stating that "every moment He is in a state (of glory)", it is clear that the history of the world is the history of the forming, deepening, and heightening of substance. It is a history that runs from chaos through countless ages of emerging cosmos. It is an evolution of time space within space-time of the growth within the res- extensa of substances of the type res-cogitans. Space and time are not only relative to the bodies and motions by which they are measured, they are relative to each other so that instead of a three-dimensional space in which matter is contained, and a one dimensional time in which changes are contained, we have a single four-dimensional continuum of "space time." This space-time is an inseparable aspect of mass and energy, which are themselves interdependent aspects of the same thing. While the time aspect continues to be regarded as infinite, the space aspect is finite though boundless.

The Quranic concept of space-time-causality is not only a problem of science, but it is in synchronicity related to the philosophy and the sociology in general and more particularly to the sociology of knowledge-sociology of science and has its own depth and level meanings. The Sura al-Asr refers to the facts enunciated above.

With the advent of Islam the types of culture, which where dominant, had to change. Not only the first principle was changed but a deep transformation of the meanings of the past cultures were also changed. The changes of meaning were experienced by the basic categories of human thought-time, space and causality etc. All these categories got an idealistically integrated meaning. Thus the above categories were related to the system of meanings and truths envisaged by the Quran in terms of Tauhid.

The Quran is the Book which has laid emphasis on the understanding of the implications of the problems of space time causality, because these categories are not only a priori principles but the conditions of the possibility of any cognition of any thinking and of any knowledge. They have to be present in human mind according to Sura al-Asr and the Hadith in order that the mind may grasp anything and know anything. There are three types of the concepts of space-time-relativity according to the three types of cultural mentalities :

1. Sensate (Polytheistic and, in our own time, the modern scientific and technological culture).
2. Ideational (People of the Book).
3. Idealistic (The Muslims).

Sensate and ideational mentalities admit that each fact or phenomenon has a cause or causes for its existence. As to what this cause is and where it is to be found, they differ. The ideational cultural mentality stresses on the super-sensory and the sensate on the sensory phenomena. Thus, ideational mentality will look only in the ideational world that lies behind or above the illusionary world of senses.

Repudiating this concept the sensate mentality will seek the cause in the sensory phenomena. Thus, for the sensate the principle of causation is to be found in the senses alone, otherwise the causal relationship would be unperceptible.

The super-sensory nature of cause (God) makes it unnecessary for ideational mentality to claim that the same cause is to be followed by the same effects. The spiritual, creature and free nature of supersensory causation agent permits to create any effect. George Berkeley is the example of the above concept. No doubt that such a conception of causality amounts to indeterminism.

Not only the People of the Book but even in some of the polytheists like the worshippers of heavenly bodies, as indicated by the Quran in the story of Ibrahim, the ideational concept of causality was widespread, but the predominant trend among them was the sensate causality. The symbolic representatives of the sensate causality were Namrod and Pharaoh. What was fore-told by the Quran centuries ago has been affirmed by the modern anthropologists and sociologists. We only refer L. Levy Brunt, E. Durkheim and L. Brunschieg. The very existence of magic and super-sensory religion among the people of the past like Pharaoh's people at the time of Moses in the form of belief in this or that deity or ceremonies of religions and magical character, in forms of sorcery; in divination; and in hundreds of similar mores and customs widely diffused among pre-historical and earlier stages of the historical people. All this is an evidence of the ideational and sensate conceptions of causality. From the detailed account of the peoples of the past during various prophetic periods in general, and Pharaoh and his people in particular it is to be concluded that the relative influences of ideational and sensate conceptions varied from people to people and was not constant among all the groups.

It has been pointed out by the Quran that there were variations even among the people of the Book. Most of them at the time of the advent of Islam were predominantly sensate and a few groups were ideational. Such a coexistence of ideational and sensate conceptions was poorly harmonized. This is why the Muslims are warned not to follow the fluctuating patterns of these people.

The Quran idealistically synthesizes between the two kinds of causes—empirical and super-sensory. God is taken ultimately as the Real Cause of what happens with and in the phenomenal world. If we are not wrong in our inference from the content and meaning of the stories of the Quran, it can be assumed that the end of each prophetic period is marked by a great shock, destruction and catastrophe of the world and man. When God sends His guidance again, at the emergence of each new prophetic era, terminating at the end of all prophets by the advent of the Last Prophet, world and mankind are reestablished in order, virtue, wisdom and values. Thus if the material cause belongs to the sensate world, the supreme final cause belongs to God. This theory of causality together with the whole system of philosophic scienticism of the Quran is an organic unity and cohesion of the transcendental, the sensate and the ideational.

The greatest contribution of the Muslims, inspired as they were by the Quran, was the replacement of the ideational conception of time-space-causality by the idealistic idea. From 15th to 20th Century the idealistic trend was changed. Through the works of Galileo, Gassendi, Pascal, Kepler, Newton and other great scientists the triumph of the sensate space-time causality was greatly facilitated. Francis Bacon, Montague, Thomas Hobbes, David Hume etc., gave further momentum to the study of the empirical causality of the empirical phenomena.

Hume opens the way for the development of the empiristic causality that passes later on through the works of Main de Biran and J. S. Mill and ends with K. Pearson's causality as a mere "routine of perception". It also paves the way for Kant's conception of causality as an a priori form of our mind. Other thinkers like Descartes, Malebranche, Spinoza, Leibnitz and Berkeley allowed the ideational cause to stay. What, however, rules their system is the sensate causality through experience or reason. In Leibnitz's Mona-dology, bodies i.e. the whole sensate universe, act as though, per impossible, there were no souls and souls act as if there were no bodies. Leibnitz freed the empirical world from the interference of super-empirical agency and declared it to be subjugated to purely mechanical laws. More than that, aptly remarks P. A. Sorokin, "that even the causation in the world of souls was greatly empiricized in spite of the formal declaration to the contrary."

In spite of solipsism, and ultimately theology. Bishop Berkeley's working conception of causality was purely empirical. Finally when Kant produced his critique he relegated the category of causality to the class of "forms of our mind", represented a dilution of the transcendentalism of the "retired Emeritus", and a complete justification of the purely empirical, purely sensate causality.

In the field of political and social science, sensate causality was given full swing by Montesquieu and Comte. In short, the 19th century sensate causality and sensate space-time conception drove entirely the ideational or idealistic conceptions from the highway of scientific and philosophical thought. In short most of the causalists assumed the principle of coexistence of a multitude of parallely developing causal claims in the world. There are different factions of sensate causality in the modern time, developing since the 19th century:

(a) Functional causality.

(b) Mathematical causality.

(c) Mechanical causality.

(d) Dynamic causality.

In recent sociology, Durkheim's conception is an example of the sensate causality. What is implied, first of all, in the notion of causal relation is the idea of efficacy of productive power, of active force. By cause is usually meant that which is susceptible of producing a determined change. Effect is the same power but actualized.

As we move from the 17th to 20th century, uniformities, with a high and low degree of probability, become dominant.

This transformation has been proceeding parallel with the growth of the functional mathematical understanding of a causal bond; and naturally parallel with the growth of empiricism, positivism, neo-positivism, agnosticism, empirico-criticism, pragmatism and epistemological and ontological relativism (Positivists beginning with Comte, Poincare Mach, K. Pearsoins, Max Well, Pareto, Heisenberg and Einstein etc.).

There is a great difference between the causal relationship and causal law understood as necessary and the causal relationship and law understood as a mere association with higher and lower probability. The Quranic idea of causality is void of the above susceptibility and skepticism. All causal relationship and law are necessary corollary of life and the phenomenal world. It is strange, indeed, that in the thought patterns of the eminent scientists like K. Pearsons, H. Poincare and Einstein, we have the extremist form of the sensate causality, that throws out everything except the data of observation and sensory perception. Like empiricism in the theory of Knowledge; temporalism in the conception of reality and relativism in ethics, it turns the world and reality into something liquid, frameless, uncertain, indeterminate and fantastic. "The development of this conception," writes Prot. P A. Sorokin, "has led to a skepticism in science, in empiricism, in the very foundations of our knowledge at the end of the nineteenth and in the twentieth century. Before our eyes this current is putting the finishing touches to its own strangulation and self destruction."

Like the conception of causality there have been three different conceptions of time-ideational, sensate and idealistic. If ideational time is an emanation or manifestation of the supersensory reality, the sensory things determined the sensate time. This unit of time in the ideational conception is not infinitely divisible, while in the sensate time, the division is mechanical and quantitative. Ideational time knows no past, present and future and it is always qualitative. After Aristotle, the Quran is in an idealistically integrated form, gave the empirical conception of time, emphasizing that movement cannot be separated from the notion of time. From the Quranic concept of Dahr and the sociological philosophy involved in the Sura al-Asr it is to be assumed that the movement is to be measured by time and time by movement. The Quranic analysis does not stop here. It is clear from the Sura al-Asr that time exists objectively outside of our mind. Every motion may be a measure of time. Considering the cosmology, physics, and finally, the metaphysics, one knows that firmament is purely empirical universe. It is, according to the Quran composed of layers of concentric spheres enclosed in one another.

> And He it is Who created the night and the day and the sun and the moon. All float in orbits"
>
> (21 : 32).

Of these spheres the ultimate spheres of the stars is the proper measure of time:

> "And certainly We have adorned this lower heaven with lamps and We make them means of conjectures for the devils, and We have prepared for them the chastisement of burning" (67 : 5).

From this the Quran goes one step further. Time is the measure of the movement of the immobile first mover who imports motion to everything else. I am persuaded to believe that the Quranic term Kun (2 : 117) has not adequately been interpreted. In its insistence that the world was created by God not in time, but with time the verse above is an indication that no time existed before the world was created. Time was created simultaneously with the universe.

The periods before the advent of Islam were the periods of ideational conception. Islam substituted this one-sided view of time with Idealistic conception and declared that space and time are inseparable from each other and also from the things with which they are connected. Time and space as categories of thought, according to the Quran, precede any cognition of any phenomena. In the time continuum things pass from sensate nonexistence to sensate existence, and then to sensate nonexistence again, which is the achievement of the end set for them and an engulfment in the super sensate world of the universality.

'Time, in the light of the Quran, may be classified into three categories :

(1) Eternal-timeless eternity where no 'becoming' exists—

(2) Intermediary between transcendental eternity and sensate tempus with accidental change—

(3) Tempus or time as merely sensate phenomenon bound with the motion and change, and as such divisible into moments :

> In its analysis the Quran lays emphasis on the ever-passing nature of time against and its divisibility into moments, so much so the prayer is hardly meaningful and perfect if it is not offered at the proper time (4 : 103).
>
> As such it is a series of changing moments inseparably bound with ever changing empirical phenomena that come and pass, are born and disappear (16 : 77).

In its empirical framework the two categories of time as Abd and Burzakh with their usual transcendental aspects, convey an idea of importance of time in human life and culture. Thus, the Quranic ideationalization goes with the sensitization of time. It does not mean the rejection of eternity.

With the human time the Quran refers to the Infinite Divine Time—Ayamallah. These conceptions of time are totally different with the conceptions of the modern scientists and philosophers like Descartes, Spinoza, Hobbes, Hime, Leibnitz,

Locke, Kant, Bergson, Minkowski and Einstein etc. As we have shown above "time is the duration of things" according to Descartes. Spinoza distinguishing duration, time and eternity, stresses eternity more than Descartes does, but gives to it a meaning somewhat remote from time. Time becomes purely empirical, a derivative of the motion or change, existing either in our mind or in the sensate world outside of it. This equally applies to Hobbes, Leibnitz, Locke, Hume, Berkeley and other thinkers.

When we pass to Newton's conception we come his absolute and relative times. The absolute is supersensory time and abstract, beyond and behind which there stands no God. In short, his concept of time is something intermediary between ideational and sensate time. Later on he went beyond this and admitted God and a duration of ideational type. Kant's critical conception of time as an a priori form of our mind or of intuition, left the reality of time per se, as open question and justified the empirical time as property of all temporal phenomena ding an sich und fur sich (thing as it is and for itself). He writes: derzeit nur die form der anschsauuing within der gegen stunde als erscheinungenist. Time is the only form exhibiting the present its background of past events.

In the modern age, not only supersensory time is rejected as absurd, but even the sensate time, stresses Prof. Sorokin, is made "dependent of the purely sensate phenomena of change without which it has no existence, no meaning,, no use". In this mentality the past, as well as the future, tended to fade away more and more, leaving only the present, and this present has tended to be reduced to shorter, and shorter, fleeting, rushing moments.

It is surprising indeed that reaction against the dichotomous concepts of sensate time of the twentieth century and the ideational time of the previous centuries in favour of idealistic concept advocated by the Quran has begun to appear. One of them is the restoration of the qualitative time by Bergson. Another is Minkowski-Einstein's "space-time continuum", which in a sense is also a revolt against the extreme sensate time.

The history of the conception of time is very old, but as a matter of fact, time was never considered either seriously or in its socio-spiritual framework. It was the Quran which for the first time invited the attention of man to think over it seriously and with socio-cultural and psycho-spiritual implications. And again, it was the Quran which logico-meaningfully related time with its interdependent element, the space. These concepts of the Quran were taken up unconsciously and unadmittedly by the modern age. So Alexander discloses this fact in this way:

> "The most characteristic feature of the thought of the last twenty five years (is) the discovery of time. I do not mean that we have waited until today to become familiar with time: I mean that we have only just begun (again I would like to add) to take time seriously."

The multiple description of the Quran in relation to the believers and the various types of faith-rejectors developed from time to time during the various prophetic ages. It is clear that the content and meanings of space varied greatly from culture to culture and period to period. These diverse conceptions of space fall easily into ideational, sensate and idealistic conceptions. The ideational concept was held by the People of the Book and the sensate by the faith-rejectors and the modern Western and American nations, in view of their adherence to sensate culture guided by the sensate cultural mentality. Islam, as an idealistic religion, advocated idealistic concept of space, uniting ideational and sensate concepts into one composite whole. And again, time and space were not categorized and identified into two different entities. They are one and the some.

The one-sided conceptions of space developed by ideational as well as by sensate culture were rejected by the Quran because for instance ideational space derived nothing from the sensory space with its three or more sensory dimensions. Ideational space is often thought of merely as a centre of supersensory phenomena, The dichotomous orientation about space in the ideational and sensate cultures, has been rejected by the Quran and this has been approved by a modern authority, P A-Sorokin, in this way :

> that for the "location" of a large portion of socio-cultural phenomena and values, sensory space is inadequate and, whether we want it or not, at least a kind of mixed (Ideational sensate) spatial system is unavoidable.

The Chinese, the Hindus and the Greeks developed ideational concept of space and time, a thing diametrically opposed to the idealistic Islamic viewpoint. This fact alone is a clear indication in relation to the fabricated view of the Western scholars, about the borrowing from the sources referred to above.

The triumph of Christianity after Chinese, Hindus and Greeks led again to the rise of the ideational conception of space. In conformity with this ideational trends cosmogenic theories of the universe and its spatial structure were developed. When these cosmogenic pictures are taken, the contrast between ideational and sensate conceptions comes out clearly. When one sees a firmament of the cosmogonies of the Church fathers like Isidore of Seville, Bede, Rhabanus, Walafrid Strabo, Honorius, Hugo St. Victor, Prstrus and others one is simply bewildered. The whole mentality is altered from one sensate atmosphere to ideational conception.

As it is said in the Holy Scripture there are waters above the firmament— these waters are, by the place they occupy, above any corporal creatures (St. Isidore).

The end of the 19th and in the beginning of the 20th century, one finds the signs of revolt against pure sensate concept of space. It is indicated by the construction of Minkowski-Einstein's four dimensional space-time continuum by Bergson and treatment of space as relaxation of the elan vital resulting in its extension. Even these modern views are not free from dichotomy and hence they are contrary to the idealistic view of space enunciated by the Quran.

However sketchy the analysis of the conception of causality, time and space may be, one is guided to conclude that in the long history of these concepts it is the Quran alone which has stressed time, space and causality as the fundamental categories of human thought, socio-cultural phenomena, spirituality and the development of society, personality, nature and culture. It is the Quran which has undoubtedly demonstrated that each of these categories—time, space and causality has indeed ideational and sensate forms, contents and meanings:

> By the declining day. Lo! man is in a state of loss. Save those who believe and do good works, and exhort one another to truth and exhort one another to endurance (104 : 1-3).

This Sura conveys another historical fact i.e. that each of these forms rose and declined (Ideational by People of the Book and Sensate by Kafiroon) with the rise and decline of the respective culture, but they are all wrong and bound to decline. The only valid and everlastingly true form is the idealistic form in which sensate and ideational concepts merge into one indivisible and continuous whole. This unity of ideational and sensate space-time has been declared in symbolic form saying that there are not two or three gods:

> "O" People of the Book, exceed not the limits in your religion nor speak anything about Allah, but the truth. The Messiah Jesus, son of Mary, is only a messenger of Allah and His word which He communicated to

> Mary and a mercy from Him. So believe in Allah and His messengers. And say not, Three-Desist! (it is) better for you. Allah is only one God. Far be it from His glory to have a son. To Him belongs whatever is in the heaven and whatever is in the earth. And sufficient is Allah as having charge of affairs".
>
> (4 : 171).

The character of the space-time system of the Islamic society and culture is to be determined by the very understanding of the nature of its socio-cultural and spiritual life and its pulsation. Its time system is always a reflection of the pulsation and beats of its socio-cultural life and is conditioned by it. In this sense, the time and space system and their units are social conventions. This symbolic unity of time and space and the representation of their social convention is to be discovered and identified in a place like mosque. The periodicity or non-periodicity of the socio-cultural process is to be measured and determined entire through time system. The meanings and the ideal of the Islamic society cannot be determined in any other way. Time system is a kind of social convention, moulded by and reflecting the real beats and pulsations of the socio-cultural and spiritual processes. It follows that any periodicity in the processes has to be in the nature of a social convention. It is detected through the conventional tools of the time units used and by its nature, it is of socio-cultural character, as one of the beats or punctuations in the flow of the socio-cultural processes.

In contradistinction to "being", any "becoming", change, process motion, movement and dynamism etc. implies time. Thus time, according to the Quran, is unavoidable to mark the beginning and end of a process, its time duration, its velocity, its location with regard to other processes. It is the greatest contribution of the Quran that instead of the blurred viewpoint of the medieval ages, the Quran gave definite concept, regarding usual time and usual space with social time and social space. As a matter of fact, for their adequate description the socio-cultural phenomena require a special category of social space, social time with their own system of coordination. This statement has been clarified by the Quran in relation to mosque as social space and prayer in relation to social time :

(a) (i) "So when you have finished the prayer, remember Allah standing and sitting and reclining. But when you are secure, from danger, keep up (regular) prayer. Prayer indeed has been enjoined on the believers at fixed times" (4 : 103).

"Keep up prayer from the declining of the sun till the darkness of the night, and the recital of the Quran at dawn. Surely the recital of the Quran at dawn is witnessed" (7:78).

"So bear patiently what they say, and celebrate the praise of thy Lord before the rising of the sun and before its setting, and glorify (Him) during the hours of night and parts of the day, that thou mayest be well pleased" (20: 130).

(ii) "Say: My Lord enjoins justice. And set upright your faces at every time of prayer and call on Him, being sincere to Him in obedience. As He brought you into being, so shall you return" (7 : 21).

(iii) "O children of Adam, attend to your adornment at every time of prayer, and eat and drink and be not prodigal; surely He loves not the prodigals" (7 : 31).

(iv) "Only Allah is your Friend and His Messenger and those who believe, those who keep up prayer and pay the poor-rate, and they bow down" (5: 55).

(b) (i) "And who is more unjust than he who prevents (men) from the mosques of Allah, from his name being remembered therein, and strives to ruin them? (As for) these, it was not proper for them to enter them except in fear. For them is disgrace in this world, and theirs is a grievous chastisement in the Hereafter"

(2 : 114).

(ii) "(It is) in houses which Allah has permitted to be exalted and His name to be remembered therein. Therein do glorify Him, in the mornings and evenings.

Men whom neither merchandise nor selling diverts from the remembrance of Allah and the keeping up of prayer and the paying of the poor-rate—they fear a day in which the hearts and the eyes will turn about" (24; 36,37).

The verses under (a) and (b) refer to the direction of a socio-cultural process. They can be reduced to four classes:

(a) Time direction (see 4 : 103,11 : 114,17: 78, 20 : 130).

(b) Space direction (2 : 114, 9: 17).

(c) Quantitative direction, and

(d) Qualitative direction (2 : 238, 29 : 45, 2 : 117).

The time specification of a process comes out in the form of duration (for instance 20 : 130). This specification is of the utmost importance from the practical point of view. The fasting in the month of Ramadan, Hajj in the month of Dhul Hijja, and the daily prayers exactly at the specified time and many other forms of time days specification of the direction of a process is one of the most important traits of the Islamic culture and the personality development of the Muslims. Time direction with either space direction (Masjid) or qualitative or quantitative direction in the forms of Rakats in prayers and apportionment of Zakat and Sadaqa, gives a series of cumulative or combined derivative directions styled by the terms velocity, tempo rhythms of the Islamic socio-cultural process called by the Quran as Deen. Except this socio-cultural system, the other socio-cultural types like the ideational and sensate are not recognized by the Quran:

> "Surely the (true) religion with Allah is Islam. And those who were given the Book differed only after knowledge had come to them, out of envy among themselves. And whoever disbelieves in the messages of Allah - Allah indeed is Quick at reckoning. But if they dispute with thee say: I submit myself entirely to Allah and (so does) he who follows me. And say to those who have been given the Book and the Unlearned (people): Do you submit yourselves. If they submit, then indeed they follow the right way; and if they turn back, thy duty is only to deliver the message. And Allah is Seer of the servants" (3: 18,19). And whoever seeks a religion other than Islam, it will not be accepted from him, and in the hereafter he will be one of the losers" (3 : 84).

There is dichotomy again in the modern concepts of space time, whereas one finds unitary concept in relation to these categories by the Quran. The space and time of the Physics are correlated and intertwined with the social space end social time. The social space and the social time originate from physical space and the physical time and in this way social space and social time become the qualitative and quantitative categories of thought and culture.

This co-relate refers to another important feature of the idealistic socio-cultural system of Islam. The time synchronicity and space adjacency in the incessant or recurring changes, as a criterion of a change in togetherness and as an evidence of the existence of causal connection between the changing variables. For instance, the prayers outside the limits and scopes of the specified time makes the prayers defective or the prayers are to be offered in the mosque, otherwise it will lose its cumulative effect and socio-cultural significance.

The contribution of Muslims to Western Science has been very great, but not acknowledged as such by the Orientalists of Europe and America, and much less recognized by the European Scientists of the present day, although the latter have based their researches and discoveries on the labours of the Muslim scholars of Medieval times. George Sarton, the great historian of Science has very ably narrated the facts relating to the contribution of the Muslims to Science during the Middle Ages. He pays a glowing tribute to Muslim scholars and their attainments when he says that:

> "The most valuable of all, the most original and the most pregnant (works) were written in Arabic. From the second half of the eighth to the end of the eleventh century. Arabic was the scientific, the progressive language of mankind. During that period anyone wishing to be well informed and up-to-date, had to study Arabic. It will suffice here to evoke a few glorious names without contemporary equivalents in the West: Jabir ibn Haiyan, al-Kindi, al-Khwarizmi, al-Farghani, al-Razi, Thabit ibn Qurra, all-Battani, Hunain ibn Ishaq, al-Farabi, Ibrahim ibn Siman, al-Masudi, al-Tabari, Abul-Wafa, Ali ibn Abbas, Abul Qasim, Ibn al-Jazzar, al-Beruni, Ibn Sina, Ibn Yunus, al-Karkhi, Ibn al-Hatham, Ali ibn Isa, al Ghazzali, al-Zaqali, Umar Khayyam—a magnificent array of names which it would not be difficult to extend. If anyone tells you that the Middle Ages were scientifically sterile, just quote these men to him : All of these scientists flourished within a relatively short period between 750 and 1100."

During the twelfth and thirteenth centuries there was a scientific renaissance in Europe and European scholars went to study Arabic Sciences in the Universities of Spain, Egypt, Syria and Morocco. By the middle of the thirteenth century innumerable Arabic works were translated into Latin and were studied with great interest and enthusiasm by the scholars of

Europe. Most of these works were prescribed as text books in their Universities, which laid the foundation of scientific enquiry and research in the West and led the scholars to make great discoveries and inventions. "It must be owned", says Moshein the author of the Ecclesiastical History, "that all the knowledge, whether of Physics, Astronomy, Philosophy or Mathematics which flourished in Europe from the tenth century, was originally derived from the Arabian scholars." In a word, the literature, arts and sciences of the Arabs formed the connecting link between the civilization of ancient and modern times.

A historian may, by his religious fervour or national bias, proclaim the intellectual superiority of his nation over the others, but a scholar or a scientist is expected to trace the source of his knowledge by which he is guided and enlightened in his studies and can well appreciate the work already carried out in the field by his precursors. But the modern scientists, barring a few honourable exceptions, do not even mention, or are ashamed to mention, the work done by others, or are quite ignorant of the labours of the early masters who laid the foundation of scientific thought and augmented on the already existing knowledge by their researches and personal observations. However in the sphere of natural and physical sciences the labours of Muslim scholars are so outstanding and conspicuous that if you take the science of alchemy alone which has greatly influenced and contributed much to modern chemistry, we may quote a veteran German scholar Julius Ruska of the Berlin University the greatest living authority on the history of Muslim Science, who says:

> "Arabic alchemy has developed so much and in so peculiar a way beyond that of the Greeks, and it had so exclusively influenced Occidental alchemy that the students of medieval sciences could not find a more attractive task than to trace the paths, until now mostly obscure, which the development once followed."

The science of alchemy was in vogue among the ancient nations: The Babylonians and Egyptians are well known for their fondness for preparing gold and silver by the alchemical process. The Greeks had also a great fascination for it. But the Muslim Arabs were the only nation who paid much attention to the development of alchemy as a science, in which they made great discoveries and invented such chemicals that are so helpful to other sciences like Mineralogy, Botany, Medicine, Engineering etc. The Muslims were so much interested in this science that it formed a part of their higher studies. According to Rhazes, or al-Razi, a man, however well-versed in philosophy, cannot be called a philosopher in the real sense unless he is well-acquainted with the science of alchemy.

From the first century of Hijra, the Muslims began to take interest in alchemy which was greatly developed at their hands for five centuries. According to H. G. Wells, in chemistry they made a good beginning. They discovered many new substances, such as potash, nitrate of silver, corrosive sublimate and nitric and sulphuric acid. The great historian Gibbon says that the science of chemistry was its origin and improvement to the industry of the Saracens.

Among the Muslim scientists that might be mentioned as cultivators of alchemy, we may recall Jabir ibn Haiyan, Zun-Noon of Egypt, Razi, Abid, Umail, Tughrai, the author of an alchemical poem, Jildaki and a host of others. Jabir, well known as Geber in the early Latin translations, is famous as the founder of alchemy. The researches and experiments carried by Jabir and his improved method for evaporation, filtration, sublimation, calcination, melting, distillation and crystallization are well known. He described the preparation of many chemical substances, e.g., cinnabar, sulphide of mercury, arsenics, oxides and others. He knew how to obtain nearly pure vitriols, alums, alkalis, sal-ammoniac and saltpetre, how to produce the so-called liver and milk of sulphur by beating sulphur with alkali. He prepared pure mercury oxide and sublimate, as well as acetates of lead and other metals. He understood the preparation of crude sulphuric and nitric acids as well as their mixture, aqua regia and the solubility of gold and silver in this acid.

Thus it was Muslim Jabir who acquainted Europe with the alchemy of the East and it is admitted by all the historians of science that he was the father of modern chemistry. Jabir was also an able theoretician and in his treatises we find remarkably sound views on methods of chemical research. A theory on the geological formation of metals, the sulphur mercury theory of metals, preparation of basic lead carbonate, arsenic and antimony from their sulphides. Jabir deals with various applications i.e. refinement of metals, preparation of steel, dyeing of cloth and leather, varnishes and water-proof cloth and protect iron, use of manganese dioxide in glass-making, use of pyrites, for writing in gold, distillation of vinegar to concentrate acetic acid. He observed the imponderability of magnetic force.

Sarton has rightly remarked that "he appears already as a very great personality, one of the greatest in medicinal science." The alchemical writings of Jabir were translated into Latin during the Middle Ages. The first such version, the Book of the composition of alchemy, was made by the Englishman Robert of Chester in A.D. 1144. The translation of the Book of the Seventy into Latin was one of the achievements of the famous Gerard of Cremona (d. 1187). A work entitled the Sum of Perfection is ascribed to Jabir by the English translator Richard Russel (1678) who described him as Geber, the most famous Arabian Prince and Philosopher.

Much evidence linking Geber of the Latin writers with the Arabic alchemist has recently appeared from the pen of Dr. E. J. Holmyard, of the Clifton College, Bristol. Among other works of Jabir there are certain works which prove that he recognized more clearly and stated more definitely the importance of experiment than any other early chemist. Thus he was able to make great advances in both the theory and practice of the subject. According to Max Meyerhoff, his influence could be traced throughout the whole historic course of European alchemy and chemistry.

After Jabir early in the ninth century the study of alchemy was prosecuted further with vigour by Muslim scientists, particularly in Persia, Egypt and Spain. The Persian physician al-Razi (d. 925) was a great alchemist who has left a lucid and logical classification of chemical substances. Although dependent partly on the same sources as Jabir, Razi excels him in his clear description of chemical process and apparatus. While other alchemists divide mineral substances into "bodies", "souls" and "spirits" al-Razi classifies alchemical substances as vegetable, animal or mineral, a conception which comes from him in modern speech. The importance of Razi's alchemical work has been brought to light during the last few years only. His great book on the art of alchemy was recently discovered. He was the first to introduce chemical preparation into the practice of medicine.

Later Muslim chemists, Ibn Umail, al-Tughrai and Abul-Qasim of Iraq, made some progress and wrote several books on alchemy. The Muslim alchemists gave to the West several chemical terms which have passed from Jabir's Arabic writings through Latin into European languages and are generally used in modern chemistry with great advantage. Their Arabic origin is recognizable prima facie in their Latinized form. Among these are: Alernbic, Alkali, Alum, Aludel, Athomor, Azymum, Cinnabar, Elixir, Tutia, Use fur, Ziniar, Alcohol and a host of others. In the history of chemistry Lavoisier is accredited with being the founder of his science, but according to the French Orientalist Dr. Lebon it must be remembered that no science either of chemistry or any other science, was discovered all of a sudden. The Arabs had established one thousand years ago their laboratories in which they used to make experiments and publish their discoveries, without which Lavoisier would not have been able to produce anything in this field. It can be said without the fear of contradiction that owing to the researches and experiments of the Muslim Scientists modern Chemistry came into being and that it produced great results in the form of great scientific inventions, viz, the Steam, the Electricity, the Telegraph, the Telephone, the Radio, the Photography, the Cinematography and so on.

The study of history of biological science from Greek to the 13th-14th centuries is linked up with a great mass of related sciences including Medicine, Anatomy and Biogeography etc. In the period under review one has to read the important works of Zakriya al-Razi (865-925), Ibn Sina (980-1037), Abu Raihan al-Beruni (973-1014), Zakriya Qazvini (d. 1283), Al-Dameri (1372), Kamal-ud-Din al-Farsi (d. 1320), Al-Ghazzali (d. 1111), together with a host of herbals specially those by Ibn Baitar and Al-Dinwari and on natural vegetation by Al-Qazwini (d. 1283). A very useful information about the animals and plants of land and sea would be obtained from the books of Al-Qazwini, Ibn Sina, Al-Razi, Al-Edrissi, Ibn Nafees Damishqui (d. 1289) and of Shamsuddin Al-Damishqi (d. 1307) edited by A. Mehran, from Copenhagen (d. 1564). The history of these sciences shows phenomenal development unparallelled ever before. We can witness a great fusion of philosophy and sciences under the common umbrella of Islamic effort to acquire knowledge from whichever source it would be available. The period under review was preceded by early years of translation followed by pooling in common resources of languages and ideas from outside. The period shows the growth of a special pattern of knowledge by all classes of people.

A complete discard of isolation and an unprecedented enthusiasm for evolving precise scientific method is a landmark of this effort. Thus in the world of Islam we get the ingredients of sciences from Greeks, Romans, Egyptians, Russians, Hindus, Chinese, Ceylonese and all localised efforts with common language as Arabic and not because it was dominated by any established dynasty but because of its great and comprehensive treasures of scientific work.

However, the stimulus come from the early days of Abbasides especially Caliph Abu Jafar al-Mansur who established a translation bureau followed by Illustrious caliphs like Harun-ur-Rashid (776-809), Mamunur Rashid (d. 833) and Al-Mutawakkil who in 1856 refounded the library and translation bureau. The pursuit of knowledge was objective, critical and constructive. All facilities and requirements for scientific research prescribed by Al-Beruni such as early education, knowledge of languages, long life, possession of means to make journeys and acquire books and instruments were amply fulfilled.

The knowledge acquired was not only exponential in nature but was even moulded into technology such as mechanics, hydraulics, agricultural and ophthalmological. In order to assist and evaluate the actual advancement of sciences and breakthrough the then existing frontiers, it is time that the original works of these authors should be examined in the light of modern works, in this way alone, it will be possible for us to trace the base line and fundamental discoveries of these centuries and find out the precise value and significance of the works of the scholars in Islamic countries.

Science during this period is neither racial, nor national, nor regional but it is a combined effort of the old world, comprising Europe, Asia and Africa. There is a real contact, collaboration and impact of sciences and scientists of all parts of the world especially from Spain, Egypt, Asia Minor and important centres of modern world located in Iran, Uzbekistan, Turkemenia, Afghanistan, India and Western China.

The spirit of investigation in these centuries is highlighted by Al-Ghazzali (d. 1111) in the following words:

> "Man has been truly termed a microcosm or a little world in himself and the structure of his body should be studied not only by those who wish to become physicians but also by those who wish to attain to a more intimate knowledge of Allah. Just as close study of the niceties and shades of language in a great poem reveals to us more and more of the genius of its author".

This is a superb exposition of Islamic point of view for seeking knowledge and with particular reference to man and his anatomy.

Works of Muslim Scholars : Apart from the books written by the famous Al-Razi, Al-Beruni and Ali lion Sina, many of which remain unpublished and unstudied, important sources hitherto neglected are Arabic works such as those written by Ali Baitar, Al-Dinwari, Al-Edrisi. Although most of these Arab writers belonged to the western Kingdoms of Islam, these works were accessible to the scholars of Central Asia. Other relatively more important sources of knowledge of plants and animals are the books of geography such as those written by Al-Masudi, Al-Beruni and Ibn Hauqal.

Very little attention has been paid to another important source of information of plants and animals contained in the book of science called cosmography. The scope of cosmography ranged from the elements of cosmology to study of physical geography, geology, oceanology and of animals and plants of land and water. In this connection one of the most important works which has attracted great interest in the Indian subcontinent and the Middle-East was that of Zakariyya bin Muhammad bin Mahmood al-Qazvini (1208 - 1263). His famous work Al-Ajaib al-Mukhluqat al-Haiwanat wal Gharaib al-Maujoodat is a treasure of knowledge. Yet another work which is of a later period but more scientifically processed and presented is that of Shams-ud-din al-Damishqui (1256-1327).

His work is known as Nukhbatul- Dahrfi Ajaib al-Barr wal Bahr. It is indeed a comprehensive treatise on animals, plant geography, minerals and cosmography. These two works deserve critical study for their elements of biological and geological sciences.

The work of Qazvini has been translated into Persian as well as Urdu. Though it contains a lot of unauthentic stories, yet the information about animals and plants is fairly reliable. It also contains interesting information about the anatomy and physiology of various organs. The second book Nukhbatul Dahr of Damishqui gives an account of the distribution of animals in the rivers of Asia and Africa with illustrations of porpoises, fishes and extensive description of water fauna, such as crocodile and octopus.

Another important book which the author has also studied is Kitab al-jamaher by Al-Beruni. It contains a description of minerals and of pearl formation.

Study of Anatomy : The study of anatomy had attracted a great many scholars in addition to Al-Razi and lion Sina. An account of the organs is given by Al-Qazvini. The organs of circulation have been described by Ibnul Nafees al-Damishqui (1208-1289) and organs of sight by Kamal-ud-Din al-Farsi (died 1320). A famous book written by Ali Ibn Isa al-Tabib from Baghdad (1000) gives also an interesting account of the organ-mostly adopted from the Greek writers.

A great break-through of the then existing knowledge in zoology, which was accumulated before the 9th century, was achieved by Al-Jahiz of Basra (868) who described the migration of birds and the life histories of locusts and bees never known before. The observations on organic evolution by Al-Beruni in his book Al-Jamaher are more precise than ever given before. The functions of heart and brain described by Aristotle have been completely refuted by Ibn Nafees al-Damishqui and Zakariyya Qazvini. According to Qazvini:

(1) The arteries arise from the left ventricle so as to infuse the pure air in the entire body and veins from the right side.

(2) Sympathetic nerve organ.

One organ is connected with the membrane of the heart and it is grown from the brain. It has two functions, one being perception. It is connected with a nerve so that it can address itself to the heart. The second function of the organ is related to emotions of grief and joy, which are incidental impacts from outside on the body. When the news of these emotions reaches the heart subsequent to their impact they should be coordinated or associated with the brain, which is the originator of perception. Hence this connecting organ has its origin from the brain.

Aeration means that pure and cool air which passes through the mouth is absorbed by the lung and is transmitted to the heart. Thereafter, the warm air is attracted towards the lung and removed to outside. It has two branches. One branch goes to the cavity (space) of the chest on the right side of the heart so as to give benefit of life until the lung is sound and the other branch provides aeration to the heart from the left if either side is damaged.

Organic Evolution : "The corals are vegetative stones or stony vegetation. In their origin they are in between plants and minerals. Hence they are the connecting links between the two. Their place is among minerals but it is in the first category of plants. Similarly "Date Palm" and Mimosa sp. are in the last category of plants and the first category of animals. Similarly apes, cats, parrots and the sea mermaids which are connecting links between Animals and Man. They are in the last place of animals and first place of mankind. Similarly the 'Wild Man (Gorilla?)' are placed in place of man and human being.

Mankind is one among the multiple species. Unit evolved from Carnivores, through Herbivores (cattle) then through apes till it was socialised.

Brain : The spirit of soul arises from the brain and emerging from the brain moves into the nerves till it covers the entire body. The brain in its length has three cavities and these three cavities have breadth or wide body. The breadth of the brain cavity (first part) has two parts. The anterior part is a perceptibly separate. The hind ventricle of the brain is also large since it is the place of origin of the spinal chord and from it arises the "Motor spirit". It is also responsible for the power of "memorisation" The middle ventricle of the brain is a perforated passage between the anterior and the posterior parts. "Veins are vessels like arteries." These contain impure blood while arteries contain pure blood.

Heart : It is covered by a fine membrane which is called (pericardium). The heart has a cavity in which blood is received from the liver and is stored. In the heart, there is a left ventricle from which gas (pure aerated air) arises. This ventricle is larger than the right ventricle, since the body needs more of aerated air than animal blood. Between the two ventricles, there is a pore across which blood flows from right to left and aerated air from left to right.

Aristotle (384-322 BC) on the other hand held that the heart was the seat of intelligence and the brain was functioning to cool the heart by secretion of phlegm and preventing its overheating. Aristotle also recognised that the arterial system duplicates the various system but failed to differentiate between arteries and veins. He believed that arteries contain air as well as blood.

Assessment of these studies on anatomy by lion Nafees al-Damishqi (1208-1289) and Zakariyya al-Qazvini (1208-1283) and also of those by Hamad al-Mastaufi al-Qazvini (d. 1340) clearly establish the fact that human anatomy was firmly founded as a modern science much ahead of Andreas Vassulius (1443), Leonardo da Vinci (1452-1516) and William Harvey (1578-1657) in Europe. The structure and function of brain as described by Zakariyya al-Qazvini show that he has recognised three parts of the brain and knew that it was the seat of perception and of emergence of motor responses as well as a controller and associator of emotions affecting heart. This knowledge was far advanced from any Greek scientist and could only be achieved through dissections and observations.

The study of the structure of heart of the connecting vessels between the heart and the lungs by Nafees al-Damishqi, Zakariyya al-Qazvini and finally by Hamad al-Mastaufi al-Qazvini (d. 1340) leave nothing to William Harvey but to work out finer details. The purification of blood in lung and the distribution of purified blood by arteries to brain by an anterior vessel and to the rest of the body by systemic artery was definitely established by these scientists in the thirteenth century.

The concept of organic evolution is vaguely and theoretically described by the Greek, Empedocles and Aristotle has also a concept of broad classification of animals.

However the above quoted extract from Al-Biruni's book, Kitabul jumahir and from that of Shamsuddin al-Damishqui (d. 1327) namely Nakhbatud Dahr finally that of Ibn Khaldun (Muqadama page 96) have a much clearer notion and understanding of organic evolution better than any of the Greek scientists. Their concepts are briefly stated below:

> Al Beruni (1014) traces the evolution of man through carnivores, then through herbivores then through primates and points out its final socialisation. Shamsuddin al-Damishqui (1327) is more elaborate in observing "Categories", "Mid-stages" and "Connecting links". He has tried to classify primates in three categories, first of monkey, second of apes like Gorilla and finally the third category man. Ibn Khaldun defines the stages in evolution of animals by depicting them as 'Horizons' which is more scientific.

He observes that the horizon of apes is followed by the horizon of man.

Development of Technology

However strange it may sound, there is hardly any conflict between the scientific achievements and the Islamic life. Islam never discourages scientific approach or the experimental method of science. What it does discourage is to consider the scientific results as the final results. True scientific method is in conformity with this belief. As a matter of fact, the Holy Quran opens its teachings with the declaration of the absence of doubt concerning the Book. In other words, the Quran claims that, you cannot in fact, doubt that the Quran is a Divine Scripture. Its teachings and diction clearly indicate that it cannot be a human speech or human composition. The Quran then guides us to doubt everything, and not to accept anything without examining it with the touch stone of reason. But we must accept that which cannot be doubted.

Islam also claims to be the natural religion advocating natural laws which need no change. While other creeds never claimed to be natural, and some of them even disregarded the spirit of nature and common sense, Islam issued all its injunctions and prohibitions in conformity with the laws of nature. Science also claims to use natural resources in a natural way. Hence, its method cannot obviously be antagonistic to Islam. But the Muslim Society of the fourteenth century cannot be regarded as simple and honest as the Muslim Society of the first century of the Hijra era. The traditional society has surely deviated from its real Islamic path, to a great extent, in course of long fourteen hundred years. This society which showed its appearance here in Pakistan, for example, cannot be considered as fresh and almost free from blemishes as that of the time of the Prophet or his companions. Coming in contact with the Persian, the Turks, the Mongols, the Afghans and the Indians, the Muslim Society underwent considerable changes from time to time and adopted many aspects which bore no impression of Islam, and could easily be discerned as un-Islamic.

Muslim institutions which have been clearly emphasized by the Quran and the Apostolic Hadith as-Salat, Sawm, Zakat, Hajj and jihad are nowadays scarcely heeded to by the Muslims. Very few people perform Salat, and still fewer keep fast. Only a limited number from among the wealthy people offer Zakat and perform Hajj jihad being entirely ignored. Even if the Muslims of the day perform these institutions they do so mechanically remaining unconscious of their actions and performances; and hence, their prayers, fasts, alms, and endeavours go in vain, and bear no fruit.

People devote their time to prayers, and fasts but at the same time, speak ill of others in their absence, disseminate hatred and ill feelings, and encourage dishonesty among the members of the community. Zakat and alms are given today mostly to those who have adopted begging as their profession, and are hardly given to the needy. Our endeavours are scarcely directed to develop brotherly affections and doing good to others; on the contrary, one does one's best in cultivating envy, enmity, malice and hatred among the community.

Islam based its society on the principle of Tawhid, Oneness of God—a conception from which follows as the day follows the night, the universal brotherhood of man inasmuch as the God of the East is also the God of the West, and the God of the White is also the God of the Black, and so on. All the members of the society have therefore been without any discrimination ordered to prostrate themselves before One and the Only God, and that they have to bear witness that Prophet Muhammad is the Messenger of Allah.

The Holy Quran, the Divine Scripture, which was revealed to the Prophet emphasizes action through which alone the inner belief in One Allah and His Apostle can be manifested and displayed.

As Islam means "submission to the laws of Allah," it enjoins its followers to obey Allah. Very often the obedience to Allah has been identified with the obedience to the Apostle. The meaning is obvious inasmuch as the Apostle supplies the necessary interpretation of the Quran. And, again, the Apostle of Allah demonstrates and illustrates the enactments prescribed by the Quran.

The Quran has prescribed the following institutions :

1. The modes of worship which require Niyyat or intention, which establish the relation of man to his Creator. These may be corporeal and spiritual, such as Salat and Sawm; social and monetary, like Zakat and all sorts of alms; and spiritual, corporeal and monetary, like Hajj jihad and the fulfillment of a votive offering.
2. The dealings instituted for organizing mutual relations between man and man, and between individuals of an Umma and the society on the basis of justice, mercy, mutual help, love and affection, removal of the causes of harm and enmity, and deriving the good and profit. These dealings include civil rights of buying and selling, giving something on lease or mortgage. Similarly, they include the personal affairs that characterize a man from his birth to death, such as marriage, divorce, 'iddat, or legal period of retirement, lineage, suckling expenses, will and inheritance, as well as the distribution of his property among his heirs.
3. Punishments prescribed for the protection of the life, honour, and wealth of the people, viz., the punishment of murder, theft, waylaying, adultery, and foul accusation, which are known as Qisas and Hudud, retaliation and criminal laws.
4. Institutions connected with the relation of the Umma to the State, and explaining the rights of the ruler against the subject, and the rights of the subject as against the

ruler, i.e., the institution of consultation, equality, justice and the obedience to the people of commandment, concerning all those affairs which require obedience, and are called in modern expression the Constitutional matters.

5. Injunctions related to jihad, endeavour, and the system of war and fighting, organizing the relation of the Muslims to non-Muslims and the affairs of prisoners, booty obtained after war and without war. These affairs are now known as international laws.

In other words, the Quran has given us laws relating to our moral, religious, personal, social, political and economic life. Some laws have been dealt with in details and some have been left to our own discretion and choice to adopt to the time and circumstances. These Quranic laws can, on no account, be ever changed or altered. All the social and criminal laws which have been explained in the Quran like those of marriage, divorce, inheritance or those of retaliation, adultery, theft, foul accusation are binding upon all followers of Islam for eternity. Nobody can challenge any part of these set-rules, A Mujtahid can only ponder over a case which has no precedent in Islam. Thus, no body can question the form of Salat, or the nisab of Zakat, Sawm can, for example, be declared as not binding in polar regions, since the purport of and complete fasting till the night, cannot be fulfilled or else the duration of the day and night will be fixed according to the timing and custom of that part of the world, and Sawm, in that region will not extend to more than the usual duration of the day considered in its neighbouring countries.

In the industrial area where the labourers attend to their work and handle machines at one and the same time, the groups of the workers can perform their prayer by turn within the scheduled period in the manner they do in relation to other natural works.

There is a misunderstanding in the European minds concerning certain Islamic institutions. Some Europeans, for example, think that since Islam allows polygamy, Islam disregards the rights of the women and treats them as cattle. This is a great injustice done to Islam inasmuch as Islam has permitted polygamy only when the man is too strong physically to be contented with one wife who is obviously to be excused for certain days in every month, or for a few months of her conception, or, again, for a period of her illness. Islam demands from every body honesty, piety and avoidance of adultery and fornication. Hence, it is essential to allow some sort of concession for a man described above, so that he can escape an immoral deed and does not follow the lead of, for example, Henry VIII, Tudor King of Great Britain, who had to break away with the Church of Rome which could not issue licence just to legalize his frequent marriages. Of course, the woman is not allowed to have more than one husband, as this would cause dissension and discord in the family over the lineage of the child she would ever bear, and over the administration of the house.

The Quran has therefore made it clear that man is the administrator over the women. Though man and woman both enjoy equal rights, man has been given a superior rank for his natural constitution and strong physique. The terms and conditions prescribed for polygamy clearly indicate that it is no licence for satisfying for one's sex instinct, but it is in fact a solution for such problems as Europe confronted in the post war period after the two world wars when the number of the male decreased and the number of the female increased.

Birth-control, the necessity of which is emphasized from the financial point of view, forms today, an inevitable doctrine of the modern culture and which encouraged, to a great extent, moral degradation, can however be defended in the light of those Apostolic sayings which permit to discharge outside, with the permission of the wife. Religious laws have a sanctity in Islam which can only be maintained by those followers who fear Allah, avoid dishonesty and self-indulgence. But those who are atheists, or who do not enjoy faith in Allah, can very well disregard such principles, violate the social and moral laws, and cause commotion and confusion and enhance the birth of unwarranted children which is the case in France and all those states where contraception is in use.

To put a stop to theft, and other crimes finally, we must enforce the Quranic Laws and severe the hand of the thief from its wrist, and stone a fornicator to death, and thus let the people live in peace and immunity from the harm done by these criminals. By ignoring the Quranic laws we have uptil now criminally encouraged the criminals and illegally disregarded our human duty towards thousands and thousands of victims whom we could have saved from cold blood and utter ruination and destruction. All this we are doing just to protect a handful miscreants from execution or making them legally disabled. All these corruptions and ethical troubles are caused by showing sympathy to a handful outlaws at the cost of peace and even life of the multitude allowed by the modern civilization and modern law.

A number of social evils have found encouragement in the form of certain arts, sports, and methods of amusement and recreation. While acting and dancing are teaching mimicry, and encouraging the eastern people to lose their faith in ethical values, the race and cinema and intellectual gambling are taxing upon the financial capacity of the individuals leading to the deplorable family troubles and unrest, and are also rousing the instincts for crime and cruelty. Though conscious of the cruelty to the animals, the modern civilization hardly cares to prevent people from the cruelty to the wife, to the children, to other relations in particular, and to mankind in general.

Turning to the system of modern education provided with in this country as well as in other neighbouring countries, it is very efficient to point out that the modern education has certainly supplied us people efficient to work in secretariates, but has surely rendered the majority of the educated people indifferent to the faith they profess in, to the fundamental principles of the society to which we claim to belong, and also to our history, culture and heritage so much so that a very highly educated University professor was, only the other day, taken aback when I stated that in spite of other draw-backs, Muslims equally treated the sons of a legal wife and a slave girl, and that the latter becomes Umm walada who cannot be sold. His surprise knew no bound when I added that Mamun al-Rashid, son of the famous Harun al-Rashid from a Persian slave-girl was accepted as a Khalifah just like his brother Amin al-Rashid, son of the famous Zubaydah, wife of Harun, and that sons of slave and slave-girls even established their dynasties not only in Egypt but also in the sub-continent of Pakistan and India.

Our education system, therefore, must include the teaching of Islamic tenets and the history of the Muslims if we want to be the faithful members of the society, and call ourselves Muslims. Is it not a sheer mimicry to imitate the West in all their walks of life and ignore the Western system of education which includes the religious education as compulsory from cradle? This is a fact and notification that the present education system of Pakistan, followed by schools and universities, has failed to make our people the intellectual of the first grade; and the Pakistanis, in particular, and the Muslims in general have fallen far behind in all branches of science and arts. This alone bears testimony as to what kind of Muslims we are Ignoring the clear teaching of the Quran, "O Lord! increase me in knowledge", no Muslim can ever prosper and thrive. While Islam had, in its heyday, rendered every mosque into a college and seat of learning open to all without demand of a fee, the modern world is making education dearer and dearer every day as it has increased the price of amenities of life in spite of all its achievements, and minimizing space and time.

Technological progress and industrialization have, no doubt, helped us a great deal to solve our problems relating to every day life, but they have, on the other hand, multiplied problems relating to our social and moral life. In order to meet these social and ethical evils it is incumbent to acquire strength of belief, and for the matter of that, honesty, sincerity, self-reliance and self-sacrifice, and we must purge the society of all sorts of corruption,. hypocrisy, dishonesty and self-indulgence. To cut short, we must rouse the martial spirit among all the members of the nation which will keep them active, and we must urge them to practise upto what they believe. The Quran repeats the expression and they acted good deeds, wherever the Quran addresses "those who believe", since mere belief is not sufficient for winning commendation and reward. It is action in conformity with belief that makes one entitled to reward and praise.

The Astronomy : Even to the naked eye the surface of the Moon appears unevenly bright, with fantastic dark patches and irregularities. Being our nearest neighbour in the astronomical world it attracted much attention from time immemorial and played a great part in the mythologies of various peoples, it was credited with all sorts of real and imaginary influences on the affairs of man on personal health as well as worldly prosperity. Any good textbook on Astronomy gives fairly adequate information about the Moon as an astronomical object, about its size and mass, its periodic movements giving rise to its apparent phases and causing tides and eclipses, but very few describe its features, which could be studied satisfactorily only after the installation of large telescopes. No wonder that ancient writers fancied there were vast seas on the Moon, to which they gave fanciful and remarkably interesting names.

In this paper we propose to give a brief general account of these lunar features and explain how enthusiasts of astronomy patiently built up more and more detailed maps of the Moon, designating its prominent features with names of past great astronomers, scientists, etc.

These features are now called 'Lunar Formations' and their names have been finally decided upon at a meeting of the International Astronomical Union in 1935. It so happens that 13 of these formations have been given the names of some well-known Muslim servants of olden days. We shall describe these 13 formations with details about their probable nature, size and location, etc., and give brief account of the lives of these distinguished scientists and their main contributions to science with special reference to astronomy. Langrenus of Brussels (c. 1600-1675) was the first to prepare a chart of the Moon in 1645 in which the largest hypothetical ocean or sea was named after Phillip IV of Spain, his patron and benefactor. In the same spirit other prominent lunar formations were given the names of Spanish princes and princesses.

Then, two years later, Hevelius (1611-87) of Danzig made another map of the Moon in which he assigned terrestrial names to lunar mountains, plains and islands, in accordance with apparent resemblance. Joannes Baptista Riccioli (1598-1671), a Jesuit professor of astronomy and philosophy in Bologna, compiled in 1651 his Almagestum Novuum, a comprehensive work on astronomy, with a map of the full Moon (prepared with the help of his friend Franciscoaria Grimaldi). An excellent feature of this map was that it discarded the names of members of the Spanish and Austrian royal families and substituted for them the names of distinguished astronomers of the Middle Ages. It was thus that ten lunar formations were designated with ten Muslim names which still continue.

Riccioli was a follower of Tycho Broke (1546-1601), the famous Danish astronomer who opposed Copernicus theory of motion of the Earth round the Sun. On Riccioli's map northern lunar formations have been given the names of olden philosophers who shared his cosmic views, like Plato and his pupils. Names of astronomers, of opposite views, generally his own contemporaries have been utilised for the southern lunar formations. A commendable feature of this system of designation, which bears testimony to Riccioli's strong sense of justice and fair-mindedness is that the most prominent mountain on the Moon is called Copernicus (1473-1543) and the brightest Aristarchus (c. 310-c. 230 b.c.)—by far the strongest supporters of the heliocentric theory.

With increased use of telescopes the number of observers of the Moon rose rapidly and after exhaustion of the more prominent formations it was found necessary to coin names for the less prominent features. It was thus that Schroter, with more powerful instruments to observe, was able to add considerably to the number of lunar names between 1791 and 1802. Later, in 1837, Beer and Medlar in their famous work Der Mond included a map of three feet, showing 427 features bearing names of famous explorers and geographers also. Al-Hasan ibn-al-Haytham (Al-hazan of Western writers), Nasir-al-Din Tusi and Ulugh Beg were additions to the names of Muslim scientists adopted by Medlar. The list prepared by the Lunar Commission of the International Astronomical Union in 1935 contains 672 names of lunar formations, 609 of which are names of distinguished persons, the rest are borrowed from terrestrial designations.

In this paper we shall point out which 'formations' are named after Muslim astronomers and scientists with brief accounts of their contributions to science and culture. We shall also state where these formations are situated on the Moon and what are their chief characteristics. An excellent method of studying the physical features of the Moon is to divide the face of the full Moon into 25 parts in imitation of Walter Goodacre (1856-1938) who spent his lifetime in the study of selenography, preparing a 60-inch chart of the Satellite in 1910 and published his book 'The Moon in 1931'.

3

Evolution and Development

Initial Achievements

The city of Gondeshapur in southwestern Persia was captured by the Arabs in AD 638; it became a center for the dissemination of Greek and other ancient philosophical and scientific knowledge throughout the new Islamic empire. Here flourished a large community of Nestorians, members of a Christian sect that had been charged with heresy and forced to flee from Christian territory late in the fifth century. The city had long supported a notable academy of scholars and physicians, many of whom spoke Greek and Sanskrit as well as Syriac, an Aramaic dialect then in wide use throughout the region. After the Arab conquest, these scholars quickly became familiar with Arabic. An intensive programme of translation into Arabic of philosophical, medical, and other scientific manuscripts was sponsored by the new Muslim caliphs, and soon this rapidly expanding enterprise spread to Baghdad and Damascus, the cultural centers of the Abbasid dynasty.

Without historical precedent, the quantity of translations produced in Gondeshapur represented from the start an ecumenical as well as an international effort, involving many Christians and Jews as well as Muslims. It was most often an enterprise prompted by royal decree, reflecting interest on the part of caliphs and other high officials of court and government not only in practical sciences such as medicine and astronomy but also in the less exact precepts of astrology and alchemy. These two exotic disciplines, of course, had already enjoyed centuries of official and public support and would continue to do so for centuries more, in both East and West.

A parallel translation programme, from Greek to Latin, was underway at the time in medieval Christian Europe. Sponsored by monasteries such as Monte Cassino and by rulers such as Charlemagne, its goal was the same as that of the effort being undertaken in the Iṣlamic lands: to produce translations of classical Greek texts. This effort, however, did not match the Muslim output in scope or quantity until the twelfth century, when imperial Islam had begun to lose some of its political and cultural supremacy.

Two centuries of Muslim translation succeeded in making the major works of Plato, Aristotle, Euclid, Archimedes, Hippocrates, Galen, Ptolemy, and many others available to Muslim scholars in settlements from Persia to Spain. Not all the translations were of the greatest fidelity or quality, but revisions became frequent as scholarship matured. Flexible and capable of accommodating new concepts, procedures, and the details of science as well as of philosophy, the Arabic language proved to be a resourceful vehicle. At the outset of this enterprise, emerged outstanding translators, such as Hunain ibn Ishaq, a ninth-century Nestorian Christian who was expert in four languages and who produced a mass of work covering much of Greek philosophy and medicine. Another eminent scientist, Thabit ibn Qurra, was particularly noted for his translations and revisions of works on logic, mathematics, and astronomy. A member of a family of distinguished scientists and scholars, he never converted to Islam; he was a member of a pagan sect, the Sabians, who were mentioned in the Quran and, thus, had protected status.

In the early selections of works to be translated, priority was given to subjects deemed most immediately useful, such as medicine, mathematics, and astronomy, the latter two needed in orientation for religious practice and for astrological prediction. However, within two centuries an encyclopaedic classical treasury was available in Arabic, embracing Greek knowledge and Hellenistic contributions. This store of cultural riches was capable of filling the intellectual needs of a new civilization even as that civilization was pursuing spiritual, political, and cultural aims radically different from those of ancient Greece and Rome. By the eleventh century, Muslim rulers had established appropriate institutions designed to preserve and maintain this treasury and put it to Islamic use.

Islam's first few centuries witnessed the establishment of great libraries and centers of learning in both East and West. The most celebrated of these were located in the seats of political or imperial power. A famous "house of wisdom" (Baitul-hikma) flourished in ninth-century Abbasid Baghdad; it was a center not only for translation but also for specialized scholarly study and investigation. Notable libraries were established in several Persian cities. In tenth-century Cairo, under Fatimid dynasty rule, one of the libraries contained forty rooms holding many thousands of works devoted to the ancient sciences. In Umayyad Spain, the great capital of Cordoba was, like Cairo and Baghdad, a center of higher learning that drew students and visiting scholars from all regions of Islam. Cairo's al-Azhar, founded late in the tenth century as a training school for preachers, later contained mosque schools (madrasa) and still flourishes today. After nearly a millennium of uninterrupted existence, it is the world's oldest university or college.

A science academy was established during the tenth century at Cordoba, and another at Toledo. Generally, however, advanced education in science was carried out on a personal rather than an institutional scale, within the confines of royal courts and royally sponsored establishments such as observatories and hospitals. A young man seeking high-level education in the sciences had to wait until he had progressed beyond elementary school and the madrasa, where he could receive instruction in basic mathematics. University curricula might include advanced mathematics, some astronomy, medicine, and natural sciences such as biology, but these subjects were treated largely within a framework of Quranic fundamentals and interpretation as well as principles of religious law. At the caliph's court, however, the young man might be fortunate enough to be admitted to a circle centered on one of the great teachers—often a person celebrated for achievement in more than one science, a philosopher-physician, perhaps, or a mathematician-astronomer.

Such high-level scholarship represented the upper track of a two-track system. On the lower track, those of the general population who went through elementary education were offered mostly the curricula and concepts that were officially deemed appropriate or adequate for the many. In addition, the procedures of traditional Muslim elementary education did not promote original speculation. Listening, reading, recitation, and preparation by rote formed a great part of the process of learning. As for prospects for young women who might be interested in learning more about the sciences or any other major academic subjects, they did not exist to any significant degree in any Islamic community until the second half of our own century.

The character of Islam's specialized scientific education can be better understood if one considers the traditional Islamic concept of knowledge and the ways in which knowledge and the curriculum were organized and classified in early Islam. Not only was the pursuit of knowledge exhorted by many Hadith, the statements traditionally attributed to Muhammad, the Quran emphasizes the value of knowledge in grasping the nature of the world around us. As previously noted, Muslim religious doctrine defines the universe as a sign of God's activity;

therefore, study of that activity is thought to provide knowledge of the right path toward the proper life on earth and salvation in the life beyond. Muslim religious leaders and educators devoted considerable time to classifying the sciences and clarifying their specific functions as they would help each person to acquire knowledge within an intellectual framework that would serve God's purpose.

Definitive classifications were attempted by such intellectual giants as Al-Farabi, Ibn Sina, and Ibn Khaldun, the greatest of the Muslim historian-philosophers. Ibn Khaldun's system reveals basic distinctions that were widely adopted. First in his schema, came the traditional religious sciences, dealing with examination and readings of the Quran, the science of tradition, sciences of jurisprudence and dialectics (argument), speculative theology, mysticism, the interpretation of dreams, and philological science.

A second major group, the philosophical sciences, included, first, Aristotelian logic; second, in a sort of umbrella category, physics, including medicine, agriculture, magic, alchemy, and other esoteric disciplines; third, metaphysics; and fourth, mathematics, covering numerical sciences such as arithmetic, calculation, algebra, commercial transactions, the apportioning of inheritances, geometrical sciences such as spherical and conical geometry, surveying, optics, and astronomy, including tabulation and astrology. Finally came music, which was considered a mathematical discipline.

Whatever the variations in degree, the different systems for the classification of learning all reflected a fundamental acceptance of the supremacy of the Islamic Revelation. Eventually there developed profound suspicion, even fear, of influences that might be exercised by intellectual disciplines inherited from the ancient world. There evolved a clear distinction between "revealed" subjects connected with religion and centered around the Quran and those not connected with religion, considered "rational" subjects. What today we would call physics, biology, agronomy, and the earth sciences belonged to this latter group. As a whole, these sciences, termed "philosophical" because they were considered accessible through human reason rather than through faith, were regarded as foreign because of their origins in classical Greece and India. Among them, philosophy in particular, at first praised as a valuable tool inherited from the Greeks, was singled out by some orthodox scholars and leaders as alien and suspect. Ironically, the eleventh-century theologian al-Ghazzali's belief in the value of logic in dealing with Islamic legal subjects helped to spread the acceptance of rational process as a valid tool in organizing knowledge.

The mosque schools and the universities' legally-oriented faculties took more or less exclusive charge of teaching the religious disciplines, leaving the philosophical, mathematical, and natural sciences to be taught mostly in the small, royal, elite groups described previously. There was little of a democratic character in medieval higher education, within or beyond Islamic lands.

A dynamic new faith, the vitality of a people freeing themselves from a struggle against the harsh elements of desert life, a pressing curiosity about the world that they encountered outside the Arabian heartland, a need for a share in that world's bounty, a language well-equipped for intellectual exploration: all these factors, binding together Muslims in greater unity than existed among any other civilization at the time, generated a powerful motive for Islam's scientific enterprise. The world, all its forms of life, and the heavens above were now subject to an unprecedented exploration and examination by Muslims and other scholars in Muslim lands. And even where spiritual motivation was less pressing than material enthusiasm and practical curiosity, there was power and material reward to be gained from learning more about what the world was made of and how such knowledge could be put to beneficial and profitable use.

In less than four centuries after the first Islamic conquest, philosophers, mathematicians, botanists, physicians, geographers, alchemists, and their peers in the other scientific disciplines, at work throughout the wide reaches of the Islamic empire, had accomplished the remarkable feat of unwrapping the vast intellectual legacy received from past civilizations, analyzing it in relentless detail, fussing with it, testing and retesting its hypotheses and answers, evolving new ones, and further revising, discarding, or reformulating many of those. From the broadest concepts of the physical universe to details of the smallest scale—including invisible processes within the human body—much was put in order and connected in ways some of which appear to reflect or to parallel the Muslim concept of cosmic unity spelled out in the Islamic Revelation. In sum, a new concept of the universe was put together, in many ways remarkably similar, or at least parallel, to the old ones, in other ways significantly simplified and clarified. More important, from macrocosmic to microcosmic element, this Islamic universe appeared, in general, orderly, functional and workable. It made sense. It represented a critical advance beyond contemporary non-Muslim concepts, most of which it would eventually affect profoundly.

What, specifically, did Islam's medieval scientists accomplish? It seems appropriate to begin the inventory with Muslim ideas about the overall cosmos and all that was in it.

Referring to *New Webster's Dictionary*, the meaning of science may be (1) "knowledge" especially of facts or principles, gained by systematic study; (2) a particular branch of knowledge especially one dealing with a body of facts or truths systematically arranged and showing the operation of general laws; (3) systematized knowledge, especially of the laws and facts of the physical or material world; and (4) skill resulting from training.

According to different scientists: Science is the systematic knowledge of natural phenomena and the mutual relations among them, it is the investigation or endeavour to find the inherent cause of any event and the knowledge obtained from such endeavour.

Thus we see that the subject matter of science are: to study or investigate the physical world or the nature created by Almighty and to understand as to how things have been created and as to what laws they are obeying. Knowledge thus acquired is applied or techniques evolved from such knowledge are used, for the benefit of mankind.

Thus, if we study different stars in the sky, we observe them to follow some laws; each of them rise in the east at a certain time and set in the west at a certain time. There are also different types of stars, some are near to us, some are located at infinite distance away, some are bright and some are not. Their arrangements in the sky are also different, they are being arranged in different ways as well. A group of infinite number of stars arranged in different forms make a galaxy. There are infinite number of galaxies located at infinite distances away from each other. Our sun, one of the stars of the galaxy, the Milky way, has its own characteristics. Some (at present nine) planets are revolving around the sun. The planets have no light of their own. They are seen shining bright because of sun's ray reflected from their surfaces. Our earth is a planet and the moon revolving around it is its satellite. The earth while revolving around the sun spins (rotates) around its own axis. The mystery of the heavenly bodies in the sky is studied in science. One of the branches of science, which deals with planets, stars, galaxies, cosmogony, etc., is the astrophysics.

There are other branches of science as well. Thus, studies of earth surface and its interior is the subject matter of geology. In this branch, different objects of the earth such as mountains, rivers, seas, different layers of the earth's crust, etc., are studied.

There is also a subject called geography to survey and study earth's surface.

Scientists' attempt to use the resources, discovered through such studies for the mankind. Crude oils, coal, different minerals, etc., discovered as a result of study are being used by the present mankind. Study of nature includes also the atmosphere that envelopes the earth's surface. Characteristics of the atmosphere, its formation, changes, uses, etc., are studied in a branch of science called "Meteorology."

Most of the earth's surface is covered by ocean. And bounties or gifts of Almighty for mankind are plenty in the ocean and beneath the ocean. Oceanography is a subject of science to study the oceans and the oceanic resources. There are ocean-related technologies studied in Marine Engineering for using ocean resources by man.

Various Branches : Some of the various branches of science are: Botany for studying plant life, Zoology for animal life. Medical science to study human beings, Chemistry for studying elements, compounds and reactions among them.

There has been widespread involvement of different types of energy in the creation of the Universe, in other words, energy is inherent in the creation processes. There has been continuous changes of energy from one type to another. The different manifestations of energy are heat, light, electric, magnetic, gravitational, nuclear or atomic, etc. Matter, different types of energy, different natural objects and the physical laws are studied in Physics. There are several branches of Physics as well.

Thus, it is observed that the main aims and objectives of scientists are to study or investigate and analyse different things of the universe and to gather or acquire knowledge from such studies and to realize the complexity of the creation of Almighty and to get benefitted from the acquired knowledge.

Nowadays with the help of the acquired knowledge from scientific studies of nature, scientists could make various devices, machines, conveyances for use. It has become possible to improve medical treatment, advent new medicines, etc. These practical or applied branches of science is the technology. Presence of scientific knowledge has given birth tc technology. Of the different technical departments, different engineering branches, electronics, computer science, communication, biotechnology are some. Because of the advancement of technology, innumerable industries and factories have been established throughout the world.

Holy Quran's Verdict : For common persons though surprising, it is true that Almighty has instructed or suggested or advised mankind to study His created world or in other words nature, to reflect and do research on different things and phenomena so that man may realize from the study complexity of creation, laws guiding them and find means for using natural bounties of Almighty. In fact, Al-Quran is an open invitation to mankind for studying the natural world and to get benefitted from it. This invitation or suggestion has been put forward in about 750 verses of total 6666 verses of the Holy Quran (about one eighth of the whole Quran). These verses have put stress on Al-tafakkur (research on natural things and natural laws) and Al-taskheer (make effort to get benefit from the natural bounties through technology). Study of nature has its inner significance also. In fact, a true observer or researcher of nature can realize Almighty, the Creator of all things. In this regard Almighty has said:

> "And how many signs in the heavens and the earth Do they pass by? Yet they turn (their faces) away from them" — (12:105)

> "On the earth are Signs for those of assumed faith, as also in your own selves will yet not then see?"
> — (51:20,21).

Morality and Ethics : It is seen in the present discussion that people are instructed or advised by Almighty to study natural things on this earth and on the sky. Man has been given this freedom and for this he has been bestowed with intellect and capacity to think. In the course of searching knowledge in scientific way, it is to be always kept in mind that knowledge gathered thus is useful for mankind, and helpful to understand Tauhid i.e. Oneness of Almighty and is not misused in various ways such as waging wars and other such activities. Al-Quran has been revealed with the aim of making or guiding man so that he may reach the goal of perfectness and he may maintain a balanced state in all earthly activities. It has not only explained basic philosophy of life. It also wants man to maintain a balance between philosophy and action in real life. Man must maintain congenial atmosphere with his fellow men and others i.e. with the environment. That is why along with private or personal activities such as faith (*Iman*), *salat* (daily prayers), fasting, etc., man has been advised to observe or study and think (research) on natural things i.e., his environment. There is no doubt that from the study of nature i.e., science, man is benefitted in this world, but the most basic aims of encouraging or advising people for studies of different subjects of science (which are nothing but studies of nature) are to let people know by themselves that:

(i) There is a Creator, only one Creator of the Universe. He is the Almighty, Scientist of scientists, Omnipotent, Omnipresent and He is Allah, (e.g. verse, 2:255)

(ii) The Universe has been created in a well organised and balanced way with different components and all objects obey natural laws as framed by Almighty (e.g. verses, 41:11, 67:3)

(iii) Man is created as a servant of Almighty. He is also a viceroy of Almighty on this earth. He has been created by Almighty with many qualities and intellect so that he may learn lessons or realise examples of Almighty on observations and studies of natural things and praise Almighty. All natural things obey Almighty's order or command (natural laws). Man also should lead his life as per commands of Almighty, (e.g. verses: 2:30-31, 51:56, 55:5-6)

(iv) A time will definitely come, when this Universe will be destroyed and every man will be given as per his performance in this world, reward or punishment in the Hereafter by Allah, (e.g. verses: 14: 48-51, 40: 16-17)

Thus, the main aim of encouraging studies of nature (science) by Almighty is not just to get benefit in this world but also in the Hereafter. The Messenger of Almighty (PBUH) has cautioned the people against using knowledge for worldly purposes only. In this regard Abu Hurrayrah reported Allah's Messenger (PBUH) as saying.

> "He who acquires knowledge, the sole purpose of which is seeking the pleasure of Allah but he does not acquire it except for gaining worldly ends, he would not smell the odour of Paradise on the Day of Resurrection." —Ahmad, Abu Daud, Ibn Majah

Do not ye see, look, reflect ?

Almighty has invited man in the Holy Quran to study science in different ways. Almighty in many verses of the Holy Quran has asked people to observe and study or think carefully different natural objects, like, stars, rivers, plants, animals, birds etc. and learn or gather knowledge from them: Thus, Almighty says:

> ".... See how Allah did originate Creation" —(29:20)

> "... See they not how Allah originates creation..?" —(29:19)

"... Seest thou not ..... ?"

—(24:43, 31:29, 39; 35:27, 39:21)

"...See ye?..."

—(25:9; 56:63, 68:5,71; 71:15-16)

"... Do they not look .."

—(16:48, 79; 32:27, 36:71; 50:6; 67:19; 88:17)

"...think..." —(86:5) "... Do they not reflect ?..."

—(30:8)

"... Do not the unbelievers see?..." —(21:30)

"... Read in the name of Thy Lord ..." — (96:1)

In this way in many other verses also Almighty has asked man to observe His created things (natural things) and reflect or apply intellect. For this Almighty, of course, has gifted man with necessary organs such as ears, eyes, brains, etc.

> "He gave you hearing and sight and intelligence and affections that you may give thanks to Allah"
>
> —(16:78)

It is known to everyone of us that all living creatures having ears are able to hear sound and having eyes can see objects. But simple hearing is not sufficient. On hearing it is necessary to understand as to what is being heard, it is necessary to study or reflect on the source of sound and act accordingly. Similarly simple observation of any thing visually is not an observation in the real sense. On seeing or observing a thing, it is necessary to study and do research on the thing to learn or get knowledge from it, and that will be the observation in the true sense. Almighty has asked people to observe natural things in the real sense.

There are many Signs, things to learn

Almighty is the supreme commander. He is the source of all knowledge and the Scientist of scientists.

In the creation of the Universe the slightest (*koon*) scientific talent and techniques, etc., of Almighty has been manifested. From the scientific studies of different natural things i.e. created things of Almighty one can get some idea of their Creator, techniques involved and glimpses of His infinite knowledge. The student of science may feel His existence in their studies. He gets amazed by the fact that beautiful scientific laws are involved in different natural phenomena. Tauhid or idea of Oneness of the Creator, Almighty becomes obvious from the studies of science as a set of laws are operating universally, one is not contradicting another. That is why Almighty has said repeatedly in the Holy Quran that there are signs or things to learn or sources of knowledge in the observation and research of His innumerable objects in nature.

In this connection the Arabic word '*aiatoon*' has been used, whose meaning may be examples, advise, signs or sentence. Analysis of the sentences using this word gives the meaning as Signs of Almighty, His scientific talent and technique, His proof of existence, etc. One can go through the following verses of the Holy Quran in this connection.

> "... Verily in these things there are Signs for those who reflect ...." —(13:3; 30:21; 45:13)

> "...... Verily in these things there are Signs for those who are wise" —(2:164; 13:4; 16:12, 67; 30:24; 45:5)

> "... There are indeed Signs for men of understanding" —(3:190)

> "... Signs for them ..." —(36:33, 37, 41)

> ".... Verily in this are Signs for all who constantly persevere ....." —(31:31)

> "... Do they not travel through the land, so that their hearts (and minds) may thus learn wisdom and their ears may then learn to hear?....." —(22:46)

"... Verily in this is a Sign for those who listen ..." —(16:65)

"…. Signs for those who fear Him …." —(10:6)

"…. And among His signs …." —(30:20-25)

"…. Signs for those who believe …." —(6:99, 45:3)

"... Signs for those of assumed faith …." —(45:4)

In the verses mentioned above and in many other verses of the Holy Quran, Almighty has invited or instructed man to observe and study various things (nature) created by Him. And from the studies one can observe His signs and realise existence and oneness of Almighty. Methods of study of Nature or finding the truth may be different for different observers. One may take the help of argument, logic or intellect to explain natural phenomena. These are theoretical explanations. For verifying such theories one may take the help of experiments i.e., real observation of the phenomena and see if the theories i.e. theoretical explanations of the phenomena are true.

Scientists take the help of both approaches (theory and experiment) for studying natural objects and phenomena. Theoretical explanation is also based on certain observations and assumptions and takes the help of mathematics and other allied branches. Experimental observations and verifications or explanations are based on real observations and takes the help of sophisticated instrumentations. Theories and experiments make a complete Science.

What else is said about Science in the Holy Quran?

Al-Quran was revealed as a guide to lead a life in the right path so that man may get benefited from this, in this world as well as in the Hereafter.

Allah has asked man repeatedly for His Ibadah as many as 82 times in the Holy Quran. This refers to daily prayers, good deeds etc. Allah has also invited or instructed man to study His creations (in natural things) and get benefited from the innumerable bounties of nature.

Study of nature has its importance in the performance of Ibadah, since it helps to understand or realize innumerable signs of Allah, His infinite scientific talent in the creation, oneness (Tauhid) of Allah, it thus brings a believer nearer to Allah. The invitation to study science (nature) has been repeated in as many as the 750 verses (about one eighth) of the whole Quran. Thus, for example, Allah said:

> "Do ye not see that Allah has subjected to your (use) all things in the heavens and on earth, and has made His bounties flow to you in exceeding measure, (both) seen and unseen?" – (31:20)

In fact Islam is not a blind faith. The Almighty has given man some faculties to use to understand things in his life.

> "It is He Who has created you, and made for you the faculties of hearing, seeing, and understanding: Little Thanks it is ye give." –(67:23)

In all ways, He has asked men to study nature: Look at the following verse:

> "Behold ! In the creation of the heavens, skies, and the earth; In the alternation of the night and the day;
>
> In the sailing of the ships through the ocean for the profit of the mankind;
>
> In the rain which Allah sends down from the skies, and the life which He gives therewith to an earth that is dead;
>
> In the beasts of all kinds that He scatters through the earth;
>
> In the change of the winds, and the clouds which they

trail their slaves between the sky and the earth; "(Here) indeed are signs for people that are wise. —(2:164)

This way the Almighty has advised man in about 750 verses to study natural things, to do research on natural phenomena and from the knowledge so gathered people may be able to use nature or harness nature for their own benefit. Studies also will enable people to realise His Signs of His might. He says:

> "And He has subjected to you, as from Him, all that is in the heavens and on earth: behold, in that are Signs indeed for those who reflect." —(45:13)

Attentive reading and analysis of the verses related to suggestions for science education reveal that in fact all branches of modern science such as Astrophysics, Space Physics, Environmental Science, Oceanography, Meteorology, Hydrology, Geology, Zoology, Botany, Medical Science, Physics, Technical Science or Engineering, etc., have been mentioned in the Holy Quran. Some are cited below:

Suggestion for Studies of Geological Science

The Almighty has asked man to study geologized science in a number of verses, for example:

> "A Sign for them is the earth that is dead: We do give it life, and produce grain therefrom, of which ye do eat." — (36:33)

> "Do they not look on the earth, for many noble things of all kinds We have produced therein?" —(26:7)

> "It is He Who has made the earth manageable for you, So traverse ye through its tracts and enjoy of the sustenance, which He furnishes:" —(67:15)

> "(Do they not look) and at the mountains how they are placed firm and at the earth How it is spread out?" —(88:192; 20)

"It is He Who hath created for you all things that are on earth" —(2:29)

Studies of earth's surface, rocks, etc., have enabled scientists to know the time of formation of the earth (age of the earth), its different stages of formation, different materials or compositions of the surface, etc. As a result, man has become successful to discover and use different minerals found on the surface and below the surface of the earth. It is surprising and unfortunate that in spite of Quranic instructions Muslims have not been successful in geological science. Even Islamic countries having rich oil deposits could not make progress in the fields of petroleum exploration, production, refining and other related industries. Scientific and technical aid is being taken from other countries by these countries for the purpose. It is possible to make progress in the fields of agriculture, mining, etc., if advancement is made in Geological science as well. The Almighty has created this earth with all the necessary things for the use of mankind. Geological studies, research and technical knowhow will help to harness and use such bounties available on the surface and beneath the surface of the earth.

Studies of Water Resources: (Hydrology and Hydrography)

It has been established by scientists of biological science that water is the essential life supporting ingredient for life and life began in water as well. In this regard Almighty the Creator of all things says:

"We made from water every living thing" —(21:30)

Water is essential for every form of life whether it is plant or animal. The connection of water with life is intimate. The basis of all living matter in the physical world; protoplasm is water, the vital power of protoplasm seems to depend on the constant presence of water. Almighty says,

"And Allah has created every animal from water" —(24:45)

> "It is He Who has created man from water"
> —(25:54)

For the sustenance of various lives on earth Almighty has arranged distribution of water throughout the world, so that all may receive its support according to needs.

> "......And We send down pure water from the sky, that with it We may give life to a dead land and slake the thirst of things. We have created, cattle and men in great numbers and We have distributed (the water) amongst them." — (25:48-50)

About 75 per cent of the earth's surface is covered by water. This means that water is predominant on our globe. Without water no living thing can survive. Such an important thing deserves studies, so that this unparallel bounty of Almighty could be realised and also could further be used by man for diverse purposes.

Regarding water, Almighty says:

> "See ye the water which ye drink? —(56:68)

The meaning of the above verse is simple. It asks man to study or do research on water and glorify Almighty for giving its diverse qualities. In this regard, there are points of reflection in the following verse:

> "Seest thou not that Allah sends down rain from the sky, and leads it through springs in the earth? Then He causes to grow, therewith, produce of various colours: then it withers; thou wilt see it grow yellow; then He makes it dry up and crumble away. Truly, in this, is a message of remembrance to men of understanding." —(39:21)

There are a few other verses in the Holy Quran about water. Nowadays, knowledge about water has been substantially increased because of scientific studies and truth has been established regarding its universal essentiality in life formation, sustaining and surviving processes. There have been extensive studies on diverse qualities of water, chemical characteristics, etc., and techniques have been evolved for drinking pure water, supplying water for agricultural purposes, for generating electricity and for using it in many other ways. Studies on water is so extensive that a separate subject, viz. "Hydrology" has been created for studying different sources of surface and ground waters and for using them.

Now the question is that despite repeated instructions given in the Holy Quran for study; research on water, do Muslims have developed or given any stress to develop Hydrology as a subject for acquiring knowledge and get benefited from it? We observe that the Muslims are not at all concerned about this type of scientific studies.

Studies of Oceanic Resources

Three fourth of the surface of the earth has been covered by sea water. In addition to this vast water resource, there are innumerable things on the sea bed. Below the sea bed there are different minerals, petrols, etc. For using these oceanic resources and also for harnessing ocean in proper ways, man must study to know qualities of ocean water, ocean bed and its geographical or geological structures, different minerals available, their distribution, etc., and man must find out or make devices or ways and means for using these resources. Gratefulness to Almighty will also be associated along with the use of Almighty's bounties available in the oceans. In this regard Almighty says:

> "It is he Who has made the sea subject, that ye may eat thereof flesh that is fresh, and tender, and that ye may extract therefrom ornaments to wear, and thou seest the ships therein that plough the waves, that ye may seek (thus) of the bounty of Allah and that ye may be grateful." —(16:14)

Again in another verse, He says:

> "It is Allah Who has subjected the sea to you, that ships may sail through it by His command, that ye may seek of His bounty, and that ye may be grateful."
> —(45:12)

In this way after getting indication or information of bounties of Almighty in the sea and instruction to harness them, no believer (Mumin) can stay away from study of sea and get benefit from it. In this modern age of science, a subject, *viz* "Oceanography" has thus been opened in many Universities. For the profession of sailing on the sea i.e. for joining the navy and also to learn techniques of harnessing oceanic resources "Marine Engineering" is taught in many institutions. Muslims of the world can be compared with other communities as to how far they have made progress in this field.

Studies of Winds or Aerodynamics

In this modern age "Aerodyanamics" has been a major subject of science for study. Detail knowledge of the atmosphere, air motion, its pressure, temperature, density and their variations, etc., is necessary for design and manufacture of modern means of communication such as aeroplanes, means of defence and offence such as aircraft, missiles, rockets, etc. Knowledge of atmosphere is also necessary to fly all these and monitor their motions through atmosphere.

In other fields of our daily activities, air or atmosphere is also used extensively. Thus, from olden days air is being used for sailing purposes. Air driven machines are also being used nowadays for generating electricity. But what is most important about air is that it is most essential for life due to the presence of oxygen in it. All these and more can be known and air can be used in proper ways if studies and researches are carried out on atmosphere. Almighty has said regarding air in the Holy Book this way:

> "Among His Signs is this that He sends the winds, as heralds of glad tidings, giving you a taste of his Mercy, that the ships may sail by His command and that ye may seek of His bounty in order that ye may be grateful." —(30:46)

In a single line of the above verse many qualities, bounties, etc., of winds have been indicated. All the benefits obtained from wind are nothing but mercy of Almighty. The winds are not only essential for surviving life, they are also means of purification and bring blessing of Almighty in terms of rain which makes the soil fertile and fills the rivers and ponds with fresh water. Air helps international business and mixing up through sea-ways (sailing) and now by air-ways (floating in air). Those who know, *i.e.* study and do research for utilising wind, with prosper and rejoice, while those who ignore or fail to understand Sign of Almighty will perish.

Meteorology

This is another branch of science which includes studies of climatic condition such as pressure, temperature of atmosphere and rainfall. All these and other informations of the atmosphere help people in various ways such as in agriculture and in communication.

Meteorological informations can be had from the studies of atmosphere. The following verse describes different phenomena occurring in the atmosphere and ask people to observe these phenomena so that people may get benefit from such observation:

> "Seest thou not that Allah makes the clouds move gently, then joins them together, then makes them into a heap?" Then wilt thou see rain issue forth from their midst. And He sends down from the sky mountain masses (of clouds) wherein is hail: He strikes therewith whom He pleases and He turns it away

from whom He pleases. The vivid flash of its lightning well-nigh binds the sight." —(24:43)

Not that winds, clouds in the atmosphere, together with the process of formation of rain drops, hails and lightning, all these topics of meteorology are mentioned in the above verse. By the words "seest thou not" and "then wilt thou see", Almighty has asked man to study all these phenomena.

Agriculture and Climate

There is intimate relation between climate of a place and its agriculture. Wind and the atmospheric condition control the formation of clouds alongwith their movement and cause rain. Proper rainfall converts a dead land into a living, fertile and beautiful land bearing a rich harvest. Allah said in this regard:

> "It is He Who sendeth the winds like herald of glad tidings, going before His Mercy: when they have carried the heavy-laden clouds. We drive them to a land that is dead, make rain to descend thereon; and produce every kind of harvest therewith."
>
> —(7:57)

For a good harvest, only rain is not sufficient, quality of land must be good. In other words, land must be fertile. Almighty has indicated this in the following verse which is the continuation of the above mentioned verse:

> "From the land that is clean and good, by the Will of its Cherisher, springs up produce, (rich) after its kind: but from the land that is bad, springs up nothing but that which is scanty, thus do we explain the Signs by various (symbols) to those who are grateful"
>
> —(7:58)

Thus, there is necessity to study and to research on climate and on quantity of land for good agricultural products. Detailled knowledge of climatic conditions enable a cultivator to know pressure, temperature, wind condition and probable rainfall in the season of the place. Detailled knowledge of quality of cultivating enables cultivators to know its fertility, moisture conditions, ground water, mineral contents, of the soil. Knowledge of climate and quality of land will, thus help the cultivators to select suitable land, help to prepare the land and help to choose proper timing for cultivation for a good harvest.

Studies of Plant Life: Botany

Almighty has advised, suggested or directed mankind through about 750 verses of the Holy Quran to study and do research on nature, *i.e.* science. In some verses, He mentioned that His creation, in some verses He mentioned natural phenomena, in some cases. He has asked man to ponder about the creation. In short, nature includes all natural things and natural laws. Modern science also includes studies of all branches of nature. Studies of plant life is a separate subject in science called Botany. Studies of plant life include all types of plants, flowers, fruits, crops, etc. Animals including birds and man depend for their survival on plants and their products. There is necessity to study these things for getting more benefit from them. Also innumerable signs of Almighty can be realised in all the phenomena of plant life. Almighty describes about His wonderful creation of plants this way:

> "It is He Who sendeth down Rain from the skies:
>
> With it We produce vegetation of all kinds:
>
> From some We produce green (crops), out of which We produce, close-compounded grain out of the date-palm and its sheaths (or spathes) come clusters of dates hanging low and near: and (then there are) gardens of grapes, and olives and pomegranates, each similar (in kind) yet different (in variety):
>
> When they begin to bear fruit; Feast your eyes with the fruit and the ripeness thereof:

> Behold! in these things there are Signs for people who believe. —(6:99)

There are many other verses of this type about plants and their products in the Holy book. It is worth noticing that instructions for study, research and reflection have been given in above verse by the sentence:

> "When they begin to bear fruit Feast your eyes with the fruit and ripeness thereof." —(6:99)

In the above mentioned verse, Almighty has invited man to study carefully the processes involved in plant growth, how flowers bloom and then fruits come from flowers and the changes taking them in the fruits. On study and reflection one can realise if not understand the complexity and sophistication of the processes involved and the inherent divine power which would make foundation of his faith in Almighty more deep rooted. Studies of Botany is also necessary in order to explain and understand various verses related to plant life. Further, there is some indication about the causes of their growth. We know in the cases of man and animals that a pair of male and female is necessary for the spread of their offsprings. Similar is the case in vegetable life and in other living organisms of which we do not know. Almighty said in this regard:

> "Glory to Allah, Who created in pairs all things that the earth produces, as well as their own (human) kind and (other) things of which they have no knowledge.
> —(36:36)

Almighty has asked man to observe or study the processes of germination and growth of plant from seeds and contemplate to find out the causes of their growth.

> "See ye the seed that ye sow in the ground? Is it ye that cause it to grow or are We the cause?
> —(:56: 63, 64)

Deep study and contemplation will reveal that only Almighty, the all powerful is behind all the phenomena.

> "It is Allah Who causeth the seed grain and the date-stone to split and sprout" —(6:95)

In the above verse the seed-grain and the date-stone are cited as examples of vegetable world. Scientists (Botanists) will notice that the seed grain includes the cereals (such as wheat, barley, rice, millet, maize, etc.) which are monocotyledons, as well as pulses (such as beans, peas, grams etc.) and other seeds which are dicotyledons. The word "split and sprout" in the above verse represents a double process: (1) the seed divides and (2) one part (plumule) shoots up seeking the light, and forming leaves and the visible parts of the future tree, and the other part (radicle) digs down into the dark, forming the roots and seeking sustenance from the soil. Thus, seed is mentioned in the above verse as one small instance of the vegetable kingdom. Studies and researches show the diversity, complexity, and supreme scientific talent involved in the processes of many other cases. In spite of such vivid and specific instructions in the Holy Quran, Muslims though followers of the Book have not shown enthusiasm to study vegetable kingdom, *i.e.* Botany and as such their knowledge in this field is also very insignificant. Other communities or nations already have concentrated in the study of Botanical science and have made progress in applying their knowledge for various purposes such as making medicines, cultivation in scientific ways and also in biotechnology.

Studies of Animals, Birds, etc.: Zoology and Veterinary Science

We should analyse whether Almighty has given any instruction for studies of animal life, i.e. zoological science or not. Almighty mentioned varieties of animals existing in nature and asked man to contemplate on their birth, different activities and the benefit obtained by mankind. He Says:

> "Allah has created every animal from water of them there are some that creep on their bellies, some that walk on two legs: and some that walk on four"
> —(24:45)

The creeping things include worms and lowly forms of animal life as well as reptiles, centipedes, spiders, and insects. Where these have legs they are small and the description of creeping or crawling is more applicable to them; fishes and sea-animals swim, their swimming is like "creeping on their bellies". Two legged animals include birds and man. Most of the mammals walk on four legs. All these include the whole animal world. This world is open for study for man. Almighty has mentioned specifically domestic animals and their use by man for carrying loads, getting milk, medicine like honey, etc. He has thus given sanction to study animal science or veterinary science.

> "And verily in cattle will ye find an instructive Sign. From what is within their bodies, between excretion and blood, we produce for your drink, milk, pure and agreeable to those who drink" —(16:66)

Again:

> "Do they not look at the camels, How they are made?"
> —(88:17)

Cattle and camels are mentioned in these verses as instances of domestic animals. Camel is specially common for Arabs, but cattle throughout the world. In the above two verses, indication for study is given by the words "ye find an instructive sign." and "Do they not look". It is indeed a matter of contemplation as to how milk is being produced in the body of the female. It is a matter of great strange that the same food, eaten by male and females, produces in the latter, the wholesome and complete food, known as milk? Also when cattle are tamed and specially bred for milk, the supply of milk is greater than is necessary for their young and it is wholesome and good diet for man. In all these there are points of contemplation. These verses encourage man to study Veterinary Science, in particular and Zoological Science, in general.

Regarding bee He says:

> "And thy Lord taught the bee to build its cells in hills, on trees and in (men's) habitations; then to eat of all produce (of the earth), and follow the ways of thy Lord made smooth: their issues from within their bodies, a drink of varying colours, wherein is healing for men.
>
> Verily in this a Sign for those who give thought."
>
> —(16 : 68, 69)

Production of honey by bee and its healing power for man are subjects of study and research. Science or Chemistry is involved in the production of milk by animals and honey by bees.

Chemical Science

It includes studies of different elements, minerals, compounds, chemicals, reactions between chemicals, etc., and synthesis of new chemicals or compounds, gases, etc. An example of chemical activities is the production of fire. Almighty says:

> "See ye the fire which ye kindle?" — (56:71)

Again:

> "(He) Who produces for you fire out of the green tree, when behold ? Ye kindle therewith (your own fire)!
>
> —(36:80)

Fire or flame or, in other words, burning of gases, petrols, kerosenes, woods, etc., involve lot of chemistry. There is intimate relation of fire with trees. Nearly for all the fire, the fuel is derived from the wood of trees. Even coal is nothing but the wood of prehistoric forests petrified under the earth through ages. Studies of all these will include chemistry of the phenomena.

Studies of Medical Science

Medical Science is a subject for studying different processes involved in birth and growth of man and diseases causing ailments and death of man. Ways and means such as medicines, operations, etc., for treatment of man, when attacked by diseases, are also taught in this subject in the field of Medical Science. Muslims are not in the forefront. For their backwardness in learning Medical Science, Muslims may have some other reasons, but there is no religious prohibition. Rather, Almighty has given instruction or invited mankind to study the life processes and to contemplate on it. Almighty says:

> "Let man but think from what he is created."
>
> —(86:5)

With a question mark Almighty has described in the Holy Quran:

> "Was he not a drop of sperm emitted (in lowly form)? Then did he become a leach-like clot; then did (Allah) make and fashion (him) in due proportion. And of him He made two sexes, male and female."
>
> —(75:37-39)

Again:

> "Has there not been over man a long period of time, when he was nothing (not even) mentioned?"
>
> —(76:1)

In the above two verses, question mark is to be specially noted. Unless one studies or knows basic phenomena involved in the processes mentioned in the two, how one can agree to or understand the answer given in the same verses. The way of expression in the verses is clearly an invitation to study various aspects of birth, growth and other related things of the human being. In the modern time, medical science has made tremendous progress in all fronts. Fertilization (conception) in the mother's womb, gradual growth and development of different organs (embryology), birth, growth after birth, different diseases and their treatment with the help of most modern techniques are all studied in Medical Science. Now it has even become possible because of the Medical Science, to transplant or replace some organs of human body, operate upon heart and produce test tube babies. Researches are going on in full swing in different laboratories of the world to discover new medicines for various diseases and for treatment of dreaded diseases. Also scientists are busy, at the same time, to know the mystery of human life itself.

Studies of Physical Laws etc.: Physics

Almighty has created innumerable things on this earth vis-a-vis- this Universe. They are subjected to certain physical laws, *i.e.* they are obeying certain laws which are commands of Almighty. Thus, for example, every particle of matter in the Universe attracts every other particle due to gravitation. The force of mutual attraction that acts between any two particles are directly proportional to the product of their masses and inversely proportional to the square of the distance between them. Planetary motion about sun is governed by such laws. Every object even movement of air, a leaf of a tree, flow of river water, etc., follows or obeys physical laws framed by Almighty.

Almighty says:

> "Seest thou not that to Allah prostrate all things that are in the Heavens and on earth." —(22:18)

Again:

> "Do they not look at Allah's Creation, among things, how their shadows turn round, from the right and the

> left, prostrating themselves to Allah, and that in the humblest manner? And to Allah doth prostrate, all that is in the heavens and on the earth, whether moving creatures or the angels: for none are arrogant....."
>
> —(16:48-49)

Prostrating means to lay flat before Almighty as a token of submission, *i.e.* worshiping Almighty. The verses, it seems, carry mystic meaning. Inanimate things even their shadows are told as recognising Almighty and humbly worshiping Him. Even their shadows turn round according to position of light and humbly prostrate themselves on the ground to celebrate the praises of Almighty.

It is known that shadows or any other things behave not on their own. They are found to obey certain laws and those laws are framed by Almighty Himself. Obeying of those laws means obeying of Almighty's commands.

By the words "Do they not look at Allah's creation," Almighty has asked man to study different laws framed by Him and obeyed by His created things including living creatures and angels. Physics include studies of these laws.

Physics, a subject of science, includes studies of different laws of natural phenomena. Further, energy is involved in the creation and maintenance of natural things. Light, heat, electricity, sound, etc., are all different manifestation of energy. Studies of these energies are also included in Physics.

Studies of Astrophysics and Space Physics

The Universe includes planets, stars, galaxies, clusters of galaxies and other bodies, all moving in controlled ways but maintaining infinite distances between any two of them. Studies of the Universe and contemplation on them enables man to realise a little of infinite scientific talent and power of Almighty, the Creator of all things of the Universe. The Holy Quran declares,

> "It is Allah Who has Created the heavens and the earth and all between them;..." —(32:4)

All these objects are subject to certain laws, as framed by Almighty:

> "He has made subject to you the night and the day: the sun and the moon; and the stars are in subjection by His Command: Verily in this are Signs for men who are wise" —(16:12)

It is indeed necessary to think or study as to how night and day happen for us; sun, moon, planets and other heavenly bodies in the sky move or what laws are obeyed by them. The sky with all these objects is full of beauty and magnificence, design and order, plainness and mystery. Almighty has asked people:

> "And (Do they not look) at the sky, how it is raised high?" —(88:18)

This way Almighty has advised mankind to observe the sky, the bodies adorned with and contemplate on their origin, physical laws obeyed by them, etc., so that man can realise the power of creativity, etc., of the Almighty.

Many people worship, out of ignorance, different objects of the sky as their gods attributing to them powers of doing good or bad for the people.

He says:

> "Among His Signs are the Night and Day, and the Sun and the Moon. Prostrate to Allah, Who Created them" —(41:37)

Studies of Astrophysics remove ignorance and prejudice from the mind and help one to identify false gods and know Almighty, the creator of all the objects.

In the modern science, Astrophysics and Space physics are two major subjects. Scientists are studying and doing research by observation and other theoretical methods on different objects of the sky and have succeeded in knowing many things: about their motion, evolution, etc. Because of such knowledge and tremendous progress in Science and Technology, it has become possible for the man to venture into outer space, to land on the moon and to send space probes to collect informations of planets, galaxies and other objects. Researches are going on in full swing in this regard throughout the world.

It is a matter of concern that of the vast Muslim population a very insignificant number of them are astrophysicists.

Space Exploration

All Praises to God, Who is the Lord of the Universe (all worlds).

One of the many aims of this book is to encourage. Muslims to come forward for science education and to remind them that Almighty has advised, instructed and also invited man to study nature or, in other words, science. Through studies of different branches of science, our knowledge increases and one can realise the complexity of our creation and hidden Signs of God, faith (Iman) of the faithful becomes more intense or deep rooted.

Nowadays scientists are not only engaged in study and research on terrestrial things and phenomena, but also have made progress in studying the earth's atmosphere. Knowledge gathered from such studies are being used by mankind. Now, not being satisfied with the study of atmosphere, scientists have ventured into outer space beyond the atmosphere. They are busy to explore outer space to study planets, stars, galaxies and other objects in the sky. This step is insignificant compared to the vastness of the Universe. Because of the infinite size of the Universe there is no possibility for man to explore or go beyond the boundary of the Universe. In fact there is no boundary of the Universe, He says:

> "O ye assembly of Jinns and men! If it be ye can pass beyond the zones of the heavens and the earth, pass ye! Not without authority shall ye be able to pass!"
> —(55:33)

This verse has given the indication of the vastness of the Universe and limited ability of man. The sun, moons, stars and other objects are created by God for the use by man, as gifts from Him. They may be studied within man's limitation and may be made useful in many ways. He has not put any condition or hindrance in studying the objects of the sky:

> "He has made subject to you the night and day; sun and the moon, and the stars are in subjection by His command: verily in this are Signs for men who are wise." —(16:12)

In the above verse, the words "subject to you" and "who are wise" are worthy of notice. Man may be more benefitted from the heavenly objects on study, reflection and applying knowledge gathered from such studies.

Technical Education

The essence of knowledge is having it, to apply it; not having it, to confess your ignorance as put by great Confucius. Studies of nature or science has given birth to Applied Science and Technical Education. For science education, many experiments are performed for observation of any phenomenon and verification of theoretical predictions or results. Experimentation needs many equipments and it is required to establish laboratories. Scientific knowledge gathered this way is used or implemented in many ways for better life style and comfort. As a result of scientific knowledge various machines, vehicles and other communication systems, ways and means for defense, etc., are being invented and being used. Industries for production of various items; whether it is medicine, food, cloth, vehicles, electronic goods, stationeries, etc., are established throughout the world. There were several messengers of Allah, the Almighty before Muhammad (PBUH) who were blessed with technical knowledge. Thus, Prophet David (Daud) was a good technologist to make various items with iron. He says:

> "And we made the iron soft for him; (commanding), "Make thou coats of mail, balancing well the rings of chain armour, and work ye right." —(34:10-11)

Manufacture of coats of mail and defensive armour are attributed to David. In this verse, with the mention of technical knowledge of David, the God had warned David and his whole people by the words "Work ye righteousness". David made the armour, but it was to be worn not only by him but all the warriors. But he and his people were to be careful to see that they did not deviate from the paths of righteousness. This warning equally applies to the modern scientists, engineers and the general people of the world. Manufacturing anything should be aimed at for righteous causes, it should not in any case create problems or misused by Governments or individual to create disturbances on this earth. Prophet Solomon was also a great engineer. He used brass for making various materials, dishes, temples known as "Temple of Solomon."

Al-Quran mentions it in this way:

> "And we made a Font of molten brass to flow for him (Solomon);...." —(34:12)

> "They (Jinns) worked for him as he desired, (making) arches, images, basins as large as wells, and (cooking) Couldrons fixed (in their places)." —(34:13)

The Almighty made violent and speedy winds available to the land of Solomon. He had miraculous power over winds and could tame them for his use.

> "(we made) violent wind flow for Solomon" —(21.81)

"And to Solomon (we made) this wind (obedient)."
—(34:12)

"Then we subjected the wind to his power, to flow gently to his order, whatsoever he willed...."
—(38:36)

Solomon used wind energy in his own way. Nowadays wind power has become one of the major sources of energy. God has granted man intelligence and faculties by which he can tame different forces of nature like winds for his use.

The story of ship-building technique or engineering may be traced back to the days of Prophet Nuh. It was to be a great flood during his time. So Nuh was instructed by Him to remain afloat in the flood, so that the righteous could be saved in it during the flood.

"And construct Ark under our eyes and our inspiration." —(11:37)

"Forthwith he (started) constructing the Ark".
—(11:38)

Thus, we see from the verses mentioned above that there was technical culture among the people of the past and several prophets were directly involved in technical or engineering activities. They possessed knowledge of metallurgy, heavy construction work, taming wind energy for useful purposes, ship-building, using iron and brass. The Holy Quran has characteristics to mention history of the past so that people can learn a lesson from them. The Prophet Muhammad (PBUH) himself showed examples in his lifetime. He never hesitated to take most modern techniques of his time for defense purposes. Thus for example, he constructed trench (Khandak) to save Medina from the attack by the enemies, the people of Mecca, which was a very new technique at that time in the whole Arab world. In the expedition to Khyber, he also adopted new techniques. He (PBUH) adopted technical tricks or knowledge whenever necessary to win a war.

Holy Prophet's Commands : Progress of any nation is judged by the number of properly educated people of the nation. One of the ways for people to become wise or educated is by study on "Nature" and reflection or research on natural things and phenomena. Educated men and women can understand or realise the vastness of the Universe, complexity of the macro as well as micro world and also realize the greatness of the creation of the God.

Muhammad (PBUH) was not literate in literal sense, but he was enlightened by the best of knowledge by Almighty Himself. He was guided and shown the best path and he could realise the creation of the Universe better than any other human body. That is why, gathering knowledge through education, and reflection were dearer to him. Because of importance and necessity he has made education compulsory for all the Muslims. Muhammad (PBUH) said: as reported by Anas:

> "The seeking of knowledge is obligatory to every Muslim" —Ibn Majah; Baihaqi

Again he (PBUH) said as reported by Anas:

> "One who goes out to search for knowledge is (devoted) to the cause of Allah till he returns"
> —Tirmidhi and Darimi

Again as Abu Umama Al-Bahili reported:

> "Allah's Messenger (PBUH) said: The superiority, of a scholar over the devout is like my superiority over one who is of the lowest rank amongst you."
> —Tirmidhi

Al-Azdi reported:

> "He Who acquires knowledge it is an expiation for his past sin." —Tirmidhi, Darimi

Studies and teachings of religious subjects are also processes of acquiring knowledge. Abu Hurrayrah reported Almighty's Messenger (PBUH) as saying:

> "Learn obligatory acts and the Quran and teach them to the people for I am mortal" —Tirmidhi

In this Hadith the Messenger (PBUH) reminded us his mortality and asked people to acquire Divine Knowledge from him and teach them to others.

Abu Hurrayrah reported God's Messenger (PBUH) as saying:

> "Verily what a believer continues to receive (in the form of reward) for his action and his virtues after his death is the knowledge which he acquired and then disseminated...." —Ibn Majah, Baihaqi

He (PBUH) said as reported by Ibn Abbas:

> "Acquiring of knowledge in company for an hour in the night is better than spending the whole night in prayer." —Darimi

There are also other Hadiths (Traditions) on the importance of *ilm* (knowledge) or on acquiring it.

In many of the Traditions, seeking of knowledge has been termed as a part of Ibadat (Prayer). By *ibadat*, as we know, the path towards Paradise becomes easier. Similar is the case with seeking of knowledge.

When we speak of knowledge, it is not meant theological or religious knowledge only. It covers all types of knowledge. Studies of all subjects lead one to earn more knowledge. To earn knowledge on different subjects such as theology, history, literature, science, etc., one should study those subjects. Similarly for administration or to rule a country, or for, trade and business studies are necessary to acquire knowledge on these topics. Studies of different subjects of science are very essential to understand natural phenomena and natural things and it becomes easier to realise science of creation. A true student of science becomes a true believer of the Creator. A knowledgeable person who is also a scholar has high place in Islam. The Messenger of Almighty (PBUH) said:

> "The superiority of the scholar over a worshipper is like that of moon in the night when it is full over the rest of the stars."
> —Ahmad, Tirmidhi, Abu Daud, Ibn Majah, Darimi

As to how much education and hence knowledge were dearer to the Prophet (PBUH), which can be guessed from the following historical incident:

In the Battle of Badr, the Muslims came victorious and there were about seventy prisoners of war. The Prophet (PBUH), holding a council decided to liberate them on payment of ransom. Four thousand *dirahms* (unit of money) was fixed as the rate of ransom for ordinary prisoners. Even the relatives of the Prophet were not exempted. In spite of all these things, the Prophet (PBUH) asked the literates among the prisoners only to teach ten Muslim boys, each how to read and write and this would be their ransom.

—(Ref. Ibn Saad Vol II / i p p14, 17, *Ibn Hanbal* Vol I, p 246, Also The Battlefields of the Prophet Muhammad (PBUH) by M. Hamidullah pp 40, 41)

From the historical fact referred to above, it can be understood that both religious and general education are essential for acquiring knowledge. At the time of Rasoolullah (PBUH), knowledge of the Islam (such as methods of daily prayer knowledge of Tauhid etc.) was given directly by him (PBUH) and his companions. In spite of that he (PBUH) realised the importance of general education and as such encouraged people to acquire knowledge through general education in addition to theological knowledge. That is why, he (PBUH) set the condition for the unbelievers (prisoners of war) to teach Muslim boys reading and writing instead of paying cash as their ransom for their freedom.

In this modern age, many institutions are being established for different disciplines. Thus, there are Madrasas for religious education, schools and colleges for studying science, literature, history, political science, and other courses, while higher institutions for medical science and engineering or technical education have also sprung up. The guardians become indecisive or get confused in selecting the type of education or institutions for their children. It is true that religious education for obligatory duties is a must for every Muslim child. There cannot be hesitation or two opinions about the urgency of Islamic education. Children must require to learn reciting Holy Quran, know necessary things of *halal* and *haram*, also know prayers and practices and, know basic things to lead Islamic way of life. In addition to religious knowledge, children should study science and also devote their time for engineering and technical education. This will help them earn more knowledge and improve their thinking capacity and family condition. The Messenger of the Almighty (PBUH) said about proper education of children in this way:

> "The best gift that a father can bestow upon his son (children) is to arrange good education and training for him." —Mishkat

The importance or usefulness of knowledge can be understood from the following description cited by Ziauddin Sardar in his arguments for Islamic science:

> "Knowledge is obligatory only in so far (it) is requisite for acting rightly. God condemns those who learn useless knowledge, and the Prophet (PBUH) said "I take refuge with thee from knowledge that profiteth naught". Much may be done by means of a little

> knowledge and knowledge should not be separated from action. The Prophet said: "The devotee without divinity is like a donkey turning a mill" because the donkey goes round and round on its tracks and never makes any advances."
>
> —(Ref *Quest for New Science* p. 47 eds. S.N. Ahmad)

More was said about the importance of practical knowledge.

> "The worst of man in the eye of Allah on the Day of Resurrection would be the scholar who does not derive benefit from knowledge" —Darimi

In fact knowledge and its application should go together. Even religious knowledge should be put into practice in religious duties. So also the case with scientific and other knowledge. Abu Hurrayrah reported God's Messenger (PBUH) as saying:

> "The knowledge from which no benefit is derived is like a treasure out of which nothing is spent in the cause of Allah" —Ahmad and Darimi

God, the Greatest Scientist : Studies of Nature or creation of God, i.e. science is a different subject. If we read the different aspects of civilisation, we come to know that from the primitive way of life and primitive stage of thinking, man has reached the present day state through continuous study and search of knowledge. In this long struggle to understand nature, innumerable mistakes were committed, correct or wrong paths or views were taken. Right conclusions or truth could be achieved after many ups and downs in the scientific search. Even now wrong or incorrect paths, views or conclusions are being corrected. In the field of politics, for example, sociology, communism, capitalism, monarchy, military or dictatorship or a system based on religious principles are being tried. Many people are not yet sure as to which system would be appropriate or universal for mankind.

The Holy Quran claims that Islam is the correct system for mankind. After many changes, rejection and acceptance, correct system may be found by man. Similar is the case in the studies of science. Scientists have some methods of their own to study nature in search of true knowledge behind any phenomena. Generally, to study or to know natural phenomena or laws, scientists may proceed in two ways:

(1) He theoretically explains or predicts and after that he establishes the truth i.e. he proves by adopting different experiments, or

(2) He observes, natural phenomena and then he finds the laws governing the observed phenomena and thus he explains as to how the phenomena happen.

If the theoretical explanation and the experimental observations of the phenomena tally, then theory is accepted as correct, if there is difference between the theoretical explanation and the natural laws or phenomena then the theory is rejected and a new theory or explanation based on certain modified assumptions are put forward by scientists. Thus, scientists sometimes adopt trial and error method to find out the truth. If we read history of science, we see commission of many mistakes and their correction.

Fundamental Particles of Matter

We can cite the examples of committing so many errors in finding the true nature of the smallest part of matter called atom. First, scientists put forward the idea that the smallest part of matter which is indivisible and fundamental or building block of matter is the atom. But afterwards as a result of more scientific studies scientists could know that atom is not the fundamental particle. It is divisible and it is made up of a number of smaller particles known as proton, neutron and electron.

In their search for atomic structure, scientists initially told us that atom is having positive as well as negative electric charges and the charges are equally distributed throughout the atom. But deep studies and researches revealed that the atomic structure is more complicated. It has a centre called the nucleus containing proton particles with positive charges, and neutron particles without any charges.

It was also found that more smaller particles called electrons with negative charges are revolving with high velocity around the nucleus on different orbits. The total number of electrons on the orbits are same as that of the number of protons in the nucleus. These findings are not the final. With the advancement of scientific studies it was later discovered that protons and neutrons within the atom are not again fundamental particles of matter. They are made up of even more smaller particles. Thus, scientists have not been successful as yet in knowing the true nature or true building block of matter. We observe that scientists have to put forward many theories to know the true nature out of which some are rejected. A sort of trial and error method is adopted. This has happened because scientists or in other words man has limitation in their thinking. Scientists in their search for knowledge can understand partially the complete phenomena of creation but can never secure the perfect knowledge. All knowledge is attributed to the Almighty only. The Holy Quran declares this:

> "To Allah belongeth the Unseen of the heavens and the earth" —(16:77)

Through studies of nature (science) one can realize the complexity of creation only, but can not understand the process of creation. Scientist should realise his weakness and his inability as well. God says:

> "Man was created weak." — (4:28)

Scientist knows that limitation and that is why he never claims finality of his research finding.

The Ideas and Knowledge of Scientists Regarding Time and Place

Initially the idea of time was that it is unchangeable and it is an absolute thing. At any time under any condition time will have the same value. This means that for an observer in motion or at rest, the length of time of any event will be the same. But after the introduction of Theory of Relativity by Albert Einstein, the notion of time has changed. According to this theory, duration of time or age of any event depends on its state of motion or its velocity. If we move with greater velocity, it will appear to us living more time compared to one at rest. This means that if we travel in space with great speed (at the speed of light for example) for sometime by a rocket or other advanced space craft and return to earth, we would see many decades already have passed on earth. This theory of relativity is not a production of mere imagination.

The truth is already established by different experiments. In Geneva (Switzerland) in the Particle research laboratory (CERN) this experiment is done easily. Here small charged particles like muon of different speeds are produced. Muons are unstable and quickly change to other particles such as electrons or neutrons. It has been observed the life times of high speed muons are larger than the life times of slow speed muons. Though it is difficult to believe that life time or age depends on speed, but it is true. Theory of Relativity changed the whole notion of time and space and the earlier idea of absolute time and space had to be abandoned.

The Uncertainty Principle put forward by Heisenberg has revealed limitation of knowledge of scientists. This theory warned us that we have limitations of knowledge by birth in knowing the absolute nature of any thing. It will be easier to illustrate this principle by an example: Thus, by an experiment if a scientist knows the absolute position (coordinates) of an electron, he can not know by the same experiment, its motion or its velocity if it is moving. If velocity of the electron is measured, it is not possible to know its position at the same time. Here lies the limitation of knowledge of a scientist.

Thus, how a scientist can boast of his limited knowledge? He can study Nature to understand creation but he can not become equal to Almighty ever, he even is not able to understand a small fraction of His infinite scientific talent. Scientist can not acquire smallest of the smallest portion of infinite knowledge. Though Almighty has invited mankind to study nature to realize His creativity and scientific talent, in reality Almighty is the Supreme, all knowing visible and invisible.

> "He knoweth the Unseen and that which is open: He is the Great, the Most High." —(13:9)

One of the greatest scientists, Ishaq Newton the inventor of the universal laws of gravitation was reported to say that he could pick up a grain of sand standing on the bank of a sea of infinite knowledge. In such a miserable situation of a scientist, religion should not have any apprehension of losing its credibility. A true scientist can not put comment or own view or change any part of the religious systems introduced by the Creator Himself. A true believing scientist, knowing his limitation of knowledge can not put suspicion on the revelation in the Holy Quran. Rather he will have more faith in the Holy Book and fear Him. The Holy Quran asserts:

> "This is the Book; in it is guidance sure, without doubt to those who fear Allah; who believe in the unseen..."
> —(2:2-3)

And the fear of God may be the beginning of Wisdom.

Religious View : Common people want to know the views of scientists in respect of religion particularly about the existence of God and also their personal believes. Opinions of a few great scientists are mentioned below:

Albert Einstein's View: Einstein, formulator of Theory of Relativity was born in Germany and was a Jew. His whole life was busy with studying natural phenomena and cosmogony and ultimately at the old age he became completely a religious person in the true sense. He was fascinated and overwhelmed with the Universe, the creation of God and he wrote this way:

> "A knowledge of the existence of something we can not penetrate, our perceptions of the profoundest reason and the most radiant beauty, which only in their most primitive forms are accessible to our minds—it is this knowledge and this emotion that constitute true religiosity; in this sense and in this alone, I am deeply religious man. I can not conceive of a God Who rewards and punishes His creatures, or has a will of the kind that we experience in ourselves."

Again he wrote:

> "I am satisfied with the mystery of the eternity of life and with the awareness and a glimpse of the marvellous structure of the existing world, together with the devoted striving to comprehend a portion, be it ever so tiny, of the Reason that manifests itself in nature."

Abdus Salam's View: From Muslim Ummah first and only Nobel Prize winner Abdus Salam was one of the forefront scientists of modern times. He was born near the city of Jhung of India (and now in Pakistan). From metric onwards he passed different examinations with position and earned Ph.D. degree in 1950 from Cambridge. He was deeply engaged in advanced research and had published more than 250 papers in different scientific journals. He was until recently Director of International Centre for Theoretical Physics, Then a research institute established by him for third world scientists. It was reported that after receiving the news of his selection for Nobel Prize, he went straight to the mosque and offered thanks giving prayer to God for the award. Abdus Salam from his childhood started studying the Holy Book Al-Quran. Afterwards as a result of studies of nature or science he became a staunt believer of the Almighty. His own words are quoted below:

> "Let me say at the outset that I am both a believer as well as a practising Muslim. I am a Muslim because I believe in the spiritual message of the Holy Quran. As a scientist, the Quran speaks to me in that it emphasises reflection on the Laws of Nature, with examples drawn from Cosmology, Physics, Biology and Medicine, as Signs for all men."

C.V. Raman's View: C.V. Raman was a great scientist of Indian subcontinent and a Nobel Prize winner in Physics. He was religious from his childhood. After becoming famous as a scientist he was religious equally. He did not leave his religious related dress, habit of vegetarian and daily religious activities. In a party after the Nobel Award ceremony, he was offered to drink alcohol. But because of his strong religious faith he politely refused to do so.

Views of other Indian scientists are more or less similar. Science studies are found to influence their religious belief. It is concluded from the analysis of personal life of scientists that their belief in Creator (Almighty) increases as a result of deep study of nature i.e. science. Thus, the apprehension that science education may detract people from religion, has no basis. There is no reason of becoming allergic to science for the Muslims.

Of course, there are some examples of scientists becoming athiests or unbelievers of Almighty. Famous scientist Darwin from his studies of fossils of animals and other things put forward theory of evolution of life on this earth. He did not believe the creation of mankind as envisaged in religion. But there are exceptions not only in the case of scientists but also in common people as well. Nonbelievers were there in the time of Rasoolullah (PBUH) also. These scientists and common people do not learn to take advise from the revelations. They do not believe in Almighty and the Hereafter.

They usually say that the universe and the life are not created. They have come into existence spontaneously. They will die and will not be created again. That means there is no Hereafter. Almighty knows these people very well and put their way of thinking in the Holy Quran this way:

> "And they say: what is there but our life in this world? We shall die and we live, and nothing but time can destroy us". But of that they have no knowledge: they merely conjecture." – (45:24)

They do not also take lessons from the innumerable signs existing in nature or creation of the Almighty. Their different organs such as of seeing (eyes), learning (ears), etc., do not work in the true sense and they do not apply their intellect in the proper way. For these people he says in the Holy Quran:

> "Those whom Allah Willeth to guide, He Openeth their breasts to Islam; Those whom He Willeth to leave straying, He maketh their breasts close and constricted." – (6:125)

In fact, there is no basic difference between science and religious belief. One is complimentary to another. Where science can not reach religion helps. Knowledge or ideas which are not realizable in science can be realized or extracted from the Holy Quran. Again revelations related to science are required to be explained or understood in the light of knowledge gathered from science studies. Thus, studies of science are necessary not only for a scientific or planned and meaningful way of life but also for understanding religious thoughts and revelations and to realize them.

Man has limited knowledge and also for him it is not possible to secure perfect knowledge. Because of this, religion puts a condition to believe the unseen, though it can not be proved by experiments. The faithful religious persons believe the revelations that the God creates every thing from nothing:

> "When He decreath a matter, He saith to it: 'Be' and it is." — (2:117)

Till now, scientists have not been able to find the solution of this i.e. unseen. Researches are going on to find the riddle of life. Only time will tell the outcome of research.

The Zenith : From the foregoing discussion we come to the conclusion that there is no religious bar or prohibition in studying science by the Muslims. Rather God has directed and advised man in different verses of Al-Quran to gather knowledge from the studies of Nature and to get benefit from it. The Messenger of God (PBUH) himself also gave much stress on seeking of knowledge from different sources.

The Muslims after his (PBUH) death have been observed to follow those instructions sincerely. Only within about two hundred years after Muhammad's (PBUH) death, the Muslims had undertaken plans and programmes to study science. In this first two centuries Muslim rulers, thoughts and energies were directed towards establishing the new Islamic states and consolidating their positions. We see in history how once Islamic science and technology flourished throughout the Islamic world and outside. Islam has always been positive force of achievement in science and technology.

During the glorious period of Islamic civilization which continued about seven hundred years, from about 700 AD to 1500 AD, Islamic science and technology flourished., Many great Muslim scientists who ushered a new horizon of science were born during this period. Some of them are:

Jabir Ibn Haytham, Abu-Bakr Ibn Zakriya, Ibn al-Haytham, Al-Beruni, Abu Sin (Abisina) and many others.

Many Muslims polymaths were also born at this period. Some of them are al-Jahiz (d 868), al-Kindi (d 873), al-Razi (d 925), al-Idrisi (b 1166), ibn Bajjah (d 1138), Umar Khayyam (d 517) , ibn Zuhr (d 1162), ibn Tufail (d 1185), ibn Rushd 91198), al-Suyuti (d 1505) and many others.

—(Ref: Ziauddin Sardar, in *Quest for New Science*, edited by R. Ahmad and S.N. Ahmad 1984, P. 55).

As put by Z. Sardar, "these scholars gave "emphasis on synthesis and interdisciplinary investigations, inultiplicity of methods and social function and accountability before God, which produced an institution which is largely unique in Islam and is unparalleled by any other civilisation."

One of the key factors of spreading and flourishing Islamic civilisation was the well planned scheme for science undertaken by the Muslim rulers at that time.

Steps taken for the pursuance of science education and research were many such as: Arabacising and translations of scientific topics from different sources, establishment of academics, observatories and libraries; patronage of scientists and conduct of scientific and technological research; as well as running of state industries and technological research.

For the Muslims, Islam and the Arabic language have always been the two unifying forces. Because of the language of the Holy Quran, Arabic became the language of all the people in the Islamic world. It became the language of daily life and the language of science and literature replacing other languages. Caliphs from the early days of the Umayyads realized the importance of learning science by the vast majority of Muslims in Arabic and Muslim scientists translated many scientific works into Arabic. The works of the Greeks, of the Near-East and of India were translated into Arabic. The technological books written by the Banu Musa brothers, al-Jazari, Ridwan, Taqi-al-Din and others are some of the examples of literature translated into Arabic.

By the end of the second and beginning of third Hijri (A.H) (8th to 9th centuries A.D.) some authoritative dictionaries and grammars were compiled for scientific and literary use by some scholars such as Abu Zaid, Ubaidah and Al-Asma. Al Kindi (ninth century A.D.) was one of the most original thinkers and philosophers of the Arab's who wrote on a variety of subjects including mineralogy and metallurgy, geology, physics, pharmacology and medicines.

Hunain b. Ishaq (d. 260 A.H./A.D. 873) was a famous translator - scientist who worked in Baghdad in Abbasid times. He translated many scientific works from the Greek manuscripts and also wrote on philosophical, meteorological, zoological, linguistics and religious subjects, besides composing original works. The work of translation and original scientific writing had begun before the Abbasids assumed power and it was Baghdad of the 3rd century A.H.: (9th century) which witnessed the earliest Islamic scientific activities. Over the next seven centuries, Islamic science flourished at different parts of the Muslim world.

Muslim rulers established many scientific academics, schools, libraries, observatories and other centres of higher education in their respective states. Some of the institutions were patronized by the rulers of the states, some by ministers, princes as well as rich men.

The caliphs or the rulers always patronized scientists, research scholars and.engineers. In all the academics, libraries, madrasas, hospitals and observatories. Financial means were provided to enable scientists to devote all their times for study and research. They were paid salaries and granted pensions.

The Caliph al-Mamun (813 AD), for example, established in Baghdad a scientific institution which was known as Baitul-Hikma (House of wisdom). Two astronomical observatories, one in Baghdad and the other in Damascus, were attached to this academy and a staff of eminent scientists were included among the members of the academy. Thus, a nucleus was formed at Baitul-Hikma at Baghdad. Later such centres were established at different major cities of the Islamic world such as Damascus, Cairo, Nishapur, Cardova, Gernada and other places.

Caliph Harun al-Rashid established a big library called Khizanat al-Hikma (library of wisdom). During the period of Fatimids (909-1171 AD) libraries were parts of palaces. In 1004 AD, al-Hakim founded Dar al-Hikma (House of wisdom) in a palace which contained a library, reading room and which was the meeting of learned scholars including doctors, mathematicians and astronomers. Houses of libraries of science, on the model of the Baitul-Hikma in Baghdad and the Dar-al-Hikma in Cairo became numerous. Some were established by public funds and others by individuals.

The mosques were always centres of learning. Libraries were attached to the mosques as well. In the early days of Islam, the mosques were the centres of teaching and learning from which madrasa type education started. Gradually such education became formal and madrasa buildings were built attached to most of the mosques. Some Universities were developed from Madrasas where teaching and researches were carried out on various subjects. Some important universities were established during the glorious time of Islamic science are: al-Azhar in Cairo, the Zaytuniyya in Tunis and Qarawiyyin in Fez. For teaching of medicine, pharmacology and related subjects Medical Schools were established attached to hospitals.

Studies of astronomical science also made progress in the golden days of Islamic science. In addition to two observatories attached to Baitul-Hikma, the observatories of Ulugh Beg in Samarqand and of Taqi al-Din in Istanbul and the Maragha observatory were at peaks in the studies of astronomy.

Muslim scientists and engineers developed their science and technology through continuous process of research, experiments and inventions. Thus, Banu Musa brothers, engaged in writing or translation in their early stage, but became researchers and inventors in later stage. Their mathematical and engineering book *Kitab al-Hiyal* (Book of Ingenious Devices) described about hundred devices out of which about seventy five were of their own designs. Similar was the case with al-Jazari in 12th century. The approach of al-Jazari was more experimental. He said in his book "Compendium of the theory and practice of the Mechanical Arts", that any industrial science is a doubtful science if that is not verified by experiments. Similar was Taqial-Din, scientist of much later time.

Great Strider

There are hundreds of thousands of Islamic manuscripts in the world's libraries, dealing with scientific works of Muslim scientists of the earlier period. Mention of a few will greatly distort or omit the general picture. Nevertheless, a brief mention of a few great Muslim scientists and their scientific works may help in focussing the Muslim achievement in the past.

Field of work of Muslim scientists were generally broad enough to include most of the sciences in those days. But in their later parts of life, each of them became, specialist in one or more of the sciences. Muslim contribution in science and technology are discussed below in a nutshell:

(i) In Mathematics Muslim scientists contributed most original work. The Indian system of reckoning using the nine Arabic numerals with a point for zero and application of decimal fractions were introduced by Muslims. Al-Khawarizimi (210 A.H./A.D. 875) laid the foundation of Algebra. The word "algorithm" came from the name of the great mathematician Al-Khawarizimi whose real name was Abu Jafar Muhammad bin Musa. Poet Umar Khayyam (d 526 A.H./A.D. 1131) also made significant contribution in Algebra. Muslim mathematicians made great contributions towards geometry. They applied geometry in surveying, construction of machines, etc., and used to solve problems and make calculations. Muslims were the inventors of plane and spherical trigonometry introducing functions of sine, cosine and tangent. Al-Battani (d. 317 A.H./A.D. 929) presented a formula involving three sides and one angle of a spherical triangle which has no equivalent in Ptolemy. Abul-Wafa (d. 388 A.H./A.D. 929) was one of the greatest Muslim mathematicians who invented secent and coseceunt, demonstrated the sine theorem for the general spherical triangle and proposed a new technique for the construction of sine tables.

(ii) In Astronomy Muslims showed much interest in the past. They gave much interest in the observation and instrumentation. Problems or contradictions found by Ptolemy in his geocentric theory were resolved by Ibn al-Shatir in the 14th century AD. Muslim astronomers developed spherical trigonometry to solve or correct astronomical problems which were equally valid in sun-centered system. They also worked on making calendar problems of time keeping and to locate the direction of Mecca (Qibla) from any place. Astronomer al-Khalili (8th century A.H) with the help of accurate trigonometrical and computational methods could give an accurate Qibla table.

(iii) Islamic contribution to Physics (science that deals with physical laws and energies) can only be appreciated by a thorough study of Muslim physics. Ibn al-Haytham

(d. 430 A.H./1039 AD) was a great mathematician and without any doubt the greatest physicist. His words had profound influence on later scientists. He had significant contributions in advanced level experimental optics. The Formats Principle which is known to modern students of optics was described by al-Haytham many centuries earlier. He discovered spherical aberration of light, explained refraction of sun rays through atmosphere of the earth. The law of inertia was originally introduced by al-Haytham. This law after many centuries became known as Newton's (1642-1727 AD) first law of motion. Unfortunately al-Haytham's name is not found in this connection even as the originator of the idea. One of his books *Kitab al-Manazir* (book on optics) was translated into Latin which had a profound influence in the Middle Ages. Al-Beruni (973-1048 AD) of Afghanistan was a great scientist well versed in mathematics, astronomy, physical science and other subjects. Al-Beruni was also a great experimentalist. He always tested his conclusions by observations and experiments. He was an instrument maker and constructed astrolabes and a geared-mechanical calendar. Al-Khazim wrote a fine book *Kital Mizan al Hikma* based on his work on specific gravity and discussed in it a theory of gravity and many instruments. His book is a fine work on mechanics, hydrostatics and physics.

(iv) In Chemistry and Chemical Industries, Muslim scientists also made significant contributions. The works of Jabir b. Hayyan (8th century AD), Abu Bakr al Razi (d-925/ A.D.), al-Kindi (9th century AD), and others were very important. Modern chemical engineering, and chemical industries of today owe much to their works. Al-Razi contributed valuable knowledge and knowhow to the modern chemists regarding distillation, solution, calcination, evaporation, crystallization, sublimation, filtration, amalgamation, creation, etc., and the various chemical processes involved in them. His book *Kitab al-Asrar* gave full account of different alchemical equipments. Al-Kindi was also a great chemist. His treatise *kitab kimya al-Itr waal Tasidat* (book of perfume, chemistry and distillation) was very useful for Islamic chemical industry. Some of the major areas in which Muslim scientists and engineers had great contributions are:

(v) Mechanical Engineering: Water raising for irrigation, drinking, domestic and industrial purposes, harnessing water power and wind power, water clocks and mechanical clocks, scientific equipments etc.

(vi) Civil Engineering : Building technology, roads and bridges, irrigation systems such as canals, dams, reservoirs etc.

(vii) Military Technology : arms such as swords, lance, bows, shields and mace, siege engines such as missile thrower, trabuchet, incediary weapons, gun powder and cannon, construction of forts, etc.

(viii) Ships and Navigation : Ship building, navigation and navies.

(ix) Chemical Industries : Chemical equipments, distillation, manufacture of perfumes, rose water, essential oils, petroleum refining (the oil fields of Baku were developed on a commercial basis by Muslims). Discovery and production of some inorganic acids: nitric acid; sulphuric and hydrochloric acids, some organic acids, alkalis, soap etc., glass making, ceramics, pottery, writing and painting materials, such as ink and pigments, varnishes, dyes, etc.

(x) Textile Industries : Works on wool, linen, cotton, silk, paper and leather manufactures.

(xi) Agriculture and Food Technology : New crops, new farming practices, agricultural implements such as ploughs, harrows, rakes, milling, production of sugar, edible vegetable oils, foods and drinks, preservation of foods.

(xii) Mining and Metallurgy : Development of mining technology; mining of most essential minerals such as gold, silver, copper, tin, iron and steel, mercury, salt, alum, coal, precious stones, exploitation of underwater resources such as pearls, etc.

The above mentioned branches of science are technological or applied science. Muslim scientists were thus active in studying nature and were serious in applying their knowledge for the benefit of the people. Engineers and architects were called in those days as 'al-muhandisun' which came from the word 'handasa' meaning engineering and architecture's. However, in many cases there was not much difference between an engineer and a scientist. Generally any scientist involved in a subject concentrated to apply the knowledge in practising fields. Thus, Jabir was a chemist and engineer, al-Kindi a physicist as well as a metallurgist and engineer, al-Razi a chemist, engineer and physician, Banu Musa brothers mathematicians, physicists and engineers; Al-Beruni an astronomer, physicist and engineer. Some like Al-Jazari devoted themselves solely to engineering.

Evolution of Islamic Science : An analysis reveals that contributions of Muslim scientists from the 8th century to the 15th century AD laid the foundation of European science to be flourished now. Muslim scientists did not leave untouched any branch of science. In medicine Ibn Sina and Al-Razi, in physical science Al-Beruni, in mathematics Al-Khawarizimi, in astronomy Al-Zarkali and Ulugh Beg, in navigation Ibn Batuta are some of many Muslim scientists whose work were the cause of progress of European science. There were many hospitals, Universities, research laboratories in Muslim countries when there was scarcity of books in science in Europe, Baghdad, Damascus, Cairo, Cordova, Gernada, etc. being the centres of Islamic science.

The Arabs studied and developed algebra, calculus, optical geometry, navigation well ahead of European scientists. It is said that the Muslims discovered America before Columbus. In fact, a Muslim was a guide of Columbus (Ref. *Quest for New Science* p. 150). Students from France, England, Portugal, Italy and Germany came to Gernada, Cordova, Madrid, etc., of Spain to study astronomy, medical science, chemistry, physics and mathematics. Roger Bacon, the father of modern science had been a student in Muslim institutions. Copernicus the great astronomer borrowed many ideas from the Muslim astronomers. Some of these students translated the works of Muslim scientists into their native languages of Europe. The influence of these books were so great that even Newton is said to read the book of Muhammad bin Musa on motion of celestial bodies and force of attraction. Many writers translated Arabic contents of science into European languages. Many centres for translation were there. Of these centres of Toleddo, Seville and Solerno were famous. An Arabic-Latin dictionary was compiled to facilitate Arabic translation. (Ref. I, *Quest for New Science* p. 150).

The Pre-Islamic civilisation from Spain to the Central Asia and northern India were inherited by Islam. Under the influence of Islam science and technology of these regions were developed and improved.

There was large scale technology transfer from the Islamic world to Europe. This is reflected by the many words of Arabic derivation that have entered into vocabularies of European languages to cite a few examples:

in textiles – muslin, sarsanet, damask, taffela, tabby;

in naval matters –arrival , admiral,

in chemical technology – alembic, alcohol, akali;

in paper – ream;

in food stuffs – alfalfa, sugar, syrup, sherbat,

in dye stuffs – saffron, kermes;

in leather works – cordovan, morocco;

Muslims were quite advanced in the fields of agriculture irrigation, hydraulic engineering etc. The Muslim ideas in these fields and others passed from Spain into Italy and northern Europe. Other installations, such as the water clocks on the bank of the Tagus at Toledo, the paper mill at Jativa near Valencia were taken over by the Christians from the Muslims. Nowadays other examples of technology transfer are given in a book *Islamic Technology* compiled by Ahmad Y. al-Hassan and Donald R. Hill. Contributions of the Muslim scientists towards Western science are more than the Greeks. The Greek philosophers mainly took the help of arguments, reasonings, etc., to arrive at conclusions or to find out the truths.

For this reason Aristotle, Pythogoras, Galen and Aristocres did not possess any laboratory for observational research. On the other hand, Muslim scientists favoured to experimental verification of arguments or reasonings and as such they established their own laboratories and observations. For experimental purposes they devised and fabricated many instruments and appliances. From excavation near Baghdad ruins of such a laboratory of Jabir bin Hayyan have already been discovered. Western historians of science have also borne, this testimony. Also instruments invented by Muslims preserved in museums prove the above mentioned facts.

Today modern science has the foundation on experiments and observations. Its sustenance has been derived from the experimental methods of Muslim scientists and not from the deductive and analogical method of the Greeks. Because of the introduction of experimental methods, different branches of science have made tremendous progress in Europe. The role of the Muslims in bringing a revolution in Europe is acknowledged by Alessandro Bausani, the Italian Orientalist, this way:

> "..... it is also true that during our middle ages the Muslim world was considered more or less like America now i.e. the world to which one had to go perfect oneself in science and technology." —(Ref. quoted by H.R. Siddiqi in his paper Science from the Muslim World into Europe.

Reverse Journey : It is clear from the discussion made above, that after the death of the Messenger of Allah (PBUH), Muslims followed instructions of the Quran and then Hadiths strictly and concentrated not only in spreading the messages of Islam but also gave much attention in learning science and for that purpose established many institutions in different parts of the Muslim world. Many Muslim rulers patronized these institutions. In course of time for various reasons unstability started in the Muslim kingdom and there had been frequent changes of rulers in many places, as a result patronization of these institutions by Muslim rulers were gradually diminished and ultimately stopped. Between the last part of the eleventh century and first part of twelfth century there was much political unstability and uncertainty and religious conflicts among the Muslims.

During this period real downfall of Islamic science started. In the beginning the determination of spreading Islamic teaching and idealism was the guiding force to the progress of science and achievement and this was at its peak when the Muslim States were stable and their economic conditions were sound. With the political disintegration of the Muslim states and the deterioration of economic life of Muslims, progress of Islamic science and achievement began to decline. Muslims were slowly deviating themselves from the teachings of the Holy Quran and Hadiths and their political power was declining one after another.

The Christians at this time started to realize their religious superstition and there was renaissance in Europe. During this period Sufisim, a new practice of Islam, unknown to the earlier Muslims was slowly introduced. After the hanging of Mansur al-Hillaj (922 A.D.), Sufism became widespread. Common people having no advanced knowledge of religion started to accept Sufism which is an advanced and mystic religious philosophy. As a result, instead of dynamic and progressive activities in the field of searching knowledge through science education a stagnant situation was developed. Muslim Ulamas also could not escape from this. The movement of religious fanaticism by the clerical factions against science was so strong that the last observatory in Islam established in Constantinople was demolished by Taqi al-Din in 1580 AD. In contrast the first observatory was established at this time by Tycho Brahe in the West.

On the other hand, after long and continuous sufferance and exploitation renaissance started in Europe. Being guided by wrong idea and wrong explanations of religion a sense of repulsion from religion was developed in the minds of these people and they could easily concentrate on materialistic aspects of life. Leaving aside the degenerated religious or theological activities, they concentrated in a full fledged way in material aspects of life and in studies and researches of science. During this period many great scientists of later period such as Copernicus, Kepler, Galileo, Pascal, Newton, and many others were born. The Europeans at this time with the advancement and discovery of science started exploring different parts of the earth and setting up of colonies.

There was industrial revolution in Europe with the advancement of science and technology. On the introduction of guns the military strength of the Europeans became far superior than the Muslims. As a result Muslims were losing their controls over their land one after another. During the 19th and 20th centuries, most Islamic lands came under colonial rule of the western powers. Western Europe during this time witnessed a scientific and industrial revolution that started in the nineteenth century and gathered momentum in the twentieth century, but during the same period the colonial dominated Islamic lands were deterred from making scientific and industrial progress.

The condition of the Muslims under colonial rule was very bad. The westerns continued to dominate them in various ways. Their West education system were imposed in the colonies.

In Muslim dominated countries also the conditions of science education were frustrating at this time of rising of European dominance: There were number of reasons for this frustration: (1) science institutions did not have any progressive outlook or planning, (2) these institutions were isolated from other institutions, (3) no encouragement or incentives were there for new scientific ideas or discoveries, (4) instructions in the Holy Quran and the Hadiths on science education were wrongly interpreted by some ignorants or vested interests to keep people away from science studies, (5) influence of Sufism was increasing at this time and many responsible Muslims and Ulamas started to give more attention to Sufism rather than science education, (6) an apprehension was growing at this time that as reasoning, rationalism, deduction, experiments, proof, etc., are the basis of science, there is a chance of science students of becoming unbelievers of Allah or religious deserters. But this propaganda had no basis, rather it was contradictory to the instructions laid down in the Holy Quran.

There were some other reasons for Muslims to show their abhorrence to science. These were some ideas or theories propagated by some scientists and social workers which were apparently against religious belief. Thus, the theory of Evolution of Darwin and the socialistic principle of Freud and Marx may be mentioned in this connection.

The theory put forward by the natural scientist Darwin to explain the appearance of life on earth ignores the role of Almighty. It apparently contradicts or opposes the ideas of creation as envisaged in the Holy book and as such many Muslims started thinking science as an ism opposed to the existence of Creator. In addition, the Ulamas became alarmed on increasing popularity of socialism of Freud and Marx. There was a wave of establishing in many European countries where science was progressing, to establish Communism based on the ideas of Marx which basically ignored religious principles of ruling the society.

In some countries infact Communism was established destroying the religious fabric of the society. Observing increasing popularity of a system based on reasoning and rationalism and material aspects, denying the Creator and the way of life framed by Him to follow, many Muslims were alarmed. No Muslim can accept a system which breaks or tends to break the foundation of faith (Iman). As a result Muslims of medieval period kept themselves away from science education. The Ulamas also did not encourage people for such education. Rather they encouraged an education system devoid of any sort of science. But in this vast universe there are exceptions in the creations of the Almighty. History bears this testimony. Darwin, Freud, Marx, etc., may be such exceptions. If theory of evolution of Darwin is seriously studied and analysed, we see that existence of God or the Creator has not been denied or it is not possible to deny God if theory of evolution is to be accepted. Because, for evolution to take place raw materials, proper environment and proper places are required. Darwin has not answered as to where from and why these raw materials were existing for evolution to take place. Darwin kept mum or silent in this regard which indirectly indicates not refusal or not denial of existence of Allah. It is true that the political and social systems envisaged by Freud and Marx were based on material aspects only. These were hypothetical systems not science. But all these created an unfavourable psychology in the minds of the Muslims.

But all the apprehensions of Muslims did not have any basis. There is no conflict between science and Islam. Rather, the whole Holy Quran contains verses based on science, justice, reasoning and truth. It invites, encourages and suggests people to study nature or science. Because of their deviation from the instruction of the Holy Quran and the Hadiths, Muslims are lagging behind in the field of general education, science and technical education.

In the Christian world before the Renaissance in Europe, there were strong differences or conflicts, between science and religion. The great scientist Galileo was punished for pursuing truth through scientific studies. Galileo proved that the earth was not the centre of the Universe. As this was against the teaching of the church, he was condemned in 1633 by a Roman Catholic Church inquisition court which sentenced Galileo to life imprisonment, later commuted to house arrest. Thus in Christian world for many centuries scientists could not pursue and publish the truth freely. Gradually people could realize this and there was renaissance throughout Europe. The Church also could realize their fault and started to change their approach towards science. At last more than 350 years after punishing Galileo, the Vatican honoured the 17th century astronomer with two stamps on May 31, 1994.

In the history of Islam such unfortunate incidents as what happened with Galileo never occurred. Many Muslims including Ulamas have realized the wrong education policy of Muslims. But it is too late. In the meantime there has been an unprecedented progress 'in the field of science and technical knowledge and the progress has been made by non-Muslims alone.

Progress in India : During the golden period of Islamic science in the Islamic world i.e. from 9th century to about 14th century India was ruled by the Muslim rulers. Though Muslims were not in majority in India, they were the vast population. India was never ruled by the Muslim rulers as per Islamic laws based on the Shariah. There were arrangements for religious education and for military training to their armies for defence of their territories and some times for conquering and territories. For religious education Maktabs, Madaris, Khankas, etc., were established at different places and they were patronized by the Muslim rulers. Sufism was also gaining popularity and it was being practised by many under famous Sufi scholars such as Nizamuddin, Moinuddin Chishti and many others. There were no institutions under the Muslim rulers to study science and to do research in a systematic way.

(i) Of course there were some progress in certain fields: the Mughals had the knowledge and practice to make arms and ammunitions which were required for defence and wars.

(ii) Also in medicine there had been some studies and progress. The Hakimi system treatment was working at that time. But there was no laboratory in the style of European chemists to improve or discover medicines.

(iii) There was some progress in the field of engineering particularly in construction and architectural engineering during the period of Muslim rulers in India. They were mainly busy in constructing palaces, forts (e.g. Red Fort of Delhi), memoirs (e.g. Taj Mahal of Agra), etc.

The conquest of many parts of the globe by the Europeans and their influence were possible mainly because of their progress in science and technology. Their strong will for studying science and their unhesitating contribution towards research for new discoveries in science were the contributing factors for further progress. After the design and fabrication of guns, the Europeans could expand their rule over many parts of the world easily. With new war tactics and new weapons, they could easily conquer scientifically backward, otherwise advanced kingdoms. The Mughals of India, though remained unparalleled in war tactics and politics for centuries in India lost to the British only because of the backwardness in science and technology. Had the Mughals been advanced in science and technology the history would have been different.

After the establishment of British rule in India, the education systems were totally changed. The British introduced science and their western education system. The Hindus without any hesitation accepted the new education system and could do progress in science education. But the Muslims under the British rule had different view about the new education system.

In an apprehension that after losing the Khilafat (the Muslim Emperors were not infact Khalifa) the religion may be lost, the Muslims rejected the education system introduced by the British. They decided instead to continue their old system of education devoid of science and technology in the schools, established and run by Muslims only. The British occupied India from the Muslim rulers and as such they considered Muslims as their rivals, they wanted Muslims to stay backward in all aspects so that Muslims can not rise against the British rule. Therefore an education system, devoid of modern subjects of that time, framed and introduced by only some Muslim Ulamas was not opposed by the British. Rather, it was supported by the British. In the same country, the Hindus and the Muslims thus adopted two education systems. As a result, in course of time, the Muslims were slowly lagging behind in education particularly in different branches of science and other modern subjects. Also as a result of constant propaganda, against learning English, science and other subjects introduced by the British, and wrong interpretation of education and encouragement to study subjects of theology only, majority of the Muslims became allergic to science education and devoted their time to learn Persian, Urdu and Arabic only in addition to Hadiths and the Holy Quran. These are some reasons of Muslims becoming backward in this part of the subcontinent.

After independence of India, the scenario started to change. The country was divided. Many educated and rich Muslims migrated to Pakistan. Majority of the Muslims who preferred to stay in India were illiterate or half educated and economically backward. They decided to live as minority with the vast majority of the Hindus. However, these Muslims got a sense of insecurity because of the apprehension that in course of time their culture, etc., may be diluted and merged with the Hindu culture and their future offspring may even leave the religion in a hostile (hostile to Islamic laws and principles) environment. Thus, many Muslims preferred Madrasa education where stresses are given on study of Arabic, Persian, Urdu, Islamic history, Hadiths and Quran. When there is a need to increase knowledge on all fronts including mathematics and science, majority of Muslim children spend time in learning some languages such as Arabic, Urdu, Persians and other theological subjects. These students after coming out from Madrasas are unable to proceed further for higher education in modern subjects because of shortage of knowledge in these subjects. Even basic education of modern subjects including science is not imparted in many Madrasas. As a result they cannot compete with the students of other communities who are already advanced in the different subjects.

There are numerous direct and indirect repercussions on the Muslim society both in social life as well as in family life for ignoring science education by the Muslims. A few are mentioned below.

Religious Work

For proper understanding of the Holy Quran, the reader should have some basic knowledge of science. Al-Quran has described briefly at many places about the natural phenomena and physical laws and asked people to ponder over them.

Knowledge of science helps to understand or at least realize the inner meaning of those verses. Knowledge is very much necessary for understanding truth of the Quranic revelations.

The Almighty says in this regards:

> "Thus do we explain the Signs in detail for those who know " —(7:32)

That the Holy Quran is easier to understand for man of knowledge (scientists are knowledgeable persons) has been said by God himself this way:

> "And that those on whom knowledge has been bestowed may learn that the (Quran) is the truth from the Lord, and that they may believe therein, and their hearts may be made. humbly (open) to it."
>
> —(22:54)

In the eyes of religion, to achieve the high position or get God's favour knowledge is also necessary: He says:

> "Allah will raise up, to (suitable) ranks (and degrees), those of you who believe and who have been granted knowledge" —(58:11)

Thus from the religious point of view, there is an urgent need of acquiring highest knowledge. Its importance can be envisaged from the fact that the Holy Quran has given stress on studying physical laws of nature (*al-tafakkur*) and control or use of nature, and natural resources or laws by inventing technical knowhow, (*al-taskheer*). In this regard, al-Quran has repeatedly advised man in about seven hundred fifty verses (one eighth of the whole Quran) to study nature (i.e. science) think or ponder over them, do research using intellect. Thus, al-Quran has advised to adopt an education policy based on science and scientific approach. The Prophet (PBUH) himself has stressed on education for acquiring knowledge and declared this task as 'Fard' or obligatory. Muslim community, in spite of such religious directions or guidance, on acquiring knowledge has not adopted a proper education policy. Guidance of al-Quran and Hadiths has not been reflected in their education policy. Studies of science subjects are essential for acquiring knowledge, but these are not included in the curriculum of education in the institutions financed community.

Many are observed to misinterpret the meaning of Islamic education which according to them is the education pertaining to learning Hadiths and Quran and other activities of Shariah only. This is not true and not supported by the Quran and the Hadiths as well. The so called Ulamas prefer a system devoid of science and they even openly speak out against science education. This may, perhaps, happen, if the Quranic injunctions on science education are not understood in their proper perspective. For persons having knowledge of all branches, it becomes easier to understand Quranic revelations based on science. Those who advocate rejection of science or do not give importance on science education perhaps have not been able to grasp the spirit or inner meaning of those verses.

To be Benefitted from Studying Science

Nature and laws governing natural objects and phenomena are studied in different branches of science such as Physics, Chemistry, Zoology, Botany, Astrophysics, Medical Science, Geography, etc. Applied sciences are the different branches of technology and engineering. Nowadays much advances have been made in the field of study and research as a result of which much has been known of the nature and natural laws. Also the mystery of creation and its complexity has been realized.

It is a fact that in this modern age progress has been made in the field of science and technology by the people of other communities except the Muslims. Knowledge obtained from the studies of nature and natural laws mostly by the people of other communities have been applied for the benefit of the people. Their endeavour could enable them to discover new medicines, communication systems and innumerable new things. In this technologically advanced age different industries are being built, where only people having science and technical degree or knowledge can work.

Muslims being ignorant of scientific education and knowledge have not been able to get jobs in such types of industries or workshops.

Even for ordinary and common jobs Muslims have been found not coping with job seekers of other communities. This is because other communities are already advanced in various subjects including different subjects of science and technology. It can be easily said that in a multicommunity system or country a community lagging in all fronts can not compete in any front with others and as such will lag further behind in the race.

Nowadays, not only in getting jobs but also in other fields such as business, cultivation, etc., there is tough competition. There have been many advancements in modern cultivation. Good seeds, advanced gadgets, etc., for cultivation have been discovered. So cultivators must also be modern and must be able to use modern machines for cultivation, use proper manure at proper season and be able to take care of the crops in a scientific manner. Any crop can be cultivated nowadays at any season of the year if scientific method is applied to cultivate it. Thus, a sort of scientific education or knowledge is necessary for cultivators as well. the Muslims, though most of them are cultivators in eastern India are completely ignorant of such a development or change.

Not only in cultivation, pattern of business has changed. In addition to buying and selling of cultivating products, scientific or industrial products are flourishing in the market. Because of research and development, hundreds of electronic goods, cosmetics, groceries, machineries, vehicles and their parts, etc., are being made and introduced in the market. For making a business, some knowledge or ideas of these goods are necessary. Otherwise it is not possible to start a business in this competitive market. In starting an industry also the same problem will be faced if knowledge of technical education is not there. The point is that the Muslims are not able to cope with or are lagging behind in all these modern fronts.

It is a fact that "the survival of the fittest" is the common principle for all. From the beginning of human history man has been trying to change, rather improve his life-style and has been making efforts to acquire knowledge for the purpose. There has been always a sense of competition among the different groups of people from the very beginning though they have originated from a single family. Many groups or tribes or community, because of their own fault, ignorance or negligence or incompetence have got defeated themselves and as per wish of the Almighty and have vanished from this world.

Some smaller groups or tribes are still there in small islands or in accessible places on the surface of the earth. These groups because of their ignorance or lack of knowledge have been living in an uncivilized way or in a primitive way. They have not been able to make betterment of their life or think for the hereafter. This way consequence of ignorance or not trying to put into action one's knowledge is disastrous God has bestowed man all human faculties and intellect to acquire knowledge, so that he can lead a life in this world to serve Him better and get the reward hereafter. This universe is created for man only so that he can study it and realize Almighty's greatness and submit before Him.

Further, he may use nature for his welfare. People of any community should put all efforts for the welfare and progress of the community. They should make their own plan and project for their own advancement. He says in this regards:

> "Verily never will Allah change the condition of people until they change what is in themselves."
>
> —(13:11)

Man is surrounded with all bounties of nature given by God. He is to put his intelligence and get benefits from His bounties in order to improve himself to change his lots. If man does not endeavour himself to improve or change his backwardness He will never change his position.

In the Islamic world, the pursuit of knowledge has historically been shaped by a number of interacting, sometimes opposing, factors, religious precept, practical need, and the powerful influence of inherited and adapted cultures among them. In particular, the intellectual treasury of classical Greece and Rome, filtered through Hellenistic thought and practice, dominated much of the heritage that was appropriated and adapted by most medieval Islamic philosopher-scientists.

4

Science in Islam

For many years we have been familiar with the phrase, "The conflict between science and religion", and we know that the war has been waged with zeal by each contending party. We have not heard very much about peace. There has been no mutual acknowledgment of complete victory for the one side or the other. Nor is it quite true to say that there have been skirmishes, although it may be true to say that of late they have been very local, and have not been conducted by the greatest minds in either camp, I think it is true to say that so far as headquarters are concerned, in either camp men have been too busy with domestic problems to undertake aggressive campaigns beyond their own territory.

Many of the old fighting men, who once tasted war and seemed to enjoy it, have passed away. Their place has been taken by younger men, who have grown up, indeed, with the knowledge that they are defending a territory—either for science or religion - but defending it from an enemy in the trenches whom they have scarcely ever seen. When they meet face to face they hardly feel that they are enemies at all, but just fellow men. It is a pity to be in trenches if you are not attacked. It is serious to be responsible for defending a territory if you do not know the appearance of the enemy- if you have lost your sense of patriotism, or are uncertain as to the rights of your country.

The conflict between religion and science has certainly become less bloodthirsty and somewhat more polite. In the meantime religion —even organised religion—has not ceased to exist. And the scientific world was not ceased to exist some would say it flourishes and is quite sufficiently confident in itself. Religion, I say, has not ceased to exist, but many have given it up, and others only hold it, not with the triumphant note of Allah-o-Akbar but with considerable misgiving, whilst yet others seem to be unconscious that there is an enemy, or has ever been a conflict, or that there is anything in Islam which is likely to be attacked, or needs to be defended.

So, too, science has not ceased to exist. Indeed, it has made wonderful progress, though some have looked askance as its achievements.

Those who hold to religion, but with some misgivings, can hardly be said to be at rest in God, even if they say they believe in Him. They are poor representatives of the noble army of martyrs who, in other ages, have confessed the Faith, and cheerfully faced the lions, the fire, and the sword.

Doubtful of the defensibility of their Creed, they ever seek to avoid a conflict and often seem eager to pretend that there is no foe, or no foe worthy of their mettle. Looking askance at science and its achievements, they do not realise its greatness, its strength, and its nobility, and are therefore seldom likely to do it Justice.

Some of us, I expect, have our misgivings about religion it is safe to admit it if such is the case. Let us remember that there are others who have no very serious misgivings at all today, (though once, perhaps, they had them. Let us one and all agree that we will not ignore or belittle men who occupy a camp which seems to be, geographically, at least, opposed to the camp of the Millat-e-Islamia. When we meet these men, they no longer use the battle cry of their grandfathers, let us have the common sense not to meet them with an array of antique weapons from the showcases of our theological museum. Times change. New men with new ideas and a new outlook call for new treatment, and the Millat will show its wisdom if it brings out of its storehouse things new as well as old.

In the last forty years or so there have been great physical scientists who, like highwaymen, have held a pistol at the head of the theist and the theist has often walked trembling. Men with a theory of materialism with reference to things that are thought to be dead, or with a conception of mechanism with reference to things that are said to be alive, have sometimes bullied society and at other times he'd it up to scorn. It is hardly too much to say that today materialism has been destroyed by the more enlightened physical scientists themselves, and that mechanism has been proved hopelessly insufficient in biology. These are two very important matters from the point of view of religion.

At first sight it is natural to think that the world as we know it is made up of matter and spirit. Common sense suggests it, but the philosopher has almost always failed to be satisfied with such a dualism. He has almost always sought for a unifying principle. He has usually come to feel that the reality of the world is spiritual rather than material, whilst the materialistic scientist has tried to solve the problem of dualism by treating matter as the all-important part of nature, and movement and life and even mental and spiritual operations as not merely resting upon a physical basis in everyday life, but as wholly and solely produced by it. It was even said in the last century that the brain secreted thought as the liver secretes bile. The soul and its religion would get scant sympathy from such thinkers. Belief in God, belief in the spiritual state, even in the limited degree that seems to be forced upon those who practise psychical research, would be viewed with suspicion. Ethics and moral responsibility would be criticised with a temper more unfriendly than that of a reverent and scholarly agnosticism. This stage of criticism is today very largely past, and its passing is due to philosophers and theologians. This is the outstanding marvel of the present situation. A deeper study of the world of Physics than was possible to the men of the last generation has convinced some of the most expert Physicists themselves that their world is not what their grandfathers thought it; indeed that it is very much more like the world of the philosophers and theologians whom their grandfathers bullied or and theologians whom their grandfathers bullied or scorned.

In the last thirty years or so, in the face of the attack upon religion made by materialistic and mechanistic science, thoughtful religious believers have found some ground for rest in the assertion that the territory lawfully occupied by physical science, and the territory lawfully covered by theology, are so distinct that it is impossible for either to disprove the other without first committing an act of trespass. Physical science, it was said (and said truly, I think), was, at the time, according to its own conceptions, merely descriptive and conscious habit of observing phenomena-things as they appeared to the observer—a conscious habit of observing them and classifying them, but in no sense dealing with their ultimate reality, their ultimate cause or their ultimate purpose; whereas it was said (and- said truly, I think) that theology had no great concern with the phenomena as described, only with the ultimate origin of the phenomena, the underlying force, and the spiritual purpose served by the series of phenomena.

According to this view, the scientist could describe the apparent process of evolution with most painstaking detail, and, it he described accurately, the theologian was not concerned to deny his statements. A theologian could still stand within his own territory and say, "The facts of nature are the acts of

God." He could say that theology teaches that God creates, whilst the scientist could describe as fully as he liked how God creates. This line of thought seems to have lost some of its attractiveness for some minds, useful as it has undoubtedly been to many harassed souls. I think it is still roughly true that the scope of physical science and the scope of religion are so different that the theologian and the scientist cannot touch one another so long as each remains in his own territory and attends to his own legitimate business; but that is precisely what neither has all times been content to do, and is not now content to do. Clever physical scientists have often been crude philosophers and ignorant of history, ethics, art, and theology, and yet they have made foolish, little, bad tempered, irritating excursions into discussions in which they were hopelessly at sea, talking a language and using methods and instruments which were manifestly unsuited to the subject-matter, or inaccurately applied. A man may be quite clever one kind of subject and yet unusually ignorant or awkward in another.

Again, theologians and philosophers, highly trained in philosophy, ethics and historical criticism, have often sallied forth in the dark, to oppose, annoy, or ridicule the chemist, the biologist, and the astronomer, and have made themselves a laughing stock by opposing a text of the Holy Scripture to an actual photograph of things in the world, or have misread the evidence of an experiment because of its supposed bearing upon the creed.

The average physical scientist has not generally been a man whose opinion was necessarily worth very much in subjects which he had not made a matter of serious study, and the philosophical theologian has often, although not as often as many are inclined to believe, been insufficiently versed in physical science to be able to criticise, without prejudice, the works of descriptive science. These two groups of excursionists from one territory into the other have often brought discredit upon their own cause, and have seriously misled the man in the street, the man in the Millat and the man in the museum or the scientific workshop.

Where theologians and scientists have kept to their own territory, each had considerable peace and liberty of late, and has made headway in domestic research. The theist, especially, has enjoyed rest in God by being able to see that the description of phenomena has no direct bearing upon what is not merely phenomenal.

But whilst it remains true that the scope of physical science is not identical with the scope of theology, and that some theologians ignore science, and some well-disposed scientists beg the theologians not to try to build his theology upon a scientific basis, and that some theologians are inclined to take the hint, and that some theologians are inclined to take the hint, and depend ever more and more upon spiritual and ethical intuition, it is becoming clear to many of both camps that there is a frontier between them which is very liable to trespass from the one side or the other. There are, therefore, borderline problems.

No one can tell where will these border-line skirmishes lead to. There may be temporary embarrassment for either party. It is not beyond the bounds of possibility that scientific thought at the moment often favouring a spiritual view of the universe may veer round again, temporarily at least. At the moment much of the best physical science comes from those more prophetic scientists who are bravely recanting the materialistic and mechanistic errors of their predecessors, or are, to change the metaphor, restoring the lambs now old sheep-stolen by their grandfathers in marauding expeditions into the Church's territory fifty years ago. There should be nothing but sympathy and admiration for those who are thus engaged.

But in view of the marvellous change of thought which has come over Physicists in their very study of Physics, we may reasonably ask that, at all times, men who have reached an experience of God by methods other than those of physical science-if there are such methods-should not be (i) regarded as fools if they suspend their judgement upon the philosophical and theological implications of some new scientific theory, at least until scientists themselves are fairly agreed upon the scientific facts, or (ii) regarded as knaves if they temporarily fall back upon their own well-verified experience, and though only as something like a working hypothesis, find rest in a belief in God.

What is needed at the present day is that the balance should be held fairly, and withal friendly, between all seekers after truth of any kind physical, mental, ethical, philosophical or theological. The theist, in view of recent history, may quite rightly refuse to be bullied. But he should be scrupulous not to take an unfair advantage of the scientist, or throw dust in the eyes of any inquirer. The revolution which is taking place in the philosophical views of physical scientists gives every encouragement that we are entering upon a new era. We have better grounds, in the eyes of the thinking world, for rest in God today than we had, say, fifty years ago, or at any period since. To argue that because a man is a physicist, or a medical man, he must necessarily be an atheist, or even sceptical or agnostic towards religions, is simply to reveal the fact that one is not up-to-date in physical and mental science. The physicist himself is often groping in the spiritual world, if not basking in its sunshine, and the really expert medical man realises the importance of physical and spiritual therapeutics.

It is not always true today that it is only the fool who hath said in his heart, "There is no God", it is certainly not true to say that a man is a fool because he believes in God. Let us rest assured of so much at least.

In the modern age of science men of religion are greatly to blame for they have failed to respond to the call of the times and have not appreciated the spirit of the modern age. They have kept the truths of religion shrouded in medieval mysteries, mythology and selfish controversy. The spirit of religion has been confined within narrow secretanian conflicts and petty squabbles. These drawbacks can be remedied by dissemination of religious knowledge on a democratic basis and by cultivating a true perspective. It is necessary that people have a true idea of both religion and the development and scope of modern knowledge.

Science is the systematised knowledge based upon practical observation. Experiment is the foundation of the development of science. In fact the aim of science is the formulation of laws behind phenomena it aims to study, because mere observation of isolated facts is no science. We have science only when we have discovered a proposition which includes all the possible infinite cases of the same class. The discovery of law is in fact the discovery of the hidden element of unit in the apparent diversity of varied phenomena. A new theory aims at introducing a further element of oneness in our knowledge by showing a sort of oneness in apparently different types of phenomena. From this point of view the aim of science is to show that the world of our common experience is not what it seems to be: it is not so complex as it appears. On the other hand, it is simple and one complete whole. It is in reality a universe and not a multiverse. Thus we see that science deals with only materialistic aspects of life, and the other aspects of life are absolutely beyond its scope. So it would be foolish to accept the lead of science in other equally important aspects of life, i.e., moral and spiritual to which it is not at all related. We will have to seek guidance in these elsewhere.

Science has influenced our mental faculties to a great extent. With the advancement of our scientific knowledge our creative faculty has also developed. We have become more inquisitive. But, unfortunately, the development of our creative faculty alone cannot give a helping hand in the solution of our social and moral problems. We produce good things with the help of our scientific genius, and hence make ourselves financially more sound but the result obtained thereof is discontentment and dissatisfaction. And other more intricate problems are also likely to arise out of it.

Uptil now the efforts of scientists to solve the eternal mystery and to understand the riddle of life have been futile. Many theories have been evolved by eminent scientists in this connection. But there is every possibility that their assumptions may be discarded today or in the near future. There is a great controversy among the scientists to accept such theories.

Science has not put before us a way of life. It has been absolutely unsuccessful in evolving a coherent system of thought which could form the basis of a complete philosophy embracing all the aspects of life. Eminent scientists have centered their attention on the material aspect of life without caring for the moral and spiritual. It can provide us every thing for our comfort but it cannot help us in leading a peaceful and happy life.

The contribution of Islam in the realm of morality is its most distinctive feature. By fixing divine pleasure as the object of human life it puts before us such a high standard of morality as will provide limitless possibilities for the moral evolution of humanity. It furnishes through the belief in God and day of resurrection a motive force which impels a person from within to observe the moral laws.

Islam takes up all the moral qualities which are commonly known; it does not pick out only some of them. It assigns suitable place to each with the sense of proper balance and proportion. In such a way it widens the fields of application of moral laws so much so that not a single cross-section of moral life is left out.

The social system of Islam is based upon the assumption that mankind belongs to one race. Islam completely discards the discrimination based on race, colour, tribe, nation, language or any other such thing. Mankind is the offspring of the same parents. So all men are equal in their capacity as human beings. And hence the social structure, whose foundation -stone is furnished by Islam, helps in maintaining peace and tranquillity.

The most important feature of Islam is its representation of the spiritual aspect of life. According to the Islamic view point the spirit is the representative of God. God has invested it with certain faculties and has upon it certain responsibilities and has endowed it with best possible physical frame. So our body is meant to assist in the exercise of the authority of the soul and the fulfilment of its duties and responsibilities. And the spirit is intended to work the machinery of the body in this world, and not outside it, to develop its potentialities. The spirit is required to utilities to the greatest extent all its faculties and potentialities to gain the Divine pleasure.

It is the privilege of Islam to be free from such absurdities which might strengthen the scientist's stand in opposition to Islam. Indeed there are certain things where the scientists hold a bit different views from those of Islam; but in those cases they have not been successful in providing rigid and concrete facts in support of their views.

No doubt, science has added much to our comforts and has enabled us to lead a luxurious life. But it has so ensured us by the multiplication of wants that in our constant struggle we can hardly get a way out; all throughout life we hanker after money, wealth and power adding thus the base of worries to the small cup of life. In spite of so much scientific progress and inventions, life is not nearer to contentment and peace than it was prior to the age of science.

Integration with Religion : Integration of science and religion is one of the major issues of our age. Some thinkers believe that their integration is possible and necessary while others contend that the two are inherently different. Much logic has been lavished on both sides but very frequently the issue has been confounded on wrong premises where one is reminded of Charles F. Kettering's saying: "Beware of logic. It is an organised way of going wrong with confidence". The issue, nevertheless, is so important and compelling that the disturbed minds of the sensitive younger generation cry for an answer that could console their agitated spirits. Whitehead has very rightly pointed out :

> "When we consider what religion is for mankind and what science is, it is no exaggeration to say that the future course of history depends upon the decision of this generation as the relations between them."

Why Integration? Only those ideas which integrate vitally can evolve into beliefs. Huxley, who regarded beliefs as important organs of cultural evolution-the only course of evolution open to man believed that they cannot be imposed by force but it is possible to encourage and promote them by helping one belief with the aid of another. He also held that there is a constant and necessary interaction between our beliefs and the facts of universe or rather between our beliefs and our knowledge of facts. According to him belief is a crystallization or fusion of emotions and feelings and knowledge into a system of ideas, which is 'always to some degree operative or effective and tends to issue in action of some sort' thus 'giving a directional set to personality' and determining an individual's 'general attitude or approach to life'.

So beliefs can live and grow only if intellectual, scientific, artistic, practical and moral ideas are integrated biologically as vital parts of an organic whole. On the other hand they degenerate if one set of ideas constantly corrodes the other. It is, therefore, simply impossible to have two types of beliefs at one and the same time. For example, if Adam and Eve of science differ entirely from the Adam and Eve of religion, the two types of concepts would give rise to a conflicting situation from where there is no escape except to abandon either clear teachings of religion or clear teachings of science. Today the young generation finds itself in a similar dilemma, thrown at the crossroads, bewildered and perplexed. Those who profess to accept this duality of thinking in their adventure of practising scientific thought while still preserving religious faith are in fact divided personalities with little prospects of finding the right path, for, faith cannot take roots in a divided mind.

Two Cultures : C. P. Snow complains that "the intellectual life of the whole of western society is being split into two polar groups, which had long ago ceased to speak to each other but they had at least managed a kind of frozen smile-across the gulf. Now even that politeness is gone, they just make faces." The cultural disintegration of a society epitomised in "two cultures" by C. P Snow is a cause of great concern for the great thinkers of the West. Renes Dubos believes that "human culture, like organisms and societies, depends for its survival on their internal integration, an integration which can be achieved only to the extent that science remains meaningful to the living experience of man." No wonder therefore that scientists like Seabourg stress the need of "integrating into our thinking and acting the full range of human wisdom", so that "the philosopher, the social scientist, the writer, the natural scientist are all intellectual brethren under the skin."

But in this age of ours "institutionalised science" has stood up against "institutionalised religion" as a rival establishing its own "sacred buildings, its mysteries, its esoteric language, its priests and acolyts, even its incantations and mummeries." Thus science has become a "metaphysical mother", a "super-human thing", and a "huge entity which has an independent existence of Its own", in which modern man believes in much the same way as his ancestors used to believe in religion. It has gradually spread its roots in all what we do and think and all what we feel and we cannot tear them out and if we do we would endanger our civilization.

Modern Mind Needs Rational Faith : In a cultural milieu permeated through and through with science, modern man has "developed habits of concrete thought which render him less capable of that type of inner experience on which religious faith ultimately rests" because he suspects it "liable to illusion". And "no one would hazard action on the basis of a doubtful principle of conduct". "Religion", said Iqbal "stands in greater need of a rational foundation of its ultimate principles than dogmas of science". In these circumstances the demand for a scientific form of religious experience is quite natural.

It was the fulfilment of this need which prompted Iqbal to reconstruct religious thought in Islam "with due regard to philosophical traditions of Islam and latest developments in various domains of human knowledge". He set himself to evolve "a method physiologically less violent and psychologically more suitable to a concrete type of mind". He found the Muslims of the twentieth century in an "extremely critical stage which immediately demanded an attempt to reconcile religion with reason". He firmly believed that the day was not far off when "Religion and science may discover mutual harmonies." His efforts at rationalization of faith but at the same time not admitting superiority of philosophy over religion, made him undoubtedly the greatest of all the Muslim thinkers of twentieth century whose appeal to the younger generation is sure and certain.

Blind Faith—A Wrong Premise : One of the basic premises, gone very deep into common religious thinking, which is responsible for the dichotomy of religion and science is the popular notion of "blind faith". It is said that faith begins where reason ends and faith has nothing to do with reason. According to this view faith in the Unseen cannot but be "blind". The argument of "blind faith" leads one to the conclusion that the name of God has no relevance to the knowable and the known. This premise has done incalculable harm and has provided strong grounds for the scientists to assume that faith is a white flag of surrender to the unknown or just another name for man's contentment with ignorance which inhibits the inquisitiveness of mind and spells doom to all scientific inquiry and endeavour. They also argue that since revelation issues from a region which is wholly inaccessible to man, the object of faith is something which is absurd to reason.

Thus human reason (science) and divine reason (religion) do not touch at any point, Huxley's assertion that, "if events are due to natural causes they are not due to supernatural causes" is rooted in the same reason. "The doctrine of personal God", says Albert Einstein, "can always take refuge in those domains in which scientific knowledge has not been able to set foot". He calls this behaviour on the part of the representatives of religion "not only unworthy but also fatal", because "a doctrine which is able to maintain itself not in clear light but only in dark will, of necessity, lose its effect on mankind" By enthroning God in the unknowable, as if He abhorred the light of human knowledge, we assign Him an extremely vulnerable position in the universe so that the ever expanding frontiers of scientific discoveries correspondingly push Him further and still further back into the ever-retreating unexplored parts of Nature. No wonder, therefore, that Russian space scientists on their first entry into space rejoicingly declared that there is no God in the Universe. How may we hope to keep the flame of faith aglow, if faith were just a sort of refuge in the nascence equating religion with darkness and Ignorance.

Clash of Ideas

Another wrong premise on which religion seeks to establish Its superiority and priority over" science is through its overemphasis on the limitations of science, The religious protagonists are in the habit of making pronouncements that science will never be able to achieve this or do that as these lie only within the competence of the "supernatural", i.e.. God.

But as Randall points out "what in the past men have called 'supernatural' might better be called 'superhuman'—that in the world which man finds lies beyond man himself, which inspires man and condemns his inadequacies". But man is a changing phenomenon in the realm of science. Ever-increasing additions in his knowledge give him more and more power over nature thus making him more and more 'supernatural' day by day.

Science has been consistently breaking its limitations and eroding the ground from underneath the superstitions, wrongly taken up as religious beliefs. Even the strongest walls, built by men of religion for the protection of their concept of God—narrowed by their own limited imaginations are being demolished one by one as science marches victoriously in her achievements. Had the imagination of the religious people been continuously broadened by new insights of science which it perpetually provides to man through new discoveries, the idea of God would have been correspondingly widened. Quran points out: "And if all the trees in the earth were pens, and the sea were ink, with seven seas more to replenish supply, the words of Allah (the facts of scientific knowledge) could not be exhausted. Lo! Allah is Mighty Wise" (31:2).

The role of science in Islam is to help cleanse religious imagination of the dross of shirk and gradually leading him to pure Godhead of Quran. "We shall show them our Signs in the expanses of the universe and within themselves until it will dawn on them that it is the Truth" (41:53). Had we allowed religion and science to intercommunicate and interpenetrate most of the conflicts between them would have been solved long ago perhaps we would have arrived at different scientific conclusions, hypotheses and theories; or perhaps our religious beliefs had been rendered more scientific by new scientific insights into the nature of truth, as envisaged in the aforementioned verse of the Holy Quran.

Almighty's Supremacy

The God of Islam is both the Manifest or the Known and the Hidden or the Unknown in the vast expanse of the universe. In the Holy Quran God offers Himself to man as much within the fold of his knowledge as beyond the range of his conceiving. In fact, God would not be God if He could be fully known and God would not be God if He could not be known at all. Now when the Holy Quran exhorts the man to toil ceaselessly to meet Him (84:6) and the man in turn determines to reach Him and be with Him. (1:4) he prays God to show him the Straight Path (1:5)—i.e., a path which passes straight through this concrete material world and does not sidetrack it. Modern mind with its habits of concrete thinking demands exactly such type of concrete living experience of God. While inviting attention to some of the natural phenomena of the material world, the Holy Quran proclaims in unambiguous words: "This Is Allah! Where are ye then led astray?" (6:96). According to the Holy Quran, all natural phenomena are 'Signs of God' indicating the activity of His Mind.

In urging its readers to observe minutely and ponder deeply over these phenomena, the Intent of Holy Quran seems to be that by keeping a close contact with the behaviour of Reality, man will sharpen his inner perception for a deeper vision of it. As Iqbal says: "It is the intellectual capture of and power over the concrete that makes it possible for the intellect of man to pass beyond the concrete". Science-based on the observation of sense data—is thus a necessary preparation for man to see God and is thus a sort of prayer.

Scientist's View : Numerous scientists have endorsed this view of Iqbal that scientific activity is a sort of religious activity. To George Washington Carver, nature Is an unlimited broadcasting system through which God speaks to us every moment if we only tune Him In. (For 'tuning Him in', Iqbal prescribes prayer as "a necessary complement to the observer of Nature"). Says Edmund W. Sinnot, "Beneath nature's surface beauties, there is a deeper beauty whose contemplation offers most profound satisfactions." "Science", declares Max Wertheimer, "is rooted In the will to truth. With will to truth it stands or falls. Lower the standard slightly and the science becomes diseases at the core. . ... The will to truth pure and unadulterated is among the essential conditions of its existence". Albert Einstein, too, is of the opinion that "science can only be created by those who are thoroughly imbued with aspiration towards truth and understanding. This source of feeling, however, springs from the sphere of religion."

Mind-an Organic Whole: Another wrong premise on which some religious thinkers seek the separation of religion from science is the idea that they come from and belong to different parts of mind and are different kinds of mental activity. They say that the fact of religion can be comprehended only through intuition, live wonder and appreciation while facts of science are learnt through observation, sensory perception, intellectual effort, reasoning and understanding. But human mind never works in such severally-isolated compartments as if it were divided into separate departments of thinking, feeling and willing. No type of mental activity can ever be imprisoned into its own confines to the absolute exclusion of others; rather they frequently walk into one another. Thus there is no such thing as pure thought or pure feeling or pure intuition.

The world cannot be divided into classes like thinkers and feelers even though there are philosophers and scientists and poets and mystics. There have been great scientists like Galvani, Perkin, Roentgen and Flemming who made their great discoveries under the flashes of intuition which came to them spontaneously; whereas a number of scientists like Lecomte du Nuoy, Teilhard de Chardin, Edmund W Sinnot, Heisenberg who caught glimpses of God during their thinking over material problems. On the one hand even great prophets having direct communion with God would, at times, need ask Him "My

Lord! show me how Thou givest life to the dead" (Ibrahim, peace be on him) or "My Lord! show me Thyself so that I may gaze on Thee" (Moses, peace be on him) or "My Lord Give me the knowledge of things as indeed they really are" (Muhammad, peace be on him).

On the other hand an ordinary human being, like the present writer's father, relates that when he was a student of Physiology he would often times fly into rapt ecstasy of a mystic while attending a lecture in the class or working in the laboratory when he felt "as if he had a direct vision of God." Thus the realms of religion and science, though clearly marked off from one another outwardly, have very strong reciprocal relationships and mutual dependencies inwardly, admitting of no departmental isolations in the human mind. A noted scientist, R.G.H. Sill has gone to the extent of saying that the sense-perception is the perception of the Absolute, it is pure suchness and no knowledge is possible unless symbolising turns it either into (i) an intuition or (ii) an Item of rational knowledge i.e., science However a deep feeling of no knowledge at the root of all knowledge makes one see God-in-the atom which in the words of Einstein inculcates in man "that humble attitude of mind towards the grandeur Incarnate In existence, which in its profoundest depths is inaccessible to man". Iqbal hits the same point when the says:

> These are all but the stages of the seeker of Truth honoured with the 'knowledge of all the names'
>
> The stage of meditation 'Scanning through time and space'.
>
> The stage of recitation: 'All praise unto Thee, my Lord the Highest'.

Islam is a strong religion. Around the year AD 610, Muhammad, a successful trader and prominent citizen of the town of Mecca in Arabia, received a revelation from God while meditating in a cave. Delivered through the angel Jibbrail, the heavenly message directly challenged local and traditional pantheistic beliefs with a broad range of spiritual and social concepts and commands that were, in part, parallel to tenets of both Christianity and Judaism. Thus was born a new faith, based on belief in one supreme and all-powerful God before whom all were equal and to whom all must submit. The word Islam itself reflects this commitment on the part of all true Muslims: it means "submission."

As a religion, Islam shares certain fundamental elements with the other two great monotheistic faiths, howsoever they vary in form and practice. Islam's holy scripture, the Quran, containing God's message to Muhammad, has its counterparts in Judaism's Torah and Christianity's Bible. All three religions venerate the city of Jerusalem as the site of momentous events and the location of sacred monuments marking their history. All three emphasize fundamental phenomena: revelation, final judgment, and salvation. All consider history as imbued with divine purpose.

The youngest of the three religions, Islam respects important elements in Judaism and Christianity. The Quran gives Ibrahim, Moses, and Jesus high and honored status as earlier prophets, and it venerates Ibrahim as the spiritual ancestor of all monotheistic worshipers. These and other shared beliefs in no way disguise or dilute the special or unique characteristics that set Muslim doctrines apart from those of Judaism and Christianity. Muslims hold that Islam is not only a continuation of the Judeo-Christian religious heritage but also an essential and comprehensive correction of its message. Muslims honor Muhammad as the most recent addition to the roster of the great prophets; they believe him to be the final messenger of God.

The fundamental doctrine of the Islamic Revelation defines the nature of God, the role of Muhammad as God's messenger, the Quran as the word of God, the hierarchy and function of Islam's angels, the categories of sin, and the final day of judgment. Five acts of worship, or duties, are required of all Muslims: known as the Five Pillars, they include the profession of faith, daily prayers, alms-giving, fasting during the month of Ramadan, and, if possible, pilgrimage to Mecca once in a lifetime. Islam possesses no single, "official" church organization in fulfilling religious obligations, each Muslim is essentially alone in the presence of God, without the mediating forms of priests and sacraments such as those found in Christianity.

Written down after Muhammad's death in the form of Islam's holy book, the Quran (Al-Quran, meaning "recitation" or "reading"), the Islamic Revelation represents, for devout Muslims, more than a set of religious beliefs and a system of worship. Together with the written record of actions or sayings attributed to Muhammad, known as Hadith, the writings of the Quran set forth fundamental Muslim religious thought. They proclaim God's purpose: to make humankind responsible for its own actions and to place each person on earth to manage its affairs prior to finding his or her destiny in the world beyond. In providing an established form of what Muslims consider the final, perfect revelation, the Quran also provides a broad range of rules covering not only religious practices but also most other phases of daily life, from family relationships and personal matters of social and sexual behavior, to proper dress, eating habits, hygiene, and the conduct of business and community affairs.

Within half a century after Muhammad's death, a fierce conflict concerning the succession of Islam's religious leadership split Muslim believers into two major sects, Sunni and Shiite. This division has endured throughout the centuries, with Sunnis claiming about four-fifths of all Muslims living today. Shiites predominate only in Iran and Iraq, although they are also found in regions of Syria, Lebanon, Pakistan, Afghanistan, the Eastern Province of Saudi Arabia, and in some of the neighboring

Gulf states. Over the centuries, the Islamic faith has come to be practiced with variations in interpretation and ritual. Both Sunni and Shiite groups long ago embraced believers who adopted the doctrines and practices of Sufi mysticism. These activities are designed to help the worshiper achieve more direct and immediate communion with God through prayer, meditation, the singing or recital of devotional texts, and, within one order, ritualistic dervish dancing. The various sectarian differences have not weakened fundamental beliefs shared by all Muslims, nor did the Sunni-Shiite controversy hinder the rapid conquest of west and east in the century after the Prophet's death.

The desire to find a better life than was possible amid the harsh struggle for existence in the Arabian heartland, as well as the lure of the spoils of conquest, might not in themselves have inspired the early and rapid growth of the Islamic empire, nor could these motives alone have long sustained vigorous Muslim rule of such a vast territory. Islam's faith was a fundamental factor in accomplishing these epic feats. At the outset, the Muslim concept of jihad – better translated as "effort" or "struggle" (for the Faith) than simply as "holy war" – helped to drive Islam's forces. But Jihad, seen as large-scale, militant struggle to advance the Faith, rarely received consistent support from Islam's leaders, especially in later centuries, when it often came to be perceived as an impractical ideal and was abandoned as an immediate option. In the Arabic-speaking world today, the term is often used to denote personal struggle to keep passion or desire under control.

What soon became the pivotal empire-building force was the generally rational, just, and humane Muslim approach to the rule and civil management of conquered territories, an approach that reflects precepts clearly set forth in the Islamic Revelation. All in all, Islamic rule encouraged cooperation on the part of local populations. Conversion became widespread in many areas, and for many people it meant less interference in their daily life than they had been accustomed to as non-Muslims or as subjects under Byzantine or Sasanid rule. Muslim law was derived from fundamental Quranic doctrine, and as such tended to promote order and justice in the daily management of city, town, and village affairs. About a third of the Quran's six thousand verses deal with matters of practical legislation.

Within a framework of ordained universal brotherhood and individual equality, the Islamic holy book prescribes mutual help as a legal duty, proscribes useless consumption as a sin, and defines moderation in all things as an essential goal. Keeping personal pledges, exercising individual or group rights, seeking conciliation and compromise, shunning reprisal: all are demanded Islamic law, like the faith it both reflects and defends, was from the beginning conceived to impart to each Muslim enough knowledge of his or her obligations and rights to maintain "right conduct" in this world while preparing for life in the next, thus carrying out God's will.

From the outset, within Muslim borders Christians and Jews who chose to pay the required tribute, thus retaining the right to follow their own beliefs, benefited from their special category as "people of the book." They were regarded by Muslims, respectful of the Bible and the Torah, as sharing parts of the same spiritual message received by followers of Islam and the Quran. At various times, some Muslims have held that the world community is split into two hostile groups, believers (Muslims) and non-believers. Of course, parochial concepts of this sort have flourished in all eras and within most great religious, ethnic, and national communities.

In any event, such prejudice did not deter Muslim empire-builders from achieving spectacularly advanced levels of civilization wherever they stayed long enough, whether in Spain, in India, or in between. Furthermore, the Islamic empire at its peak embraced a population that was more ethnically and culturally diverse, as well as socially stable, than the people of earlier or later empires such as those of Rome and imperial Russia.

During the early centuries of Islam's empire, the religious and political community—the Arab word is Ummah—was considered by Muslims to be the center of existence, recognizing its possession of God's truth and acceptance of Shariah, God's law. For several centuries, notable travelers and other worldly scholars were the only Muslims to discern much of significance in the institutions and ways of life of non-Muslim peoples. However, as both commerce and conflict expanded contacts between the Islamic world and the lands beyond its boundaries, the Muslim leadership became acquainted with other types of political and social organization.

Increasing contact with European societies reshaped by the Renaissance, the Reformation, and the Enlightenment led Muslims to reexamine Western constitutional and parliamentary systems of rule, which their leaders had long considered suspect and dangerous. Some of what they learned was appropriated and adapted for local use. More than any other factor, however, growing experience with imperial governance stimulated Muslim leaders to develop their own ways of applying the law to meet the increasingly complex, practical needs of communities in all parts of the Islamic realm. Their solutions to legal problems of everyday life often developed in ways that differed from those banned by religious scholars bound by holy law.

In the most traditional Muslim belief, there can be no real demarcation between religion and state or government, let alone between government and society; nor can morality be separated from politics. No earthly power has the right to invalidate or even amend Quranic law, let alone act outside it. The duty of rulers consists only in maintaining and enforcing it. Legal interpretation can be allowed, but it is only to be undertaken by those doctors of law or other learned individuals officially qualified for such an intricate task. The traditional view maintains that there can be but one earthly goal for all in government: justice, a society in harmony, its component parts in perfect balance within a divinely ordained system. Such a view has prevailed for centuries within orthodox Islam. However, in time, opposition between rulers and religious scholars has generated considerable flexibility involving compromise and temporary shifting of ascendancy from one group to the other.

Over the centuries, the Muslim legal picture has changed in many ways. By the end of the ninth century, the views of differing theologians had brought about the development of four schools of law, each with its own interpretation of the Shariah, and the split between Sunni and Shiite sects generated further interpretations. Eventually, courts of appeal were created with the power to overturn Shariah court judgments, and Ottoman sultans and Mughal rulers issued their own edicts to supplement the Shariah. Today, the Shariah remains the official foundation of law and government only in Saudi Arabia and some of the Gulf states, but its influence continues to be strong in a number of Muslim countries that have not fully adopted Western legal procedures. Moreover, the currently increasing force of Islamic fundamentalism among many Muslim communities around the world has stimulated new support for traditional Shariah a concepts.

Islamic law often employs analogy in dealing with its subjects; that is, it reasons through comparison. Thought-by-analogy or association is reflected in the structure and style of Arabic speech. Whether spoken or written, the Arabic language is the second fundamental bond that, together with Islam's faith, has held the worlds Muslim community together for fourteen centuries. Rarely if ever have faith, thought, and expression of feeling been served by a more appropriate and uniquely resourceful instrument.

Religious Angle

Arabic, the most important Semitic tongue, is today the common language of more than two hundred million people. Its alphabet is derived from the Nabataean script, which itself came from Aramaic, a language dating back as far as the fourteenth century BC. Arabic is the sacred language of Islam and of the Quran. In its classical, or Quranic form, it still serves religious, literary, artistic, and other formal needs. Classical Arabic differs in many ways from its descendant, the vernacular Arabic spoken, with considerable variation in dialect, by Muslim populations around the world.

Classical Arabic's syntax and grammar do not have the "subject . . . object" structure of Indo-European languages, nor does Arabic require the verb "to be." Most words stem from simple roots of three letters and have both specific meanings as well as universal ones drawn from their roots. The basic meaning of a root is provided by consonants (Arabic has twenty-eight of them) and is modified by changing or omitting vowels and by adding prefixes and suffixes. Short vowels appear as symbols above or below consonants. Case endings allow great variety in sentence structure. Arabic is read right to left; varying the order of words in a sentence permits a change in emphasis while retaining the basic meaning. With these characteristics, the Arabic language is an enormously fluid and flexible instrument for all kinds of written and spoken discourse, sacred or profane, philosophical or technological.

Classical Arabic has retained its original character over the years to a far greater extent than has, for example, English or French. This stability may result from its having remained for so long almost exclusively the language of religion and ritual throughout the territories dominated by Muslims. Furthermore, for at least six centuries, from the eighth through the thirteenth, Arabic was the most important language of international diplomacy and commerce. It was, at that time, also the principal language of philosophers, scientists, and poets, much as Latin was during the centuries of imperial Roman domination and as Greek was in the great age before Rome. Even today, while Muslims around the world speak in the many different tongues and dialects of vernacular Arabic, many of them read and write the same classical Arabic script, employing various Arab, Turkish, Persian, and other verbal modes and calligraphic styles.

The words used by the angel Jibbrail in dictating the Revelation to Muhammad—sacred Arabic words subsequently preserved for all time in the Quranic text— retain a living and relevant power in themselves. Indeed, devout Muslims believe the Quran can truly be read only in Arabic. Furthermore, reverence for the language is matched by reverence for the written script, an attachment reflected in the major role played by various styles of Arabic calligraphy in all forms of Islamic art for more than a thousand years.

Medieval Arabic's international importance was gained in good part through its adaptability: from Islam's early centuries onward, the language was stretched and augmented to serve an increasingly wide range of commercial, technological, scientific, philosophical, and literary purposes. As the basic vehicle of communication throughout the Mediterranean and Near Eastern territories, Arabic spread contemporary knowledge among people of diverse national and ethnic origins at all social levels. Quickly expanding communication between major Muslim intellectual centers in Spain and the Middle East acted as a spur to intellectual advance of every kind. Even as Muslim rule embraced more and more populations speaking different languages, from local Arabic, Persian, and Turkish dialects to those of neighbouring, non-Muslim peoples, Arabic retained its central importance throughout most Islamic lands. Today it retains this power to serve the Muslim world's intellectual needs and to unite that world's peoples spiritually and emotionally.

From the start, Muslims faced the task of building a society that was not only multinational but multiethnic. Forward-looking caliphs encouraged non-confrontational contacts, especially commercial ones, with other societies. The expansion of Muslim trade helped to open Islam to outside influence, particularly from India and, to a lesser degree, China, and such traffic helped to promote advances in education and reinforced a sense of intellectual adventure. Fortunately, spiritual encouragement for such an enterprise was at hand in the Hadith. These collected sayings, traditionally attributed to the Prophet and highly revered, include strong endorsements of learning.

"He who pursues the road of knowledge God will direct to the road of Paradise. . .. The brightness of a learned man compared to that of a mere worshiper is like that of the full moon compared to all the stars.. . . Obtain knowledge; its possessor can distinguish right from wrong; it shows the way to Heaven; it befriends us in the desert and in solitude, and when we are friendless; it is our guide to happiness; it gives us strength in misery; it is an ornament to friends, protection against enemies. . . . The scholar's ink is holier than the martyr's blood... . Seeking knowledge is required of every Muslim. . .."

The assertions and recommendations contained in the Hadith reveal the exalted position historically accorded to knowledge by the shapers of Islamic thought. Muslim religious doctrine promotes a concept of the entire material universe as a sign of God's activity, a creation by God, which God upholds. Thus, in order to understand God, it is necessary to investigate every aspect of his creation—all phenomena that exist in the world of animals, vegetables, minerals, and the elements in which people must live. This pursuit, of course, includes humankind itself as a subject. In traditional Muslim belief, such an effort to comprehend is essential in attaining the just and righteous life that forms the earthly part of a person's purpose as proclaimed by the Prophet. A simpler, more expressive spiritual motivation for scientific inquiry, let alone metaphysical investigation, is difficult to imagine.

In the early centuries of Islamic civilization, the broadest possible learning was widely supported by orthodox Muslim precepts. However, in time, an opposing doctrinal trend gained strength. Not only the limitations but also the "dangers" of knowledge were increasingly described by religious authorities and pious philosophers, who declared that gaining knowledge for its own sake could never be legitimate for Muslims – it must be acquired solely as a means of gaining understanding of God, serving his will, and working to solve the problems of Islamic society. Limits to the scope of permissible learning eventually came to be defined by religious scholars, and philosophical and scientific investigation came under increasing attack as potentially destructive to faith and society. This fundamental ideological conflict has waxed and waned in other civilizations. Fortunately, during the early development of the Islamic realm, the near-obsession with the acquisition of knowledge was for a time relatively unfettered.

Another and eternal element was crucial in motivating the extraordinary intellectual expansion of the Muslim world during the early golden age of the ninth, tenth, and eleventh centuries: simple human curiosity. This drive, together with the new civilization's faith, its Quranic teachings about the world, and its increasingly resourceful language, impelled Muslims to set about investigating everything around them. They were equipped to make remarkable sense of their world, and this they did, with an enthusiasm and energy rivaled only in the heydays of Renaissance Italy, the Scientific Revolution, the Age of Enlightenment, and the early period of the Industrial Revolution. The cultural result of this effort was soon evident, and it amounted to notable and unique accomplishments in both the arts and sciences. In these pages; a broad survey of the Islamic scientific enterprise, in particular, can best begin by looking at the intellectual landscape in which medieval Muslim scientists undertook their work.

Islam was born without what the Western world recognizes as "philosophy." However, from the very beginning, Muslims, like all others in all times and places, sought answers to questions about every aspect of existence, about God, the creation of the universe, the destiny of humankind, and the proper organization of individual and community life on earth. For traditional Muslims, the Quran—the holy text—has always embraced the basic answers to these questions, answers that are beyond dispute, if not always beyond interpretation. Quranic statements are subjected by orthodox Muslims to kalam, a theological discipline involving rationalist dialectical examination, parallel in some ways to the kinds of argument that have been associated with Western theological and philosophical debate since the beginning of intellectual speculation in classical antiquity. From the earliest days, Islamic scholars showed great zeal in uncovering and exploring in depth the intellectual heritage they came upon in the newly conquered non-Muslim regions. In those lands, first of all, lay a treasury of philosophical writings setting forth older systems of thought, notably those of ancient Greece, India, and Persia.

The rapid expansion of imperial Muslim rule was followed by the conversion to Islam of many Christians, Jews, and others. Arab Muslims were thus exposed to ways in which thinkers holding to other faiths and ideologies approached the fundamental questions of life and being. The early Muslim philosophers came to see that their own thinking could be enhanced—or, at least, made more orderly and productive—if they adapted to their own purposes some of the speculative processes and systems of philosophical and physical classification established centuries earlier.

The works of Pythagoras, Socrates, Plato, Aristotle, the Stoics, and Epicurus appealed to Muslim philosophers. Here was a rich intellectual accumulation that they felt they could and should put to Islamic use. By the time the Islamic empire had been established, this legacy amounted to an unusually eclectic blend of philosophical concepts and argument. Ready at hand were the Socratic belief in knowledge as good and as within reach of humankind, as well as Plato's emphasis on the geometric structure of the material world and the ultimate authority of divine principles over natural laws. Here also were Aristotle's views of causality, his belief in design and purpose as the focus of all natural process, his original and comprehensive system of logic, applicable to all thought, and his macroscopically to microscopically arranged methods of classifying everything in the material universe.

To be sure, this treasury of thought had undergone some evolution: major Platonic and Aristotelian concepts had become somewhat blended with mystical elements set forth by the third-century philosopher Plotinus, as well as with features of Persian, Egyptian, Jewish, and Christian belief. Ultimately called Neoplatonism, this extraordinary hybrid philosophy profoundly influenced not only most of Islam's philosophers but also many medieval Christian theologians, attracting them in varying degrees toward an overall detachment from the everyday or "real" world. During the Islamic civilization's early centuries, this new found classical and Eastern treasury of knowledge often appeared to orthodox believers as "wisdom mixed with unbelief."

Traditionalists could only view with alarm the gradual dilution of faith with rational speculation. Charges of heresy came to be leveled at such Muslim groups as the Mutazila, a ninth-century school of thinkers who wanted to apply reason to matters of faith and who held some clearly unorthodox views concerning the creation of the Quran, free will, and predestination. The Mutazilites eventually fell into strong disfavor and were suppressed. As for those, the Arabs called falasifa, philosophers who were loyal, in particular, to the principles contained in a Hellenistic version of Aristotelian thought as a whole, their view of God's nature and role and of the world's creation was not easily nor substantially accommodated by orthodox Islam. In sum, their philosophy rested on speculation dependent on human faculties and thus directly challenged the supremacy of divine Revelation.

During Islamic civilization's first few centuries, the Muslim attachment to philosophical speculation was strong and adventurous enough to survive periodic attempts to purge concepts that were less than purely Islamic. Elements of Hellenistic philosophy soon penetrated Muslim thought deeply and permanently. In the long run, even amid intermittent religious-philosophical confrontation and conflict, philosophy in medieval Islam remained sufficiently vigorous to produce a number of outstanding giants who rank among history's great intellectual movers and shakers. Five of these stand out, in particular. One way or another, all provoked controversy, and most earned strong orthodox opposition.

First and greatest of the Arab philosophers, Al-Kindi, who was active in ninth-century Baghdad, developed a system of thought that encompassed religion, politics, and the sciences, achieving something of a bridge across the chasm between belief and reason. One of the first to sponsor translation of the works of Aristotle, Al-Kindi was also one of the earliest Muslim polymaths, gifted in physics, or "natural science," mathematics, optics, music, and cosmology, as well as philosophy. Islamic civilization produced many such polymaths, much as a later age produced Leonardo da Vinci and the other artist-scientists known as Renaissance men.

Al-Kindi was Islam's first major music theorist, and his universal interests also included meteorology. His deep involvement in the workings of the physical, or "real," world around him was to remain a significant element in mainstream Islamic philosophy throughout its period of greatest vigor.

Convinced of the value of rational thought, al-Kindi was one of the first noted Muslim philosophers to become suspect in the eyes of rigidly orthodox believers.

Known as the "second teacher" (after Aristotle), Abu Nasr al-Farabi, a Turk who died in the tenth century, was particularly interested in reconciling Aristotelian and Platonic ideas. He found areas of accord between classical Hellenistic philosophy and prophecy. Accepting the validity of both the Quran and the philosophy of Plato and Aristotle, he reasoned that both must agree, and he worked to clarify the reconciliation. His work Al-Medina al-fadila (The Good City) set forth ways of gaining happiness through politics and showed the relation between Plato's ideal community and Islam's divine law.

Like Al-Kindi, Al-Farabi defended rational thinking. In his Kitab Chsa al ulum (Catalog of Sciences), after listing and describing the various sciences, he placed philosophy at their head, claiming that it guarantees the truth of knowledge gained by clearly proven reasoning. Al-Farabi and Al-Kindi did much to set the main course of Islam's philosophy, and the great majority of great Muslim philosophers and scientists who followed them were, essentially, their intellectual descendants. One of the most conspicuous differences between science in the medieval Islamic world and twentieth-century science in the Western world is the prominent role of philosophy in providing most medieval Muslim scientists with an almost tangible framework for their work.

The eleventh-century Persian philosophical and medical genius Ibn Sina, known in the Western world by the Latin name Avicenna, dealt with most of the eternal questions posed by rational philosophy as well as by religious faith. In dealing with the eternally challenging nature of universals—fundamental qualities, characteristics, or properties of things—he tried to reconcile Platonic with Aristotelian concepts. At times, his unorthodox beliefs, along with his worldly life-style and elitist arrogance, aroused controversy—after his death his books were burned by an Abbasid Caliph. However, Ibn Sina's all-embracing vision took effect far beyond Islam, ultimately influencing the evolution of the scholastic philosophy that dominated the medieval theological philosophy of the Christian West.

The eleventh-century jurist-theologian-philosopher Al-Ghazzali played a pivotal role in reinvigorating Islamic thought. His two greatest texts dealt with what he termed a revival of the religious sciences and the incoherence of the philosophers. He placed the mystical thinkers, the Sufis, above the philosophers in their ability to reach the truth. Yet, like the dialectical theologians, he accepted the role of reason in explaining divine concepts. As a result of the work of Al-Ghazzali, the Muslim world became more receptive to Sufism, and Islamic thought became more inclusive, more harmonious, better able to integrate philosophical, theological, and mystical elements. His work greatly influenced subsequent Christian and Jewish theologians and philosophers.

Finally, Ibn Rushd, also known as Averroes, was the brightest light of the cultural zenith that was achieved in Muslim Spain during the eleventh and twelfth centuries. He became the most celebrated of all commentators on Aristotle. Like Aristotle and some Muslim dialectical theologians, he held God's existence to be provable on rational grounds alone. Ibn Rushd came to be regarded by some as the father of free thought or even unbelief, yet his influence was not hindered by this prejudicial label, and he left a mark on both Christian and Jewish thinking.

In the development of Islamic philosophy, both within and beyond Quranic boundaries, there can be seen a sort of double standard concerning the dissemination of philosophical wisdom to the public. This is particularly evident in the thinking of both Al-Kindi and Ibn Rushd: these two concluded that the educated elite could be guided by reason, the less-advantaged masses only by faith. More specifically, the Quran could be interpreted allegorically for the intellectual minority but should be delivered more as literal truth for the majority, whose faith might be undermined by "unsuitable" speculation and doubt. An unequal distribution of doctrine such as this is, of course, also characteristic of some Christian practice. In any event, as it evolved, Islamic thought endeavored to accommodate elements of worldly philosophy while retaining the directness and simplicity of the Faith as first proclaimed. Striving to have it both ways undoubtedly has as a long history as does philosophy itself, and the result never seems to include a long-lasting resolution. In the case of medieval Islam, this often complex and sophisticated endeavor was destined to continue through both fruitful and lean times into the modern age.

Although Muslim scholars gave close attention to the manuscripts of classical philosophy that they found stored in their newly won lands, what first attracted their interest were works devoted to medicine and astronomy, in which more than one of the greatest Greek philosophers had excelled. These texts offered vital guidance in practical matters given high priority by the Muslims: health, travel, and precise orientation in time and space in connection with religious practice. Notwithstanding the Muslim concern for preparing for life in the hereafter, Muslim scientific effort, from the very beginning, focused most immediately on gaining knowledge that could be applied in making life better and more efficient on Earth. This effort seems, in the light of history, to have been perfectly timed.

In the eighth century most of the civilized Mediterranean and European world languished in generally low estate. Today, no serious historian dealing with that world refers to the dozen-odd centuries of medieval times as simply constituting the Dark Ages, but it remains reasonable to claim that the first few of those centuries saw little of the light of civilization. Soon after the Muslims had reached as far as Spain and India, some illumination began to be restored. At first, much of it was the result of ancient fires being relit, but new light was soon to come as well, all of it generated by the vigorous and enterprising civilization that had begun in the desert communities far away on the Arabian peninsula.

Religion and science, the two words have vast connotations. Religion is generally understood to mean the recognition of the existence of a supernatural ruling power, the creator and controller of the universe, who has given to man a spiritual nature which continues to exist after the death of the body, and of man's duty to be obedient to this power. As a concept of life, it is all-encompassing. Science, on the other hand, is the study of the perceptible world. Both are extremely broad-ranging subjects, and their respective spheres are in many aspects quite separate from each other. It is not intended here to go into the details of these two subjects, but to deal only with the clash — real, or unreal — which has taken place between science and religion on an academic level, and certain of its consequences. One of the reasons for this clash is the claim that scientific discoveries have proved religion baseless, and it is principally this point on which attention has been focused here.

The traditional conflict between science and religion made itself felt in the eighteenth and nineteenth centuries. It was during this period that, in the light of new scientific discoveries, many came to feel that there was no further call to believe in God. One of the most compelling reasons for believing in God, amongst others, was that without this belief, the universe was inexplicable. The antagonists of religion were quick to point out that we no longer required the 'God' hypothesis when there was no aspect of the universe which could not be explained quite easily by the findings of scientific research. To them, the idea of God was redundant and, therefore, it was baseless.

This claim was quite flimsy from the academic or logical point of view even at the time it was made, and now science itself has admitted, directly or indirectly, that it had no satisfactory ground for making such a claim.

Of what nature was this discovery of science which attempted to convince people that there was no further need for the concept of God? It was no more than the discovery that the universe is bound by certain laws. In ancient times, man had simply believed that all happenings in the world were directly attributable to God. But modern findings revealed that behind every event there was a cause which was discoverable by observation. For instance, Newton observed that all the stars and planets in the vastness of space are bound by certain immutable laws and move in strict accordance with those laws. Darwin's research showed that man had not come into existence through an act of special creation but had evolved, in-consonance with general material laws, from the lower species and had gradually developed into *homo sapiens,* i.e. man as we now know him. Similar observational studies showed that all events seemed to occur as part of a known system called the 'Law of Nature.' Significantly, this law of nature functioned with such effective regularity that it was considered entirely predictable.

These discoveries were taken to mean that the universe, which we had regarded as God's domain, was in fact subservient to a set of material and physical laws. When these laws were applied, they yielded consistent results, and this further convinced members of the educated elite that they were right in embracing atheism. The German philosopher, Kant, declared: 'Give me matter and I shall demonstrate how the world is made out of matter.' Haeckel even went so far as to say that, given water, chemical elements and time, he would be able to create a man. Nietsche proclaimed with triumphant finality, 'God is dead.' Another belief had it that the creator and sustainer of this universe was not an alive, intelligent being possessing power; that the universe, from beginning to end, was material.

All movements and all manifestations of the universe, whether related to life or to lifeless matter were nothing but blind material processes. The world discovered by science evinced no signs whatsoever of the hand of God — which is surely the basis of all religions. Then how could it be considered rational to believe in God?

All the heroes who had discovered the laws of nature were believers in God, but, ironically, when their research was brought before the public, it was thought that their discoveries had rendered meaningless the very existence of God. Since, in order to explain events, one had only to have recourse to the causes and laws of the material universe, there seemed to be no need to postulate the existence of a God who was extraneous to that universe. It was said, for example, that the rising and setting of the sun had not been properly understood until telescopes had been made and mathematics developed. The former ascription of these phenomena to the will and power of supernatural beings had been due merely to man's poor comprehension of these matters. And now that astronomy had proved that there was a universal system of gravitation which controlled the movements of the sun, moon and stars, there was no further need to believe in God. Gradually, all those happenings in nature, which were supposed in ancient times to have invisible superhuman forces at work behind them, were shown to be the results of the action and reaction of the forces of nature. It was as if, after the natural causes of events had been described in modern scientific terms, belief in God should automatically cease. Julian Huxley, in his book, *Man in the Modern World,* says:

> If the rainbow is generated by the refraction of the sun's rays on falling rain, it is not set in the sky as a sign by God. If the plague is inevitably generated by the Bacillus pestis and spread by rat-fleas, an outbreak of plague can no longer be looked on as sign of divine wrath. If animals and plants have slowly

> evolved through hundreds of millions of years, there is no room for a creator of animals and plants, except in a metaphorical sense totally different from that in which the word was originally and is normally used. If hysteria and insanity are the natural results of disordered minds, there is no place remaining in them for possession by devils.

After presenting this piece of 'reasoning' with great conviction, he says that the ascription of such events 'to supernatural beings is merely due to man's ignorance combined with his passion for some sort of explanation.' He then sums up with: 'If events are due to natural causes, they are not due to supernatural causes' (pp. 18-19).

There is a serious weakness inherent in such arguments of the anti-religionists, which can be best understood through illustrations. Think of the railway engine speeding along the track. How do its wheels revolve? If we attempt to answer this question by studying the different parts of the engine and their movements, we shall arrive at the conclusion that the movement of the wheels is an extension of the functioning of the locomotive's mechanism. But would we be justified in believing that the reason for their movement is the engine and its various parts? Obviously, we would not. We should first have to consider the respective roles of the engineer who designed the engine and the engine driver who set it in motion. Without their instrumentality, the engine could neither exist, nor move. The engine and its parts are not then the final reality. The final reality is the mind which has brought the engine into existence, and runs it at will. A Christian scholar, Cecil Boyce Hamann, has aptly said: "Nature does not explain, she is herself in need of explanation." This is because, as he puts it, nature is a fact, not an explanation.

Let us consider, for example, how a chick comes into this world. In embryo, it develops inside the smooth, hard shell of an egg, then it emerges when the shell breaks up. How does it come about that the shell breaks up at the right moment and the fledgling, which is no more than a small lump of flesh, finds its way into the outer world? In the past, the obvious answer was: "It is the hand of God." But now, microscopic studies have shown that on the completion of twenty-one days, when the chick is ready to emerge, there appears on its beak a small, hard horn with which this 'lump of flesh' is able to break through the walls of its cell. The horn, having done its job, falls off a few days later. This observation, from the point of view of the anti-religionists, contradicts the old concept that it is God who brings the chick out of the shell, because the microscope has clearly shown that a twenty one day law exists which is responsible for creating conditions which make it possible for the chick to emerge from the shell. This is a mere fallacy. What modern observation has done is to add a few more links to the chain of factors which lead up to an event.

It does not tell us the real cause of the occurrence. It has just shifted the problem of the breaking up of the shell to the development of the horn. The breaking of the shell by the chick is simply an intermediate stage in the occurrence rather than its cause. Will the cause of the event be understood only when we learn what made the horn appear on the chick's beak? In other words, when we have traced the event back to primary cause, the cause which 'knew' that the chick required some hard instrument to break through the shell and, therefore, in exactly twenty-one days, compelled a hard substance to appear on the beak in the form of a horn and to fall off after having discharged its function?

'How does the shell break?' was the question that faced man previously. Now, in the light of recent observations, instead of an answer, we have another question: 'How does the horn develop?' In the context of perceived phenomena, there is no difference in the nature of these two questions. At the most, questions of the type that lead us from one link to another in the chain of cause and effect demand an extension of the observation of facts, if they are to be answered at all. On this basis, they do not elicit any valid explanation.

The discoveries held by the atheists to be an explanation of nature and, as such, an alternative to God, can just as easily be thought of as being the way nature works. We can, quite rationally, say that God implements his will through these laws, only parts of which man, with his limited skills, has been able to discover. Let us suppose that religious-minded people, who believe that it is God who causes the ebb and flow of the tides, are confronted with the scientific explanation that the tides are actually caused by the gravitational pull of the moon and vary according to the geographical configuration of the seas and land surfaces. There would be no need for them to deny this explanation in order to uphold their belief in God's instrumentality. They could accept it without causing the slightest harm to their religious beliefs. It is true that tides do occur in consonance with geographical configuration and as a result of gravitational pull. But, after all, what are these things? They too are God's creations. It is through these phenomena that God acts. As John Wilson observed: This does not destroy my belief. It is still God (working through these things') who is responsible for the tides.'

Similarly, in the field of biology, the theory of evolution implies that biological processes no longer demand the existence of metaphysical realities. In other words, in order to understand the nature of life, we do not need to believe in a conscious God, modern studies having 'proved' that life automatically patterns itself along certain material lines: reproduction, variation and selective survival. That is, through reproduction, living creatures continue to be born, certain congenital variations go on developing, then after a long and complicated process of mutation, an altogether new species comes into being. Thus, according to the antagonists of religion, the application of Darwin's principle of natural selection in biology has made it not only possible but imperative to reject outright the concept of God's hand in life's development.

The supposition that the various species of living creatures have come into being through a gradual process of evolution has yet to be established as a fact, but even were we to give credence to this theory, it could still be said with equal conviction, that this is God's chosen way of creation, rather than its being the result of a blind, automatic force. Mechanical evolution can easily be proved to be a creational evolution. This being so, those anti-religionists who refer to science for support have no genuine basis on which to reject this argument of creational evolution.

This is far from being all that there is to the matter. The truth is that the 20th century science has lost its ability to convince. Today, Newton has been replaced by Einstein, and the theories of Planck and Heisenberg have overthrown those of Laplace. Now the anti-religionists, at least on an academic level, can no longer claim that science has arrived at the ultimate truth. Indeed, the Theory of Relativity and the Quantum Theory have led scientists to the conclusion that it is impossible in science to separate the observer from the observed. This means that we can see only certain external manifestations of reality; we cannot apprehend it in its essence. The revolution that has occurred in science in the twentieth century has itself proved the importance of religion from the scientific point of view.

In his book, *The Limitations of Science,* J.N. Sullivan states the case thus: What is called the modern "revolution" in science consists of the fact that the Newtonian outlook, which dominated the scientific world for nearly two hundred years, has been found insufficient. It is in process of being replaced by a different outlook, and, although the reconstruction is by no means complete, it is already apparent that the philosophical implications of the new outlook are very different from those of the old one. We are no longer taught that the scientific method of approach is the only valid method of acquiring knowledge about reality. Eminent men of science are insisting, with what seems a strange enthusiasm, on the fact that science gives us but a partial knowledge of reality.

This change in the scientific outlook seems to have taken place suddenly. It is not yet sixty years since Tyndall, in his Belfast Address, claimed that science alone was competent to deal with all man's major problems. But, in truth, so far as these remarks sprang from the conviction that the sole reality is 'matter and motion,' their foundations had already been undermined. The attempt to represent nature in terms of matter and motion was already breaking down. That attempt was at its most triumphant by the end of the eighteenth century, when Laplace was emboldened to affirm that a sufficiently great mathematician, given the distribution of the particles in the primitive nebula, could predict the whole future history of the world. The fundamental concepts isolated by Newton had proved themselves so adequate in the applications that had been made of them that they were regarded as the key to everything.

The first indication that the Newtonian concepts were not all sufficient when men tried to fashion a mechanical theory of light. This endeavour led to the creation of the ether, the most unsatisfactory and wasteful product of human ingenuity that science has to show. For generations this monster was elaborated. Miracles of mathematical ingenuity were performed in the attempt to account for the properties of light in terms of the Newtonian concepts. The difficulties became even more heartbreaking until, after the publication of Maxwell's demonstration that light is an electromagnetic phenomenon, they seemed to become insuperable. For it had dawned on men of science that there was, after all, nothing sacrosanct about the Newtonian entities. After a certain amount of hesitation, and a few last desperate efforts to make electricity mechanical, electricity was added to the list of irreducible elements.

This may seem to have been a simple step to take, but it was, in reality, of profound significance. For the Newtonian concepts were all of a kind that one seemed to understand intimately. Thus the mass of a body was the quantity of matter in it. Force was a notion derived from our experience of muscular effort. Nevertheless, we supposed that we knew the nature of what we were talking about. But in the case of electricity its nature is precisely what we did not know. Attempts to represent it in familiar terms — as a condition of strain in the ether, or what not — had been given up. All that we knew about electricity was the way it affected our measuring instruments. The precise description of this behaviour gave us the mathematical specification of electricity and this, in truth, was all we knew about it. It is only now, in retrospect, that we can see how very significant a step this was. An entity had been admitted into Physics of which we knew nothing but its mathematical structure.

Since then other entities have been admitted on the same terms, and it is found that they play precisely the same role in the formation of scientific theories as do the old entities. It has become evident that so far as the science of Physics is concerned, we do not require to know the nature of the entities we discuss, but only their mathematical structure. And, in truth, that is all we do know. It is now realized that this is all the scientific knowledge we have even of the familiar Newtonian entities. Our persuasion that we knew them in some exceptionally intimate manner was an illusion.

With this realization it is no long step to Eddington's position that a knowledge of mathematical structure is the only knowledge that the science of Physics can give us. Leaving out all aesthetic, ethical, or spiritual aspects of our environment, we are faced with qualities such as massiveness, substantiality, extension, duration, which are supposed to belong to the domain of Physics. In a sense they do belong; but Physics is not in a position to handle them directly. The essence of their nature is inscrutable; we may use mental pictures to aid calculations, but no image in the mind can be a replica of that which is not in the mind. And so in its actual procedure Physics studies not these inscrutable qualities, but pointer-readings which we can observe. The readings, it is true, reflect the fluctuations of the world-qualities; but our exact knowledge is of the readings, not of the qualities. The former have as much resemblance to the latter as a telephone number has to a subscriber.

The fact that science is confined to a knowledge of structure is obviously of great "humanistic" importance. For it means that the problem of the nature of reality is not prejudged. We are no longer required to believe that our response to beauty, or the mystic's sense of communion with God, have no objective counterpart. It is perfectly possible that they are, what they have so often been taken to be, clues to the nature of reality. Thus, our various experiences are put on a more equal footing, as it were. Our religious aspirations, our perceptions of beauty, may not be the essentially illusory phenomena as they were supposed to be. In this new scientific universe even mystics have a right to exist (pp. 138-42).

Such explanations from scientific philosophers now abound. Morton White in his book *The Age of Analysis,* points out that 'the philosophically-minded scientists of the 20th century have started a new crusade, the names of Whitehead, Eddington and James Jeans are the most prominent among them.' He then bears out this notion of a 'crusade' with highly pertinent quotations from each of them.

'Nature is alive' (p. 84). Such was the interpretation of modern information by the English mathematician and philosopher, A.N. Whitehead (1861-1947).

The stuff of the world is mind stuff (p. 134). So said the English astronomer, Sir Arthur Eddington (1882-1944), deriving this conclusion from his studies in science.

The English mathematical physicist, Sir James Jeans (1877-

1946), interprets modern research thus: 'The universe is a universe of thought' (p. 134).

The views of the most perceptive scientists, can be summed up in J.W.N. Sullivan's words: 'The ultimate nature of the universe is mental' (p. 145).

The thoughts of these scholars clearly negate any material interpretation of the universe, their special virtue being that they have been advanced in the context of modern findings in the field of physics and mathematics. That the proponents of such ideas have had to make courageous, herculean efforts to overcome the materialistic outlook is aptly expressed by Morton White with reference to Whitehead: 'He is a heroic thinker who tries to beard the lions of Intellectualism, Materialism and Positivism in their own bristling den' (p. 84). Morton White may have said this only about Whitehead, but this applies to all the scientists mentioned above.

This philosophical question as to the final reality being mind or matter is actually concerned with the question of whether the universe has developed independently and spontaneously through some material process, or whether there is a non-material being who has created it at will. If we accepted the former proposition, it would be just like saying that, in the last analysis, a machine is simply a fortuitous compound of iron and petrol. That is to say, that the machine started off as iron and petrol, but owing to some blind, automatic process, it took on the form of a machine. All a pure accident! A machine, as we all know, is the product of an engineer's mind. That mind, quite distinct from the matter, existed before the machine. It conceived it, designed it, and brought it into being. The machine's existence was clearly consequent upon the exercise of mind and will.

In determining the nature of the mind, differences can be found among those who believe the mind to be the final reality, just as believers in God have diverse concepts of God. Even so, the conclusion arrived at by academic study that the final underlying reality of the universe is mind, testifies by its very nature to the truth of religion and amounts to a rejection of atheism. The truly significant change in modern science is not to be found in its increased powers to aid man's religion and science progress, but in the change in its metaphysical foundations.'

The best exposition of this viewpoint is to be found in *The Mysterious Universe,* by Sir James Jeans. By pure scientific argument, the writer has come to the conclusion that in the light of modern physics, 'The universe cannot admit of material representation, and the reason, I think, is that it has become a mere mental concept.'

He later goes on to say that "if the universe is a universe of thought, then its creation must have been an act of thought" (pp. 133-34).

He holds that the modern concept which interprets matter in terms of waves of electrons is quite unconceivable to human thought, because these 'waves' could be only the 'waves of probabilities' without having any material existence. Such reasons have compelled Jeans to conclude that the substance of the universe is thought, not matter. Now where is this thought situated? His answer is that it exists in the mind of a great 'mathematical thinker? Because the structure of this thought that comes to our mind is a completely mathematical structure. The 'great Architect of the Universe thus begins to appear as a pure mathematician,'

Sir James Jeans then states the entire case with great precision: It seems at least safe to say that the river of knowledge has made a sharp bend in the last few years. Thirty years ago, we thought, or assumed, that we were heading towards an ultimate reality of a mechanical kind. It seemed to consist of fortuitous jumble of atoms, which was destined to perform meaningless dances for a time under the action of blind purposeless forces, and then fall back to form a dead world. Into this wholly mechanical world, through the play of the same blind forces, life had stumbled by accident. One tiny corner at least, and possibly several tiny corners of this universe of atoms had chanced to become conscious for a time, but was destined in the end, still under the action of blind mechanical forces, to be frozen out and again leave a lifeless world.

Today there is a wide measure of agreement, which on the physical side of science approaches almost to unanimity, that the stream of knowledge is heading towards a non-mechanical reality; the universe begins to look more like a great thought than like a great machine. Mind no longer appears as an accidental intruder into the realm of matter; we are beginning to suspect that we ought rather to hail it as the creator and governor of the realm of matter — not of course our individual minds, but the mind in which the atoms out of which our individual minds have grown exist as thoughts.

The new knowledge compels us to revise our hasty first impressions that we had stumbled into a universe which either did not concern itself with life or was actively hostile to life. The old dualism of mind and matter, which was mainly responsible for the supposed hostility, seems likely to disappear, not through matter becoming in any way more shadowy or insubstantial than heretofore, or through mind becoming resolved into a function of the working of matter, but through substantial matter resolving itself into a creation and manifestation of mind. We discover that the universe shows evidence of a designing or controlling power that has something in common with our own individual minds — not, so far as we have discovered, emotion, morality, or aesthetic appreciation, but the tendency to think in the way, which, for want of a better word, we describe as mathematical.

In spite of this complete about-face in science from the academic point of view, it is a fact that, in practice, there have been no noticeable changes in the attitudes of anti-religionists. On the contrary, they are engaged in seeking new arguments to support their theory. The reason for this is not to be found within any academic framework. No, the reason is to be traced, alas! to a biased mentality. How often have we seen educated people refuse to accept the truth when ample proofs have been offered to them, simply because of deeply-rooted preconceived ideas. It was just such a prejudiced attitude, in the seventeenth century, which had prevented Italian scholars from accepting Galileo's theory as an alternative to Aristotle's, although a ball thrown from the Leaning Tower had demonstrated quite conclusively that Galileo was right. Again, it was this bias which caused scholars at the end of the nineteenth century to ridicule Berlin Professor Max Planck when he gave a physical explanation of light,— the quantum theory, — which proved the Newtonian concept wrong. Planck's theory was not accepted for many years, but today it is considered one of the most important principles in physics.

There is a common belief that it is only laymen who are guilty of prejudice and not scientists; we should do well, therefore, to mark the words of A.V. Hills, himself a scientist: I should be the last to claim that we, scientific men, are less liable to prejudice than other educated men.

Sir James Jeans underscores this when he says, 'Our modern minds have, I think, a bias towards mechanical interpretation.'

Now, in a world where prejudice holds sway, how can we hope that a concept will be accepted only because it has been proved academically? The often-repeated experiences of history show that man has all along been governed by his emotions rather than by his intellect, in spite of the fact that academically and logically, reason occupies the higher position. More often than not, reason has played into the hands of emotion. It has seldom happened that it has gained a positive control over the emotions. Indeed, the intellect has always coined arguments to support the emotional and thus tried to prove that emotional attitudes were rational. Man finds it a psychological necessity to cling to his emotional being, even at the cost of remaining blind to reality. We must remember, therefore, that we are not dealing with machines, which ought to respond to the mere flicking of a switch. What we have to address ourselves to is man, and man accepts something only when he himself is willing to do so. If he is not, no argument, however sound it may be, will convince him. Arguments are not, sad to say, electric switches. That man, with all his capacity for reasoning, should so seldom, himself, be amenable to reasoning, is perhaps the greatest tragedy of human history.

Failure of Science : Modern scholars have come to the conclusion that we may have succeeded in making great discoveries about inanimate matter, but that we cannot be certain of having been successful in discovering the facts of man's nature and existence, for there exists a strange disparity between the sciences of inanimate matter and those of life. The sciences which concern themselves with the inanimate part of our world differ from the biological sciences in that the former are subject to definite laws whereas the latter are, to quote Dr. Alexis Carrel, inextricably lost 'in the midst of a magic forest whose countless trees unceasingly change their place and shape.' Unlike material phenomena, biological phenomena cannot be defined in terms of algebraic equations.

The sciences of the material world are confined to description, a lower form of science altogether, because they do not unveil the ultimate nature of things, but only convey certain qualities such as weight and spatial dimensions. They do give us the power to predict future events, and often to determine at will their occurrence; in learning the secret of the constitution and properties of matter, we have gained the mastery of almost everything which exists on the surface of the earth – excepting ourselves. The science of living beings in general, and of the human individual in particular, has not made such spectacular progress. It still remains at the descriptive stage, while the elucidation of the real nature of living beings requires much more than mere description.

The Nobel prize winner, Dr. Alexis Carrel, who achieved unique fame in biological research at the Rockfeller Institute in New York, elaborates at some length in his book, *Man, the Unknown,* on what is meant by man:

> Man is an indivisible whole of extreme complexity. No simple representation of him can be obtained. There is no method capable of apprehending him simultaneously in his entirety, his parts, and his relations with the outer world. In order to analyze ourselves we are obliged to seek the help of various techniques and, therefore, to utilize several sciences. Naturally, all these sciences arrive at a different conception of their common object. They abstract only from man what is attainable by their special methods. And those abstractions, after they have been added together, are still less rich than the concrete fact. They leave behind them a residue too important to be neglected. Anatomy, chemistry, physiology, psychology, pedagogy, history, sociology, political economy do not exhaust their subject. Man, as known to the specialists, is far from being the concrete man, the real man. He is nothing but a schema, consisting of other schemata built up by the techniques of each science.

He is, at the same time, the corpse dissected by the anatomists, the consciousness observed by the psychologists and the great teachers of the spiritual life, and the personality which introspection shows to everyone as lying in the depth of himself. He is the chemical substance constituting the tissues and humours of the body. He is the amazing community of cells and nutrient fluids whose organic laws are studied by the physiologists. He is the compound of tissues and consciousness that hygienists and educators endeavour to lead to its optimum development while it extends into time. He is the homoaconomicus who must ceaselessly consume manufactured products in order that the machines, of which he is made a slave, may be kept at work.

But he is also the poet, the hero, and the saint. He is not only the prodigiously complex being analyzed by our scientific techniques, but also the tendencies, the conjectures, the aspirations of humanity. Our conceptions of him are imbued with metaphysics. They are founded on so many and such imprecise data that the temptation is great to choose among them those which please us. Therefore, our idea of man varies according to our feelings and our beliefs. A materialist and a spiritualist accept the same definition of a crystal of sodium chloride; but they do not agree with one another upon that of the human being. A mechanistic physiologist and a vitalistic physiologist do not consider the organism in the same light. The living being of Jacques Loeb differs profoundly from that of Hans Driesch. Indeed, mankind has made a gigantic effort to know itself. Although we possess the treasure of the observations accumulated by the scientists, the philosophers, the poets, and the great mystics of all times, we have grasped only certain aspects of ourselves. We do not apprehend man as a whole. We know him as composed of distinct parts. And even these parts are created by our methods. Each one of us is made up of a procession of phantoms, in the midst of which strides an unknowable reality.

In fact, our ignorance is profound. Most of the questions put to themselves by those who study human beings remain without answer. Immense regions of our inner world are still unknown. How do the molecules of chemical substance associate in order to form the complex and temporary organs of the cell? How do the genes contained in the nucleus of a fertilized ovum determine the characteristics of the individual deriving from that ovum? How do cells organize themselves by their own efforts into societies, such as the tissues and the organs? Like the ants and the bees, they have advance knowledge of the part they are destined to play in the life of the community. And hidden mechanisms enable them to build up an organism both complex and simple.

What is the nature of our duration, of psychological time, and of physiological time? We know that we are a compound of tissues, organs, fluids, and consciousness. But the relations between consciousness and cerebrum are still a mystery. We lack almost entirely a knowledge of the physiology of nervous cells. To what extent does will power modify the organism? How is the mind influenced by the state of the organs? In what manner can the organic and mental characteristics, which each individual inherits, be changed by the mode of life, the chemical substances contained in food, the climate, and the physiological and moral disciplines?

We are very far from knowing what relations exist between skeleton, muscles, and organs, and mental and spiritual activities. We are ignorant of the factors that bring about nervous equilibrium and resistance to fatigue and to diseases. We do not know how moral sense, judgement, and audacity could be augmented. What is the relative importance of intellectual, moral, and mystical activities? What is the significance of aesthetic and religious sense? What form of energy is responsible for telepathic communications? Without any doubt, certain physiological and mental factors determine happiness or misery, success or failure. But we do not know what they are. We cannot artificially give to any individual the aptitude for happiness. As yet we do not know what environment is the most favourable for the optimum development of civilized man. Is it possible to suppress struggle, effort, and suffering from our physiological and spiritual formation? How can we prevent the degeneration of man in modern civilization? Many other questions could be asked on subjects which are to us of the utmost interest. They would also remain unanswered. It is quite evident that the accomplishments of all the sciences having man as an object remain insufficient, and that our knowledge of ourselves is still most rudimentary. This passage more than adequately demonstrates that we still have not formulated a true science of man. About the material part of human existence we are fairly well informed, but we are completely ignorant of who or what controls it. Life is still a mystery to us, and until it is unveiled, there can be no proper apprehension of what, in essence, it is. Alexis Carrel's book, *Man, the Unknown,* is an attempt to make scientific approach to its discovery.

Today man can split an atom; he can make icy lands habitable; he has walked on the moon and sent probes into outer space. Such instances of advanced technological progress give the impression that if man can learn so much about his material environment that he is able to exploit it at will, he should certainly be able to discover himself and, in the process, set right whatever ails him. But there are strong indications in our known world that man can never be understood in the same way that matter can. Let us look at this entity, called man, on a purely physiological basis. He is composed of millions and millions of cells of protoplasm. And what is protoplasm? We can say with certainty that it is a viscous, translucent, homogeneous, structureless substance endowed with contractility and a chemical composition allied to that of albumen: it is the physical basis of life and, clearly, we know a great deal about it as such. Yet we have to concede that we do not know why it should have this unique property of life, or how this came to be so. Moreover, it is a fact that the methods we employ to study the material world cannot be applied to protoplasm in any way which should elicit an answer to these awesome questions. All that is visible to us is a compound of certain things.

If we had the means and the resources, we should be able not only to destroy but also to create such compounds. Indeed, science has discovered the elements of which protoplasm is composed and the particular proportion of those elements have also been learnt. But it is in vain that we join together the two distinct forms of protoplasm, the nucleus and the cytoplasm, albeit in the correct proportions, for no protoplasm is thus formed which has the property of life. While other chemical compounds can be formed by combining their elements in the correct proportions, (e.g. one molecule of water is made up of one atom of oxygen and two atoms of hydrogen) the life-giving matter which is the main constituent of a human being's body can in no way be brought into existence by human agency. Our powers of creation extend only to inanimate matter, never to living entities.

This is the area in which we are the most helpless, and we have no option but to admit it. The greatest irony is that although all our physiological studies are concerned with the living man, the results they yield bear more relevance to this cadaver. Science has discovered both the elements which constitute protoplasm and their correct proportions, yet the particular order or arrangement which is responsible for the life-property of protoplasm has still to be revealed. The moment this arrangement disintegrates, the protoplasm is rendered lifeless. It is as if a particular arrangement was responsible for the existence of soul in the protoplasm. But the difficulty that confronts us is that so long as we keep this arrangement intact, the protoplasm cannot be chemically analysed. The moment we break it, life vanishes. Whenever protoplasm is subjected to chemical analysis, the soul has already left it. And this will always be the case. Science will always remain in the dark regarding the reality of life. But this is not the end of our problem. It goes much deeper than this.

Let us suppose someone sets out to unveil reality, thus disclosing to man the law of life, and, to this end, he begins the study of human settlements. After prolonged examination of different societies, he comes to the conclusion that, since society is composed of human beings, he had best concern himself with the individual, the better to understand the group. So he reduces his focus accordingly. His first preoccupation then is with psychology. But he soon realizes that no single philosophy emerges, because there are several schools of thought on the subject, all arriving at different conclusions. One school claims that the senses are central to all human actions while others say that all man's responses are reactions to impressions received consciously or unconsciously from the external world. Yet others say that it is sexual desires which provide the stimulus for all of man's actions. A different type of study shows that an unrecognized urge to realize a certain set of ideals keeps man active.

Some schools of thought take consciousness to be a reality and explain the whole of man's being in relation to this; others hold that the mind and intellect, have no existence, and that there is no central power commanding the various parts of the body. Rather the parts which receive most attention are better developed and that is what makes it possible, for example, for one man to be highly skilled in dancing, another in archery and yet another in profound reflection. These differences in thinking in the field of psychology go to such extremes that one might be led to wonder if there was any such unified science as psychology. On seeing this jungle of ideas, our inquirer thinks of studying another aspect of human existence – biology – in order to come to more cogent conclusions. But in this discipline he finds that man is treated as an amalgam of the metabolism, the respiratory system, the blood circulation, and so on. These systems are based on certain chemical changes and, judging from their action and reaction, it would appear that the different parts of the whole bodily system are sub-functions of the metabolism.

After deep reflection, he comes to the conclusion that since the existence of the human body and its development are related to chemical actions and reactions, the principles according to which chemical changes take place should first of all be properly understood, failing which no really satisfactory information about man could ever be discovered. So he engrosses himself in the study of physics and chemistry and, indeed, devotes the major part of his life to it. This branch of study leads him on to an investigation of the molecule and the atom, from which he proceeds to study the electrons and protons of which the atom is composed.

The realization then comes to him that the whole universe is nothing but electric waves, and he becomes immersed in the study of the latest discoveries in nuclear science. He thus collects a huge mass of facts, but at the end of it all, he fails to arrive at any firm conclusions about the reality of man. He has become lost in a world which, in spite of being visible, has remained impenetrable. According to Dr. C.E.M. Joad, matter is something unreal which cannot be grasped. It is a part of the four dimensional space-time continuum, a network of electric waves, or a wave of probability which perished on being looked at; and it has even been considered an extension of the observer's consciousness instead of something solid and tangible.

This pathetic end to the quest for the secret of life in the material sciences shows that the secret of life is not discoverable by man. Now just as a sick man cannot treat his disease himself and is forced to consult a doctor, so a man who is in need of spiritual sustenance cannot provide this for himself without turning to God. The fact that he cannot discover the secret either of life or of his own nature is a sure indicator that he is in need of the God who created him in the form in which he exists. Just as God has created man in such a way that he needs oxygen and then has given him oxygen in abundance, He has made him yearn to know the secret of life and then has sent His messengers to him so that all veils should fall from reality and the man becomes fully aware of what the God Almighty and the nature is.

5

Contribution of Arabs

By Arabian Science or Arabian Medicine mean that body of scientific or medical doctrine which is enshrined in books written in the Arabic language, but which is for the most part Greek in its origin, though with Indian, Persian and Syrian accretions, and only in a very small degree the product of the Arabian mind.

Its importance, as has long been recognized, lies not in its originality, but in the fact that in the long interval which separated the decay of Greek learning from the Renascence, it represented the most faithful tradition of ancient Wisdom, and was during the Dark Ages the principal source from which Europe derived such philosophical and scientific ideas as she possessed.

The translation of the Greek books into Arabic, either directly or through intermediate Syrian versions, was effected for the most part under the enlightened patronage of the early Abbasid Caliphs at Baghdad between the middle of the eighth and ninth centuries of our era by skilful and painstaking scholars who were for the most part neither Arabs nor even Muhammadans, but Syrians, Hebrews or Persians of the Christian, Jewish or Magian faith.

Some four or five centuries later, European seekers after knowledge cut off from the original Greek sources, betook themselves with ever increasing enthusiasm to this Arabian presentation of the ancient learning, and rehabilitated it in a Latin dress; and for the first century after the discovery of the art of printing the Latin renderings of Arabic philosophical, scientific and medical works constituted a considerable proportion of the output of the European Press; until the revival of a direct knowledge of the Greek originals in the first place, and the inauguration of a fresh, fruitful and first-hand investigation of natural phenomena in the second, robbed them to a great extent of their prestige and their utility, and changed the excessive veneration in which they had hitherto been held into an equally exaggerated contempt.

Embryology of Science

For sometime, in recent years, however, when the interest and importance of what may be called the Embryology of Science has obtained recognition, the Arabian, together with other ancient and obsolete systems of Medicine, has attracted increasing attention, has formed the subject of much admirable and ingenious research, and has already produced a fairly copious literature.

The chief Arabic biographical and bibliographical sources, such as the Fehrist or "Index" (377/987), al-Qifti's History of the Philosophers (c. 624/1227), Ibn Abi Usaybia's Classes of Physicians (640/1242), the great bibliography of Haji Khalifa (1068/1658) and the like, have been made available in excellent editions, while their most essential contents have been summarized by Wenrich, Wusten-feld, Leclerc, Brockelmann and others; the general character and relations of Arabian Medicine have been concisely yet adequately described by Neuburger, Pagel, Withington and Garrison, to name only a few of the more recent writers on the history of Medicine; while amongst more specialized investigations, to mention one branch only of the subject, the admirable works of Dr P. de Koning and Dr Max Simon have accurately determined the anatomical terminology of the Arabs and its equivalence with that of the Greek anatomists. For the pathological terminology much more remains to be done, and I have been greatly hampered in my reading of Arabic medical books by the difficulty of determining the exact scientific signification of many words used in the ordinary literary language in a looser and less precise sense than that which they evidently bear in the technical works in question.

Nor is much help to be derived from the medieval translations of the " Latino-Barbari," who too often simply preserve in a distorted form the Arabic term which they pretend to translate. Thus, the first section of the first discourse of the first part of the third book of Avicenna's great Qanun is entitled in the Latin Version Sermo universalis de Soda, but who, not having the original before him, could divine that soda stands for the Arabic , the ordinary Arabic word for a headache, being the regularly formed "noun of pain" from the verb "to split"?

Now the history of Arabian Medicine can only be studied in connection with the general history of Islam, which, as you all know, first began to assume political significance in A.D. 266. In that year, Muhammad, whose real miracle was that he inspired the warring tribes of Arabia with a common religious and social ideal, welded them into one people, sent them forth to conquer half the-then known world, and founded an Empire destined to rival and replace those of Caesar and Chosroes, transferred the scene of his activities from Mecca to al-Medina. This event marks the beginning of the Muhammadan era known as the Hijra or "migration" from which 1338 lunar years have now elapsed. About the middle of this period, viz. in the seventh century of the Flight and the thirteenth of our era, Arabian or, more correctly speaking, Muhammadan Civilization suffered through the Mongol or Tartar invasion an injury from which it never recovered, and which destroyed for ever the

Caliphate, the nominal unity of the Arabian Empire, and the preeminence of Baghdad as a centre of learning.

Even before this, however, partly in consequence of the triumph of the narrower and more orthodox doctrines of the Ashari over the more liberal Mutazila school of theology, partly in consequence of the gradual displacement of Arabian and Persian by Turkish influences in the political world, science, and particularly philosophy (which was so closely connected with medicine that the title Hakim was, and still is, indifferently applied alike to the metaphysician and the physician), had ceased to be cultivated with the same enthusiasm and assiduity which had prevailed in "the Golden Prime of good Harunur-Rashid" and his immediate predecessors and successors. This Golden Age of Arabian learning culminated in the century between A.D. 750 and 850, the century succeeding the establishment of the 'Abbasid Caliphate' with its metropolis at Baghdad.

Of the ten Caliphs who reigned during this period, the second, al-Mansur, and the seventh, al-Mamun (whose mother and wife were both Persians, and in whose reign Persian influences, already powerful, reached their culminating point), were conspicuous for their intellectual curiosity and for their love and generous patronage of learning, and for a broad tolerance which scandalized the orthodox and led one of them to change the Caliph's title of "Commander of the Faithful" (Amirul-Muminin) into that of "Commander of the Unbelievers" (Amirul-Kafirin). To the ancient learning, especially that of the ancient Greeks, they were enthusiastically attached; by purchase, conquest or exchange they possessed themselves of countless precious manuscripts, Greek and other, which they stored in the Royal Library or Baitul-Hikmat ("House of Wisdom") and caused to be translated, by the most competent scholars they could attract to their court, into Arabic, either directly from the Greek, or through the intermediary of the Syriac language. In the Fehrist or Index (i.e. of Sciences), an Arabic work composed in A.D. 987, more than a century after what I have spoken of as the "Golden Age", we have at once a mirror of the learning of that time, and an indicator of the appalling losses which it afterwards sustained, for of the books there enumerated it would hardly be an exaggeration to say that not one in a thousand now exists even in the most fragmentary form. The hateful Mongols—"that detestable nation of Satan," as old Matthew Paris (writing in A.D. 1240) calls them, "who poured forth like devils from Tartarus so that they are rightly called 'Tartars'"—did their work of devastation only too thoroughly, and the Muhammadan culture which survived the sack of Baghdad and the extinction of the Caliphate in A.D. 1258 was but a shadow of that before it.

Muslim Civilization

The chosen, term is "Muslim Civilization," which, for reasons to be given shortly, I prefer to "Arabian." As Latin was the learned language of medieval Europe, so was (and to some extent is) Arabic the learned language of the whole Muhammadan world. There is no objection to our talking of "Arabian Science" or "Arabian Medicine" so long as we never lose sight of the fact that this simply means the body of scientific or medical doctrine set forth in the Arabic language, for it is not until the eleventh century of our era that we begin to meet with what may be called a vernacular scientific literature in Muhammadan lands, a literature typified by such works as al-Beruni's Tafhim on astronomy (eleventh century) and the Dhakhira or "Thesaurus" of Medicine composed for the King of Khwarizm or Khiva in the twelfth century.

Literary Contribution

No doubt, the scientific literature in the Arabic language was for the most part produced by Persians, Syrians, Jews, and in a lesser degree by Greeks, but only to a very small extent by genuine Arabs. Ibn Khaldun, who composed his celebrated Prolegomena to the Study of History—one of the most remarkable books in Arabic—about A.D. 1400, judges his countrymen very harshly. He declares that every country conquered by them is soon ruined, that they are incapable of evolving a stable and orderly system of government, that of all people in the world they are the least capable of ruling a kingdom, and that of all people in the world they have the least aptitude for the arts. Goldziher, one of the profoundest Arabic scholars of our time and himself a Jew, rightly says that Lagarde goes too far when he asserts that "of the Muhammadans who have achieved anything in science not one was a Semite"; yet he himself is constrained to admit that even in the religious sciences (exegesis of the Quran, tradition, jurisprudence, and the like) "the Arabian element lagged far behind the non-Arabian."

Much more evidence of this might be adduced, but I will content myself with one instance (hitherto, I believe, unnoticed in Europe) of the mistrust with which Arab practitioners of medicine were regarded even by their own people. The anecdote in question is related to that most learned but discursive writer Al-Jahiz (so called on account of his prominent eyes) in his "Book of Misers" (Kitabul-Bukhala) and concerns an Arabian physician named Asad ibn Jani, who, even in a year of pestilence, and in spite of his recognized learning, skill and diligence, had but few patients.

Being asked the reason of this by one of his acquaintances he replied: "In the first place, I am a Muslim, and before I studied medicine, nay, before ever I was created, the people held the view that Muslims are not successful physicians. Further my name is Asad, and it should have been Saliba, Marail, Yuhana or Bira [i.e. a Syriac or Aramaic name]; and my kunyat is Abul-Harith, and it should have been Abu Isa, Abu Zakriya or Abu Ibrahim [i.e. Christian or Jewish instead of Muhammadan]; and I wear a cloak of white cotton, and it should have been of black silk; and my speech is Arabic, and it should have been the speech of the people of Jundi-Shapur" [in S.W. Persia].

The scepticism of the Arabs was not confined to matters of religion, avenged themselves to some extent by disparaging verses about doctors, such as the following on the death of Yuhana ibn Masawayhi (the Mesues of the medieval writers) in A.D. 857:

> *"Verily the physician, with his physic and his drugs,*
> *Cannot avert a summons that hath come.*
> *What ails the physician that he dies of the disease*
> *Which he used to cure in time gone by?*
> *There died alike he who administered the drug, and he who took the drug,*
> *And he who imported and sold the drug, and he who bought it."*

Similar in purport are the following verses from the popular romance of Antara, the old Bedouin hero:

> *"The physician says to thee, I can cure thee,*
> *'When he feels thy wrist and thy arm;*
> *But did the physician know a cure/or disease*
> *Which would ward off death, he would not himself suffer the death agony."*

Now, in considering the genesis and development of the so-called Arabian Medicine, of which, though the main outlines are clearly determined, many details remain to be filled in, we may most conveniently begin by enquiring what was the state of medical knowledge, or ignorance, amongst the ancient Arabs before the driving force of Islam destroyed their secular isolation, sent them out to conquer half the-then known world, and brought this primitive but quick-witted people into close contact with the ancient civilization of the Greeks, Persians, Egyptians, Indians and others. We have to distinguish three periods antecedent to what I have called the Golden Age, viz,:

(1) The Jahiliyyat, or Pagan Period, preceding the rise and speedy triumph of Islam, which was fully accomplished by the middle of the seventh century of our era.

(2) The theocratic period of the Prophet and his immediate successors, the Four Orthodox Caliphs, which endured in all, from the Hijra or "Flight" to the assassination of 'All' less than forty years (A.D. 622-661) and which had its centre at al-Medina, the ancient Yathrib.

(3) The period of the Umayyad Caliphs, whose immense Empire stretched from Spain to Samarqand, and whose court at Damascus speedily began to show a luxury and wealth hitherto utterly undreamed of by the Arabs.

Presently, it is hardly necessary to consider separately the first and second of these three periods, those namely which preceded and immediately followed the rise of Islam, and which, however widely they differed in their theological, ethical and political aspects, were, as regards scientific knowledge, almost on the same level. The life of the old pagan Arabs was rough and primitive in the highest degree—very much what the life of the Bedouin of Inner Arabia remains to this day;—the different tribes were constantly engaged in savage wars fomented by interminable vendettas; only the strong and resourceful could hold their own, and for the weak and sick there was little chance of survival.

On the other hand, they were intelligent, resourceful, courageous, hardy, chivalrous in many respects, very observant all natural phenomena which came within the range of their observation, and possessed of a language of great wealth and virility of which they were inordinately proud, so that to this day, when they still praise God "who created the Arabic language the best of all languages," the poems of that far-off time, describing their raids, their battles, their venturous journeys and their love affairs, remain the standard and model of the chastest and most classical Arabic. Most of these warring tribes acknowledged no authority save that of their own chiefs and princes; only on the borders of the Persian and Roman Empires respectively, in the little kingdoms of Hira and Ghassan, the elements of civilization and science can be witnessed.

First Arab Doctor

In fact, the first Arab doctor mentioned by those careful biographers of philosophers and physicians, al-Qifti and Ibn Abi Usaybia, is al-Harith ibn Kalada, an elder contemporary of the Prophet Muhammad, who had completed his studies at the great Persian medical school of Jundi-Shapur, and who had the honour of being consulted on at least one occasion by the great Persian King Khusrau Anushirwan (the Kisra of the Arabs and Chosroes of the Greeks) who harboured and protected the Neo-Platonist 'philosophers driven into exile by the intolerance of the Emperor Justinian. An account of this interview, authentic or otherwise, fills a couple of closely-printed pages of Arabic in Ibn Abi Usaybia's Classes of Physicians, and the substance of it is given by Dr Lucien Leclerc in his Histoire de la Medicine Arabe.

It consists almost entirely of general hygienic principles, sound enough as far as they go, but of little technical interest. A certain tragic interest attaches to Nadr, the son of this al-Harith, who like his father seems to have had some skill in medicine and a Persian education. This led him to mock at the biblical anecdotes contained in the Quran, these being, he did not hesitate to say, much less entertaining and instructive than the old Persian legends about Rustam and Isfandiyar, with which he would distract the attention and divert the interest of the Prophet's audience. Muhammad never forgave him for this, and when he was taken prisoner at the Battle of Badr—

the first notable victory of the Muslims over the unbelievers—he caused him to be murdered.

Having studied the Prophet's own ideas about medicine and hygiene (partly derived, very likely, from the above-mentioned al-Harith) we can form a fairly accurate idea from the very full and carefully authenticated body of traditions of his sayings and doings which, after the Quran, forms the most authoritative basis of Muhammadan doctrine. These traditions, finally collected and arranged during the ninth and tenth centuries of our era, are grouped according to subjects, each subject constituting a "book" (kitab) and each tradition a "chapter" (bab). If we take the Sahih of al-Bukhari, the most celebrated of these collections, we find at the beginning of the fourth volume two books dealing with medicine and the sick, containing in all 80 chapters.

This looks promising; but when we come to examine them more closely we find that only a small proportion deal with medicine, surgery or therapeutics as we understand them, and that the majority are concerned with such matters as the visitation, encouragement and spiritual consolation of the sick, the evil eye, magic, talismans, amulets and protective prayers and formulae. Although the Prophet declares that for every malady wherewith God afflicts mankind. He has appointed a suitable remedy, he subsequently limits the principal methods of treatment to three, the administration of honey, cupping, and the actual cautery, and he recommends his followers to avoid or make sparing use of the latter. Camel's milk, fennel-flower (Nigella saliva), aloes, antimony (for ophthalmia), manna, and, as a styptic, the ashes of burnt matting, are amongst the other therapeutical agents mentioned.

The diseases referred to include headache and migraine, ophthalmia, leprosy, pleurisy, pestilence and fever, which is characterized as "an exhalation of Hell." The Prophet advises his followers not to visit a country where pestilence is raging, but not to flee from it if they find themselves there. The scanty material furnished by these and other traditions (for the Quran, apart from some mention of wounds and a vague popular Embryology, contains hardly any medical matter) has been more or less systematized by later writers as what is termed Tibbun-Nabi, or the "Prophet's Medicine," and I am informed that a manual so entitled is still one of the first books read by the student of the Old Medicine in India, along with the abridgment of Avicenna's Qanun, known as the Qanuncha.

Ibn Khaldun, whom we have already had occasion to mention, speaks slightingly of this "Prophetic Medicine" and of the indigenous Arab Medicine which it summarized and of which it formed part, but judiciously adds that we are not called upon to conform to its rules, since "the Prophet's mission was to make known to us the prescriptions of the Divine Law, and not to instruct us in Medicine and the common practices of ordinary life." A propos of this he reminds us that on one occasion the Prophet endeavoured to forbid the artificial fecundation of the date-palm, with such disastrous results to the fruit-crop that he withdrew his prohibition with the remark, " You know better than I do what concerns your worldly interests." "One is then under no obligation," continues our author, "to believe that the medical prescriptions handed down even in authentic traditions have been transmitted to us as rules which we are bound to observe; nothing in these traditions indicates that this is the case. It is, however true, that if one likes to employ these remedies with the object of earning the Divine Blessing, and if one takes them with sincere faith, one may derive from them great advantage, though they form no part of Medicine properly so-called."

Enough has been said to show how wide was the difference between what passed for medical knowledge amongst the early Arabs of the pagan, prophetic and patriarchal periods, and the elaborate system built up on a Hippocratic and Galenic basis at Baghdad under the early 'Abbasid Caliphs'. The facts here are certain and the data ample. More difficult is the question how far this system of Medicine was evolved under the Umayyad Caliphs in the intermediate period which lay between the middle of the seventh and the middle of the eighth centuries of the Christian era. These Umayyads, though, indeed, purely Arab, were by this time accustomed to the settled life and the amenities of civilization, and already far removed from the conquerors of Ctesiphon, the Sasanian capital, who mistook camphor for salt and found it insipid in their food; exchanged gold for an equal amount of silver—"the yellow for the white," as they expressed it;—and sold an incomparable royal jewel for a thousand pieces of money, because, as the vendor said when reproached for selling it so cheap, he knew no number beyond a thousand to ask for.

Under these Umayyads, the Arabian or Islamic Empire attained its maximum extent, for Spain, one of their chief glories, never acknowledged the 'Abbasid rule'. In Egypt and Persia, as well as in Syria and its capital Damascus, where they held their court, they were in immediate contact with the chief centres of ancient learning. How far, we must enquire, did they profit by the afforded opportunities?

With the progress of their theology, as Von Kremer has shown', they were almost certainly influenced by John of Damascus, entitled Chrysorrhoas, and named in Arabic Mansur, who enjoyed the favour of the first Umayyad Caliph Muawiyyah. The first impulse given to the desire of the Arabs for knowledge of the wisdom of the Greeks came from the Umayyad prince Khalid the son of Yazid the son of Muawiyyah, who had a passion for Alchemy. According to the Fehrist, the oldest and best existing source of our knowledge on these matters, he assembled the Greek philosophers in Egypt and commanded them to translate Greek and Egyptian books on this subject into Arabic; and these, says the author of the

Fehrist, " were the first translations made in Islam from one language to another." With this prince is associated the celebrated Arabian alchemist Jabir ibn Hayyan, famous in medieval Europe under the name of Geber.

Many, if not most, of the Latin books which passed under his name in the Middle Ages are spurious, being the original productions of European investigators who sought by the prestige attaching to his name to give authority and currency to their own writings. The Arabic originals of his works are rare, and the only serious study of them which I have met with is contained in the third volume of Berthelot's admirable Histoire de la Chimie au Moyen Age, where the 'text and French translation of one of his genuine treatises are given. Berthelot points out, what, indeed, has long been recognized, that though the chief pursuit of the old alchemists was the Philosopher's Stone and the Elixir of Life, they nevertheless made many real and valuable discoveries. How many of these, we owe to the Arabs, is apparent in such words as alcohol, alembic and the like, still current amongst us. It is indeed generally recognized that it was in the domains of chemistry and materia medica that the Arabs added most to the body of scientific doctrine inherently.

Development of Medicine

If we talk of medicine proper, we find little trace amongst the Arabs at this period, only three or four physicians being specifically mentioned, mostly Christians, and probably non-Arabs. One of them was Ibn Uthal, physician to Muawiyyah, the first Umayyad Caliph, who was murdered by a man of the tribe of Makhzum on suspicion of having, at the instigation of the Caliph, poisoned an obnoxious relative named Abdur-Rahman. Another, Abul-Hakam, also a Christian, lived to be a centenarian, as did also his son Hakam. In the case of the latter, we have a fairly detailed account of his successful treatment of a case of severe arterial haemorrhage caused by an unskilful surgeon-barber. Neither of these men seems to have written anything, but to Isa the son of Hakam is ascribed a large Kunnash, or treatise on the Art of Medicine, of which no fragment has been preserved. Mention is also made by the Arab biographers of a certain Theodosius or Theodorus, evidently a Greek, who was physician to the cruel but capable Hajjaj ibn Yusuf, by whom he was held in high honour and esteem.

Some of his aphorisms are preserved, but none of the three or four works ascribed to him. The short list of these medical practitioners of the Umayyad period is closed by a Bedouin woman named Zainab, who treated cases of ophthalmia. That somewhat more attention began to be paid to public health is indicated by the fact recorded by the historian Tabari that the Caliph al-Walid in the year 88/707 segregated the lepers, while assigning to them an adequate supply of food. Amongst the Bedouin the recourse was still to the old charms and incantations, often accompanied by the application to the patient of the operator's saliva. An instance of this is recorded in connection with the poet Jarir, who gave his daughter Umm Ghaylan in marriage to a magician named Ablaq who had cured him in this fashion of erysipelas. The practice of medicine amongst the genuine Arabs of Arabia, both Bedouin and dwellers in towns, at the present day is succinctly described by Zwemer in his book Arabia, the Cradle of Islam; and his description, so far as we can judge, fairly represents its condition at the remote period under discussion.

The question which demands consideration before we pass on to the great revival of learning under the early Abbasid Caliphs at Baghdad in the eighth and ninth centuries of our era. Leclerc in his Histoire de la Medicine Arabe maintains that already, a century earlier, when the Arabs conquered Egypt, the process of assimilating Greek learning began. In this process he assigns an important part to a certain Yahya an-Nahwi, or

"John the Grammarian," who enjoyed high favour with Amr Ibnul-Aas, the conqueror and first Muslim governor of Egypt, and whom he identifies with John Philoponus the commentator of Aristotle. This Yahya, of whom the fullest notice occurs in al-Qifti's "History of the Philosophers" (Tarikhul-Hukama), was a Jacobite bishop at Alexandria, who subsequently repudiated the doctrine of the Trinity, and consequently attracted the favourable notice of the Muslims, to whose strict monotheism this doctrine is particularly obnoxious. He was, according to the well-known story, now generally discredited by Orientalists, who was the ultimate though innocent cause of the alleged burning of the books in the great library at Alexandria by the Muslims, a story which Leclerc, in spite of his strong pro-Arab and pro-Muhammadan sympathies, oddly enough accepts as a historical fact.

This Yahya, at any rate, was a great Greek scholar, and is said by al-Qifti to have mentioned in one of his works the year 343 of Diocletian (reckoned from A.D. 284) as the current year in which he wrote. This would agree very well with his presence in Egypt at the time of the Arab conquest in A.D. 640, but would prove that he was not identical with John Philoponus, who, according to a note added by Professor Bury to Gibbon's narrative of the event in question, flourished not in the seventh but in the early part of the sixth century after Christ. The precious library of Alexandria had, as Gibbon observes, been pretty thoroughly destroyed by Christian fanatics nearly three centuries before Egypt destroyed by the Muslims.

Of the fate of the Alexandrian library and the identity of the two Johns or Yahyas are, however, quite subordinate to the much larger and more important question of the state of learning in Egypt at the time of the Arab conquest. Leclerc's view is that the School of Medicine, once so famous, long outlived that of Philosophy, and continued, even though much fallen from its ancient splendour, until the time of the Arab conquest. This is a difficult point to decide; but Dr Wallis Budge, whose opinion I sought, definitely took the view that the Egyptian writings of this period at any rate, so far as they touched on these topics at all, showed little or no trace of medical science, Greek or other. At the same time we must give due weight to the well-authenticated Arabian tradition as to the translation of Greek works on Alchemy for the Umayyad prince Khalid ibn Yazid in Egypt, and must admit the possibility, if not the probability, that these translations included other subjects, philosophical, medical and the like, besides that which constituted the prince's special hobby mentioned above.

It was in the middle of the eighth century of our era and through the-then newly-founded city of Baghdad that the great stream of Greek and other ancient learning began to pour into the Muhammadan world and to reclothe itself in an Arabian dress. And so far as Medicine is concerned, the tradition of the old Sasanian school of Jundi-Shapur was predominant. Of this once celebrated school, now long a mere name, with difficulty located by modern travellers and scholars on the site of the hamlet of Shahabad in the province of Khuzistan in S.W. Persia, a brief account is as follows.

The Sasanian monarch Shapur I founded the city the son and successor of Ardashir Babakan who founded this great dynasty in the third century after Christ, and restored, after five centuries and a half of eclipse, the ancient glories of Achaemenian Persia. Shapur, after he had defeated and taken captive the Emperor Valerian, and sacked the famous city of Antioch, built, at the place called in Syriac Beth Lapat, a town which he named Veh-az-Andev-i-Shapur, or " Shapur's ' Better than Antioch," a name which was gradually converted into Gunde Shapur or in Arabic Jundi Sabur Another" Better than Antioch " was founded in the sixth century of our era by Khusrau Anushirwan, the Chosroes of the Greeks and Kisra of the Arabs, which, to distinguish it from the first, was called Veh-az-Andev-i-Khusrau. This latter town, by a practice which prevailed in Persia even until the sixteenth century, was chiefly populated by the deported citizens— especially craftsmen and artisans—of the foreign town after which it was named; and it seems likely that Jundi-Shapur also received a considerable number of Greek settlers, for the Greek translations of Shapur's Pahlawi inscriptions carved on the rocks at Istakhr in Fars prove that Greek labour was available at this time even in the interior of Persia.

Forty or fifty years later, in the early part of the fourth century, in the reign of the second Shapur, the city had become a royal residence, and it was there that Mani or Manes, the founder of the Manichaean heresy, was put to death, and his skin, stuffed with straw, suspended from one of the city gates, known long afterwards, even in Muhammadan times, as the "Gate of Manes." There also, as appears probable, Shapur II established the Greek physician Theodosius or Theodorus whom he summoned to attend him, and whose system of medicine is mentioned in the Fehrist as one of the Persian books on Medicine afterwards translated into Arabic and preserved at any rate until the tenth century of our era. This physician, who was a Christian, obtained such honour and consideration in Persia that Shapur caused a church to be built for him and at his request set free a number of captives of his own country.

However, the unforeseen and unintended result of that Byzantine intolerance which in the fifth century of our era drove the Nestorians from their school at Edessa and forced them to seek refuge in Persian territory was the great development of the school of Jundi-shapur. In the following century the enlightened and wisdom-loving Khusrau Anushirwan, the protector of the exiled Neo-Platonist philosophers, sen this physician Burzuya to India, who, together with the game of chess and the celebrated Book of Kalila and Dimna, brought back Indian works on medicine and also, apparently, Indian physicians living in Persia.

At the time of the Prophet Muhammad's birth, the school at the height of its glory. There converged Greek and Oriental learning, the former transmitted in part directly through Greek scholars, but for the most part through the industrious and assimilative Syrians, who made up in diligence what they lacked in originality. Sergius of Rasool-'Ayn, who flourished a little before this time, was one of those who translated Hippocrates and Galen into Syriac. Of this intermediate Syriac medical literature, from which many, perhaps most, of the Arabic translations of the eighth and ninth centuries were made, not much survives, but M. H. Pognon's edition and French translation of a Syriac version of the Aphorisms of Hippocrates, and Dr Wallis Budge's Syriac Book of Medicines, enable us to form some idea of its quality. To the Syrians, whatever their defects, and especially to the Nestorians, Asia owes much, and the written characters of the Mongol, Manchu, Uyghur and many other peoples in the western half of Asia testify to the literary influence of the Aramaic peoples.

Teaching of Medicine

Although the medical teaching of Jundi-Shapur was in the main Greek, there was no doubt in underlying Persian element, especially in Pharmacology, where the Arabic nomenclature plainly reveals in many cases Persian origins. Unfortunately the two most glorious periods of pre-Islamic Persia, the Achaemenian (B.C. 550-330) and the Sasanian (A.D. 226-640) both terminated in a disastrous foreign invasion, Greek in the first case, Arab in the second, which involved the wholesale destruction of the indigenous learning and literature, so that it is impossible for us to reconstitute more than the main outlines of these two ancient civilizations. Yet the Avesta, the sacred book of the Zoroastrians speaks of three classes of healers, by prayers and religious observances, by diet and drugs, and by instruments; in other words, priests, physicians and surgeons. As regards the latter, one curious passage in the

Vendidad ordains that the tyro must operate successfully on three unbelievers before he may attempt an operation on one of the "good Mazdayasnian religion." And, of course, Greek physicians, of whom Ctesias is the best known, besides an occasional Egyptian, were to be found at the Achaemenian court before the time of Alexander of Macedon.

The medical school of Jundi-Shapur seems to have been little affected by the Arab invasion and conquest of the seventh century of our era, but it was not till the latter half of the eighth century, when Baghdad became the metropolis of Islam, that its influence began to be widely exerted on the Muslims. It was in the year A.D. 765 that the second Abbasid Caliph al-Mansur, being afflicted with an illness which baffled his medical advisers, summoned to attend him Jurjis the son of Bukht-Yishu' (a half-Persian, half-Syriac name, meaning "Jesus hath delivered"), the chief physician of the great hospital of Jundi-Shapur. Four years later Jurjis fell ill and craved permission to return home to see his family and children, and, should he die, to be buried with his fathers.

The Caliph invited him to embrace the religion of Islam, but Jurjis replied that he preferred to be with his fathers, whether in heaven or hell. Thereat, the Caliph, laughed and said, "Since I saw thee I have found relief from the maladies to which I had been accustomed," and he dismissed him with a gift of 10, 000 dinars, and sent with him on his journey an attendant who should convey him, living or dead, to Jundi-Shapur, the "Civitas Hippocratica" which he loved so well. Jurjis on his part promised to send to Baghdad to replace him one of his pupils named Isa ibn Shahla, but declined to send his son, Bukht-Yishu' the second, on the ground that he could not be spared from the Bimdristan, or hospital, of Jundi-Shapur.

For six generations and over 250 years, the Bukht-Yishu' family remained pre-eminent in medicine, the last (Jibbrail son of 'Ubaidullah son of Bukht-Yishu' son of Jibbrail son of Bukht-

Yishu' son of Jurjis son of Jibbrail), who died on April 10, 1006, being as eminent and as highly honoured by the rulers and nobles of his time as the first. That a certain exclusiveness and un-willingness to impart their knowledge to strangers characterized the physicians of Jundi-Shapur may be inferred from the treatment received at the beginning of his career by the celebrated translator of Greek medical works into Arabic, Hunain ibn Ishaq, known to medieval Europe as "Johannitius." He was a Christian of Hira with a great passion for knowledge, and acted as dispenser to Yuhana ibn Masawayh (the "Messues" of the Latino-Barbari), whose lectures he also followed.

But he was prone to ask too many troublesome questions, and one day his master, losing patience, exclaimed, " What have the people of Hira to do with medicine? Go and change money in the streets!" and drove him forth in tears; "for," says al-Qifti, "these people of Jundi-Shapur used to believe that they only were worthy of this science, and would not suffer it to go forth from themselves, their children and their kin." But Hunain, more resolved than ever on pursuing knowledge to its source, went away for several years to learn Greek.

During this period one of his former acquaintances, Yusuf the physician, one day saw a man with long hair and undipped beard and moustaches reciting Homer in the street, and, in spite of his changed appearance, recognized his voice as that of Hunain. He, being questioned, admitted his identity, but enjoined silence on Yusuf, saying that he had sworn not to continue his medical studies until he had perfected himself in knowledge of the Greek language. When he finally returned, Jibbrail ibn Bukht-Yishu', to whom he attached himself, was delighted with his Greek scholarship and declared him to be a miracle of learning, and Ibn Masawayh, who had formerly driven him out with contumely, sought Yusuf's good offices to effect a reconciliation with him.

Later, he gained high favour with the Caliph, who, however, was minded first to prove his professional honour by a hard test, for he bade him concoct a poison for one of his enemies, offering him rich rewards if he would do so, but severe punishment—imprisonment or death—if he refused. He refused and was imprisoned for a year, when he was again brought before the Caliph and bidden to choose again between compliance and a rich reward, or the sword of the executioner. " I have already told the Commander of the Faithful," replied Hunain, "that I have skill only in what is beneficial, and have studied naught else"; and being again threatened with instant death he added, "I have a Lord who will give me my right tomorrow in the Supreme Uprising, so if the Caliph would injure his own soul, let him do so." Then the Caliph smiled and declared that he had only desired to assure himself of Hunain's probity before yielding him implicit confidence.

So the incident ended satisfactorily, but it serves to show that the position of Court Physician at Baghdad in early Abbasid times was sometimes a trying one; a fact brought out in the well-known story of the physician Duban and King Yunan (which, however, had a much more tragic ending) in the Arabian Nights.

Hunain was not only the most celebrated but the most productive of these translators. Of the ten Hippocratic writings mentioned by the author of the Fehrist' as existing in Arabic translations in his time, seven were his work and three the work of his pupil Isa ibn Yahya, while the "sixteen books" of Galen were all translated by him or his pupil Hubaysh. Generally, as we learn from the Fehrist, Hunain translated the Greek into Syriac, while Hubaysh translated from Syriac into Arabic, the Arabic version being then revised by Hunain, who, however, sometimes translated directly from Greek into Arabic. All three languages were known to most of these translators, and it is probable, as Leclerc suggests, that whether the translation was made into Syriac or Arabic depended on whether it was primarily designed for Christian or Muslim readers.

At the present day, comparatively few of these Arabic translations are available, even in manuscript; but good MSS. of the Aphorisms' and Prognostics' exist in the British Museum, besides an epitome of the "sixteen books" of Galen ascribed to Yahya-an-Nahwi, or "John the Grammarian." Of the Aphorisms in Arabic, there is an Indian lithographed edition, which, however, I have not seen. This dearth of texts is very unfortunate for the student of Arabian Medicine, who is thereby much hampered in the solution of two important preliminary questions, viz. the accuracy and fidelity of these early Arabic translations, and the development of the Arabic medical terminology, often unintelligible without reference to the Greek original.

As regards the first question, Leclerc is apparently right in his opinion that the translation from Greek into Arabic was generally effected with much greater skill and knowledge than the later translation from Arabic into Latin, and that he who judges Arabian Medicine only by the latter will inevitably undervalue it and do it a great injustice. Indeed, it is difficult to resist the conclusion that many passages in the Latin version of the Qanun of Avicenna were misunderstood or not understood at all by the translator, and consequently, can never have conveyed a clear idea to the reader.

Another group of great translators from Greek into Arabic was provided by the city of Harran, the classical Charrae, which remained pagan down to the thirteenth century, and, by reason of the high degree of Greek culture long maintained there, was known as Helleno-polis. How the inhabitants of this city came to be known as "Sabaeans" from the ninth century onwards, though they had nothing to do with the true Sabaeans of Chaldaea (of whom a remnant, known to be the

Muhammadans as al-Mughtasila from their frequent ceremonial bathings and washings, and to Europeans, for the same reason, as "Christians of St John the Baptist," exist to the present day near Basra and along the banks of the Shattul-'Arab), is a very curious story, exhaustively set forth, with full documentary evidence, by Chwolson in his great work Die Sabier und Sabismus. Of these learned Harranians, the most celebrated were Thabit ibn Qurra (born A.D. 836, died A.D. 901), his sons Ibrahim and Sinan, his grandsons Thabit and Ibrahim, and his great-grandson Sinan; and the family of Zahrun. Mention should also be made of another contemporary translator, though his predilection was for mathematics rather than medicine, Qusta ibn Luqa, a Christian of Baalbek in Syria, who died about A.D. 923.

Great Contributions

Thus, by the tenth century, the Muslims, to all of whom, irrespective of race, Arabic was not only the language of Revelation and Religion, but also of science, diplomacy and polite intercourse, had at their disposal a great mass of generally excellent translations of all the most famous philosophical and scientific writings of the Greeks. For Greek poetry and drama they cared little, and of the Latin writers they seem to have known nothing whatever. Of the Greek medical writers, besides Hippocrates and Galen, their favourites were Rufus of Ephesus, Oribasius, Paul of Egina, and Alexander of Tralles; and, for materia medica, Dioscorides.

In some cases Greek, writings, lost in the original, have been preserved to us in Arabic translations. The most notable instance of this is afforded by the seven books of Galen's Anatomy (ix-xv), lost in the original Greek but preserved in the Arabic, of which the text, with German translation and full apparatus criticus, has been published by Dr Max Simon with an admirable Arabic-Greek-German vocabulary of technical terms, to which reference has already been made.

Were the materials accessible, it would be interesting to compare those Arabic translations made directly from the Greek with those which first passed through the medium of Syriac. Of the few Syriac versions preserved to us, I cannot myself form an opinion, being unfortunately unacquainted with that language, but they are rather harshly judged by M. Pognon, of whose edition and translation of the Syriac Aphorisms of Hippocrates I have already spoken. "The Syriac version of the Aphorisms contained in my manuscript," he writes, "is a very faithful, or rather too faithful translation of the Greek text; sometimes, indeed, it is a literal translation absolutely devoid of sense. This, unfortunately, does not allow us to determine the epoch at which it was made, since to render too literally has been the defect of many Syrian translators."

"I will not venture to say," he continues, "that the Syrians never possessed clear translations written in a correct style, but in most of the translations which have reached us, the style is often obscure, the construction incorrect, and words are often employed in a sense not properly belonging to them, this generally arising from the desire of the Syriac translator to reproduce the Greek text too faithfully. The Syrian translators, when they found a difficult passage, too often contented themselves with rendering each Greek word by a Syriac word without in any way seeking to write an intelligible sentence. Thus, we find in their translations many incorrect sentences, and even expressions which have absolutely no meaning. In short, I believe that when they did not understand the meaning of a Greek word, the translators did not hesitate to transcribe it in Syriac characters, leaving their readers to conjecture the meaning of these barbarisms which they had created."

The translation of the Aphorisms, with which he is specially concerned, M. Pognon characterizes as "detestable," and adds: "Whenever the translator comes across an obscure passage, his translation is obscure; and whenever he meets with a passage which is susceptible of several different renderings, his translation can be interpreted in several different ways." This assertion he proves by numerous examples.

The Arab mind, on the other hand, is clear and positive, and the Arabic language nervous, virile and rich both actually and potentially. The old Arabs were an acute and observant people, and for all natural objects which fell under their notice they had appropriate and finely differentiated words. To render the medical works of the Greeks into their own language, they had, of course, in many cases, to invent new terms translated or imitated from the Greek, and often only to be understood by reference to the Greek originals; but they already possessed a fairly copious anatomical vocabulary, which, moreover, they were fond of using in ordinary life, even in their poetry. Thus, the Umayyad Caliph Yazid ibn Abdul-Malik, who, in 105/723-4, died of love for the slave-girl Habbaba, was deeply stirred by her singing of the following verse:

"Between the clavicles and the uvula is a burning heat
Which cannot be appeased or swallowed down and cooled."

The poet al-Mutanabbi (tenth century) has a poem on a fever by which he was attacked in Egypt in Dhul-Hijja 348 (February 960), and which left him—

"Sick a body, unable to rise up, vehemently intoxicated (i.e. delirious) without wine."

He compares the fever to a coy maiden who will only visit him under cover of darkness:

"And it is as though she who visits me were filled with modesty,
For she does not pay her visits save under cover of darkness.
I freely offered her my linen and my pillows,
But she refused them, and spent the night in my bones.
My skin is too contracted to contain both my breath and her,
So she relaxes it with all sorts of sickness.

When she leaves me, she washes me [with perspiration]
As though we had retired apart for some forbidden action.
It is as though the morning drives her away,
And her lachrymal ducts are flooded in their four channels.
I watch for her time [of arrival] without desire,
Yet with the watchfulness of the eager lover.
And she is ever faithful to her appointed time, but faithfulness is an evil When it casts thee into grievous sufferings."

Under such astonishing imagery are clearly depicted the delirium and regular nightly recurrence of the fever, the rigors which mark its onset, and the copious perspiration with which it concludes, the latter being fantastically likened to the weeping of a woman torn from her lover's arms.

That in the days of the Caliphate every educated person was expected to take some interest in Medicine and to know something about Anatomy is shown by the curious story of the equally fair and talented slave-girl Tawaddud in the Arabian Nights. The girl is offered to the Caliph Harunur-Rashid for an enormous price (10,000 dinars) by her bankrupt master Abul-Husn, and the Caliph agrees to pay this sum provided she can answer satisfactorily any questions addressed to her by those most learned in each of the many branches of knowledge in which she claims to excel. Therefore, the most notable professors of Theology, Law, Exegesis of the Quran, Medicine, Astronomy, Philosophy, Rhetoric and Chess examine her in succession, and in each case, she not only gives satisfactory replies to all their questions, but ends by putting to each of them a question which he is unable to answer.

Lane describes this story, which provides material for six of the '1001 Nights', as "extremely tiresome to most readers," but it is very valuable as indicating what was regarded by the medieval Muslims as a good all-round education.

The medical portion of the examination includes the outlines of Anatomy and Physiology, according to Arabian ideas, diagnosis from signs and symptoms, humoristic Pathology, Hygiene, Dietetics and the like. The enumeration of the bones is fairly complete, but that of the blood vessels very vague. Of the branches of the Aorta, says Tawaddud, "none knoweth the tale save He who created them, but it is said that they number 360"—a mystical number, 12 x 30, which still plays a great part in the doctrines of certain Muhammadan sects, by whom it is called "The Number of All Things" for reasons which it would be tedious to enumerate in this place.

6

Progress in Various Disciplines

Mathematics

The achievements of Muslims in the field of mathematics are extremely remarkable. A regular study of this science, like all other sciences, was begun during the reign of the second Abbasi Caliph, Al-Mansur in the second half of the eighth century A.C. During this period the work on mathematics was exclusively done by Muslims. Some stimulus came from Indian and Greek works which were later translated into Arabic. The investigations were carried out and until the end of the fifth century A.H./the 11th century A.C, nearly all of the original and creative work was done by Muslims, and even the non-Muslims wrote all the works on mathematics in Arabic. In the 12th century the Christians and jews started the work of translation from Arabic into Latin and Hebrew, and also began to conduct research in this field. But until the end of the 13th century no mathematical work comparable to that of Muslims could be done by the Christians or Jews.

The Muslims used numerals including zero for counting in contrast with writing the amounts in words, or counting with the letters of alphabet. Thus, they made arithmetic simple and applicable to the problems of everyday life in connection with commerce and trade and the division of estates and inheritance. The zero has a great importance in arithmetic. Without zero it is not possible to indicate the figures like tens, hundreds, etc. If zero is not used it becomes necessary to use a table (named abacus) with columns of units, tens, hundreds, etc., to keep each figure in its place. The zero was used by the Muslims centuries before it was known in the West. The Latin word *ciphar* for zero is of Arabic origin; the Arabic word for it being *sifr,* meaning empty or nil.

The West learnt the use of numerals from the Arabs, and, therefore, called them the 'Arabic numerals'. The Arabs themselves termed them as 'Hindi numbers' *(al-Adad-al-Hindi).* The word *Hindi* has been translated as Indian by some writers, for, as they suggest, the numerals are of Indian origin. But this translation of the word *Hindi* does not seem to be correct, for, the word *Hindi* is sometimes written in place of *Handasi,* i.e., what relates to *Handasah* which means geometry and the art of engineering. Thus, the numerals called *Hindi* may simply mean 'the mathematical characters'. There are some such instances in which the word *Hindi* may be considered to be a substitute for *Handasi* such as in astronomy wherein a graduated circle called *Daira-e-Hindi* may better be translated as 'Mathematical (Geometrical) Circle'.

The diffusion of the Arabic numerals in Christian Europe was very slow. The Christian mathematicians either used the old Roman numerals and the abacus, or used the Arabic numerals together with their old system. It was only in the 12th century that after learning from the Muslims the Western scholars were able to produce some literature on the numeral system, without columns, and completed by zero. It was Leonardo of Pisa who after travelling in Muslim lands and studying the Arabic system of numerals there, published a work which is mostly responsible for the introduction of that system into Europe. This system was named algorithm (or algorism) which has been derived by the Latin writers from the patronymic Al-Khwarizmi (a native of Khwarizm) who was a distinguished Muslim mathematician, astronomer and geographer of the ninth century A.C. He flourished under the Caliph Al-Mamun. His full name was Abu Abd Allah Muhammad ibn Musa-al-Khawarizimi. This name gained so much popularity that it was included in many languages of the world. Till the end of the 18th century the science of numbers (1, 2, 3, etc.) was called by the Latin writers as algorism whereas in Spanish it was termed as Guorismo. The English poet Chaucer named zero as augrim.

The Muslims made advancement in arithmetic. They wrote books on the arithmetic of every day use. They also wrote on commercial arithmetic.

Algebra was made by them an exact science. Al-Khwarizmi named his book dealing with this subject as *Kitab-al-Jabr Wal-Muqabalah* (the book of restitution and comparison). The word *Jabr* means 'restitution'. It is the adding some thing to a given sum or multiplying it so that it becomes equal to another. The word *Muqabalah* means comparison. This term is applied for the comparison of the two sides of an equation as a + b = 5. It seems that the word *Al-Jabr* was originally used for these simple operations i.e. addition and multiplication, but later on it came to mean the whole subject.

***Analytical Geometry* :** The Muslims founded analytical geometry as well as plane and spherical trigonometry. The latter which in the early stage of its development was considered to be a part of astronomy, was made a separate branch of mathematics in the 13th century when it became sufficiently advanced.

Under the Caliph Al-Mansur, the centre of the Muslim Caliphate was transferred from Syria to Persia. The plans of the new capital, Baghdad, were drawn under the direction of the celebrated Minister, Khalid ibn Barmak for making measurements preliminary to the building of Baghdad. A Persian astronomer and engineer, Naubakht, and an astronomer named Masha Allah were appointed for this purpose. To Masha Allah is ascribed a book dealing with the prices of the wares, which is extant in Arabic. It is the first work of its kind in Arabic literature. A book on astrological judgements, *Kitab-al-Ahkam,* was written by Naubkht.

The Caliph gathered around him a number of learned men at his court. His court mathematician, Muhammad Ibn Ibrahim-al-Fazari and Yaqub Ibn Tariq were the first to introduce Hindu mathematics to Arabs through an Indian astronomical and mathematical work, *Siddhanta.*

Al-Hajjaj Ibn Yusuf who flourished sometimes between 786 and 833 probably in Baghdad, was the first to translate *Euclid's Elements* into Arabic. This work was twice translated, first under the Caliph Harun-al-Rashid and again under his son Al-Mamun. The second Arabic version was translated into Latin."

Abu Said Al-Darir-al-Jurfani (d. 845), who was a Muslim astronomer and mathematician, wrote a treatise on geometrical problems.

The Muslim mathematician, astronomer and geographer, Abu Abd Allah Muhammad Ibn Musa-al-Khwarizmi (d. 850) gathered Greek and Hindu knowledge, and through his arithmetic (later translated into Latin), the Muslims and the Europeans were introduced to the Hindi system of numerals. His influence on mathematical thought has been more than that of any other medieval writer. He wrote an encyclopaedic work dealing with arithmetic, geometry, music and astronomy. In one of his books he discusses the question of the origin of numerals.

In his book on Algebra, Al-Khwarizmi first of all deals with the problems of the second degree equations. After that he describes multiplication and division, he also discusses the measurement of surfaces. A section of the book deals with the problems of inheritance. The equations of the first degree are illustrated by numerical examples. The author distinguishes the following six cases of the equations of the second degree. Squares equal to roots, $ax^2 = bx$; squares equal to numbers, $ax^2=c$; roots equal to numbers $ax = c$; squares & roots equal to numbers, $ax^2 + bx = c$; squares and numbers equal to roots $ax^2 + c = bx$; roots and numbers equal to squares, $bx + c = ax^2$. The author gives an analytical solution of linear and quadratic equations. From his way of treatment of the equations the idea of positive and negative signs seems just to emerge. The author also gives a geometrical solution, illustrated with figures, of quadratic equations as $x^2 + 10x = 30$. Such equations have been repeated by the later writers.

In his book, Leonardo of Pisa, enumerates the six cases of quadratic equations just as Al-Khwarizmi does. He comments that the Arab method is superior to the method of Pythagorus.

The three brothers, Ahmad, Muhammad and Hasan, called Banu Musa (the sons of Musa), who flourished during the reign of Al-Mamun, wrote many mathematical, mechanical and astronomical works. Ahmad was especially interested in mechanics and Hasan in geometry.

The third brother, Aba Jafar Muhammad, who was also a logician and a student of Euclid and Almagest, was probably the most prominent. Among their works the most important ones are their treatises on the balance (*Frastun* or *Qarastun)*, on the measurement of the sphere and on the trisection of the angle and the determination of two mean proportions between two given quantities (later translated into Latin) Banu Musa described the kinematical trisection of the angle and the so-called gardener's construction of the ellipse (by means of a string attached to the foci).

The encyclopaedic scientist and the philosopher of the Arabs, Abu Yusuf Yaqub Ibn Ishaq, popularly known as Al-Kindi

(Latinized as Al-Kindus) because he belonged to the Kindah tribe, wrote 270 works, some of which deal with mathematics. He wrote four books on the use of Hindi numerals. The writings of Al-Khwarizmi and Al-Kindi were the main channels through which the numeral system became known to the West.

The Specialists : In the second half of the ninth century A.C, the number of Muslim mathematicians increased considerably. Some of them specialised in arithmetic, some in geometry and the others, who were astronomers as well, showed particular interest in trigonometry. During this period the use of the numerals became common. It was due to the fact that at that time the trade of the Muslims was flourishing in every part of the world. This active trade accelerated the diffusion of numerals throughout the world. The earliest Muslim documents bearing the numerals date from 874 and 888 A.C.

A great mathematician and astronomer of this century was Abu Abd Allah Muhammad Ibn Isa-al-Mahani, that is from Mahan, Kirman, Persia (d. 844 A.C). He wrote commentaries on Euclid and Archimedes, and improved the translation made by Ishaq Ibn Hunain of Menelaos's Spherics. He tried in vain to solve an Archimedian problem which was to divide a sphere into two segments being in a given ratio.

It led to a cubic equation, $x^3 + C^2b = cx^2$, which was called Al-Mahani's equation. This problem became a classical Muslim problem.

Hilal-al-Himsi translated the first four books of Apollonios into Arabic for Ahmad, one of the three sons of Musa. Ahmad Ibn Yusuf who was a secretary of the Tulunis, the rulers of Egypt from 868 to 905, wrote a book as an ode, a commentary on Ptolemy's Centiloquium, and a book on proportions. The latter is of special importance because it influenced the medieval thought and through it Western mathematicians became aware of the theorem of Menelaos (about the triangle cut by a transversal).

Al-Fadl Ibn Hatim-al-Nairizi (Latin Anaritius) who flourished under Al-Mutadid (d. 922) wrote commentaries on Ptolemy and Euclid, which were translated into Latin. He used the tangent as a genuine trigonometric element.

Thabit Ibn Qurrah (d. 901) improved the theory of amicable numbers (if-$p = 3.2^n - 1$: $q = 3.2^{n-1} - 1$; $r = 9.2^{2n-1} - 1$; and if p, q and r are prime together, $2^n pq$ and $2^n r$ are amicable numbers). His mensuration of parabolas and paraboloids are very remarkable.

Al-Battani (d.´ 929) devoted the third chapter of his astronomical work to trigonometry. He uses sines considering them to be superior to the Greek chords. He completed the introduction of the functions *umbra extensa* and *umbra versa* (whence our cotangents and tangents which are among the fundamental elements of trigonometry), and gave a table of cotangents by degrees. He gave the relation between the sides and angles of a spherical triangle which is expressed by the formula, $\cos a = \cos b \cos c + \sin b \sin c \cos a$.

In the 10th century A.C, all the creative work on mathematics was done exclusively by Muslims and all the writings were produced in Arabic. By the end of this century the number of mathematicians increased immensely. Abu Kamil, who was one of the distinguished mathematicians of this period, perfected Al-Khwarizmi's work on algebra. He determined and constructed both roots of quadratic equations. He made a special study of pentagon and decagon with algebraic treatment, and of the addition and subtraction of radicals, corresponding to the formula $\sqrt{a} \pm \sqrt{b} = \sqrt{a + b \pm \sqrt{2ab}}$. He mentioned the multiplication and division of algebraic quantities as well. He resolved systems of equations of up to five unknowns. His work was studied and greatly utilised by Al-Karkhi and Leonardo of Pisa.

The Muslim physician and mathematician Abu Uthman Said Ibn Yaqub-al-Dimashqi who flourished at Baghdad under the Caliphate of Muqtadir (295-320/908-932) translated into Arabic the works of Aristotle, Euclid and Galen on temperament and pulse, etc. The most important translation made by him was that of Book X of *Euclid*, together with Papus' commentary on it. He was the superintendent of the hospitals of Baghdad, Mecca and Medina.

The astronomer and mathematician, Abu Ishaq Ibrahim Ibn Sinan wrote commentaries on the first book of *Conics* and on *Almagest.* Many papers on geometrical and astronomical subjects (for example, on sundials) are ascribed to him. His quadrature of parabolas was much simpler than that of Archimedes. In fact, it was the simplest ever made before the invention of the integral calculus. Ibrahim's father Sinan was also an astronomer and mathematician. Both of them embraced Islam. The Muslim mathematician and astronomer, Ali Ibn Ahmad-al-Imrani (d. 955) wrote a commentary on Abu Kamil's algebra.

Abu Jafar Al-Khazin (d. 961) wrote a commentary on the *Tenth Book of Euclid.* Other mathematical and astronomical writings are also ascribed to him. He solved, by means of conic sections, the cubic equation, called Al-Mahani's equation which Al-Mahani himself could not solve.

Al-Kuhi, who was the author of many mathematical and astronomical works, made investigations on the Archimedian and Apollonian problems leading to the equations of a higher degree than the second. He solved some of these equations and discussed the conditions of solvability. These investigations are among the best ones made on geometry by Muslims.

The mathematician Abu Said Ahmad-al-Sijzi (951-1024) made a special study of the intersection of conic sections and circles. He replaced the old kinematical trisection of an angle by a purely geometric solution (intersection of a circle and an equilateral hyperbola). Al-Saghani (d. 990) also made a study of the trisection of the angle.

Abul Wafa Muhammad-al-Buzjani, who was an astronomer and one of the greatest Muslim mathematicians, flourished in Baghdad where he died in 997 or 998. He was one of the last Arabic translators and commentators of Greek works. He wrote commentaries on Euclid, Diophantos, and Al-Khwarizmi, and a practical arithmetic entitled *Kitab-al-Kamil* (the complete book). A book on applied geometry named *Kitab-al-Handasah* is also ascribed to him. He gave the solution of geometrical problems with one opening of the compass. He described the construction of a square equivalent to other squares, and approximate construction of regular heptagon (taking for its side half the side of the equilateral triangle inscribed in the same circle). He described regular polyhedron, and gave the construction of parabola by points. He gave the geometrical solution of $X^4=a$ and $X^4 + ax^3 = b$.

Abul Wafa's contribution to the development of trigonometry is remarkable. He was the first to show the generality of the sine theorem relative to spherical triangles. He gave a new method of constructing sine tables, the value of sin 30' being correct to the eight decimal places. He knew relations for sin (a+b) and also the relation equivalent to $2 \sin^2 \frac{a}{2} = 1 + \cos a \sin a = 2 \sin \frac{a}{2} \cos \frac{a}{2}$ He introduced the secant and cosecant which are among the six fundamental elements of trigonometry. He made the study of tangent, and compiled a table of tangents. He had the knowledge of those simple relations between the six trigonometric lines, which are now often used to define them.

Abu Mahmud Hamid-al-Khujandi (d. 1000 A.C.) proved imperfectly that the sum of two cubic numbers cannot be a cubic number. He may be considered to be the discoverer of the sine theorem relating to spherical triangles.

Abu Nasr Mansur Ibn Ali, the teacher of Al-Beruni, was one of the three to whom goes the credit of the discovery of this theorem. He gave an improved edition of Menelaos's spherics. He is the author of many trigonometrical and astronomical works.

Maslamah Ibn Ahmad wrote on commercial arithmetic a book entitled *Al-Muamalat.* He spoke of the erotic power of the amicable numbers.

Progress in Mathematics : Let us now discuss the progress made in mathematics in the 11th century. Giving an account of the development of this branch of science in the Latin and Muslim world, George Sarton writes: "A little stream of mathematical thought may be detected in the Latin writings, a stream which will gradually increase, but which will not become truly significant until the 13th century when a sufficient amount of Arabic water will have flowed into it". He further writes: "Let us pass on to Islam. It is almost like passing from the shade to the open sun and from a sleepy world into one tremendously active". In the East the work on mathematics was done in Egypt, and in the West in Spain, Morocco, Tunis and other places.

Ibn Yunus (d. 1009) introduced the first of those formulae which were indispensable before the invention of logarithms, namely, the equivalent of $\cos \pm \cos {}^{2} = \frac{1}{2} [\cos (\pm - {}^{2}) + \cos (\pm + {}^{2})]$. He gave the approximate value of $\sin 1° = \frac{1}{3} \cdot \frac{8}{9} \sin (\frac{9}{8})° + \frac{2}{3} \cdot \frac{16}{15} \sin (\frac{15}{16})°$.

The Persian mathematician Kushyar Ibn Labban made valuable contribution to the development of trigonometry. He continued the investigations which Abu Jafar started on the tangent and compiled a table of tangents.

Abu Jafar Muhammad Ibn-al-Hussain wrote a memoir (translated into French) on rational right angled triangles, and another on the determination of two mean proportionals between two lines by a geometrical method vs. kinematic method, that is by the use of what the Muslims called *Al-*

Handsah-al-thabit, "fixed geometry". He gave the solution of the equation $X^2+a=Y^2$.

Abu Bakr Muhammad Ibn-al-Hasan (or Hussain) Al-Hasib-al-Karkhi flourished in Baghdad during the Ministership of Abu Ghalib Muhammad Ibn Khalaf Fakhr-al-Mulk (d. 1016). He was one of the greatest Muslim mathematicians. He wrote a book on arithmetic entitled *Al-Kafifil-Hisab* (the sufficient on calculation). This book is largely based on Greek knowledge. Instead of using the numerals, the author wrote the name of numbers in full. He wrote a book on algebra entitled *Al-Fakhri* which he dedicated to the Minister. He gave with proofs the complete solution of quadratic equations and mentioned the reduction of equations of the type $ax^{2p} + bx^p = c$ to quadratic equations. He also described the addition and subtraction of radicals, $\sqrt{8}+\sqrt{18}=\sqrt{50}; {}^3\sqrt{54} - {}^2\sqrt{2} = {}^3\sqrt{16}$ and summation of series:

$$\sum_1^{11} i^2 = (\sum_1^{11} i)(2n+1)/3$$ (with geometrical

$$\sum_1^{11} i^2 = (\sum_1^{11} i)^2$$

proof) / He gave the solution of Diophantine equations including twenty five problems which are not found in Diophantos.

The Persian mathematician Abul Hasan Ali-al-Nasawi, who flourished under the Buwayhid Sultan, Majd-al-Dawlah (d. 1029) and under his successor, wrote a practical arithmetic in Persian, and translated it into Arabic. In his arithmetic called *Al-Mughnifil Hisab-al-Hindi*, he explains the division of fractions and the extraction of square and cubic roots. His replacement of sexagesimal by decimal fractions is remarkable, e.g. $\sqrt{17°} = 1/100\ \sqrt{170.000°} = (1/100)\ 412° = 4°\ 7'\ 12''$.

Ibn-al-Haitham conducted research in catoptrics which contains Alhazen's problem, it is as follows:

> "Draw lines from two points in the plane of the circle which meet the circumference at a point and make equal angles with the normal at that point".

This problem leads to the equation of the fourth degree. Ibn-al-Haitham solved it by the help of a hyperbola intersecting a circle. He also solved Al-Mahani's (cubic) equation in the same way.

The encyclopaedist Abu Raihan Muhammad ibn Ahmad-al-Beruni (d. 1045) who was a mathematician, astronomer, philosopher, geographer and traveller, made a good contribution to mathematics. He was one of the greatest scientists of all times. He spent a considerable time in India. He translated a number of works from Sanskrit into Arabic, and also transmitted Muslim knowledge to the people of India. Many works on various scientific subjects are ascribed to him. He gave a very clear account of Arabic numerals and a method for the trisection of the angle. He solved many problems (later called Alberunic problems) which cannot be solved with ruler and compass alone.

Now we come to the mathematical work of Umar Ibn Ibrahim-al-Khayyam who was one of the greatest Muslim mathematicians and astronomers of the Middle Ages. His algebra marks a considerable advance on the work of the Greeks and on that of Al-Khwarizmi and other Muslim algebraists, and indicates an advanced stage of the development of this science.

While Al-Khwarizmi deals only with quadratics, Umar-al-Khayyam mostly discusses the cubic equations. He makes a remarkable classification of the equations, which are based on the complexity of the equation, i.e. on the number of different terms which they contain. Since the beginning of the 17th century the modern classification has been made on the basis of the degree of the equation. But it may be noted that the higher the degree of an equation, the more different terms it can have. The author classified the cubic equations into 27 classes which are subdivided into four categories. He tried to solve them and discussed the limits of the solution. He gave a partial geometrical solution of a number of them. He also investigated Euclid's postulates and generalities. The algebra of Umar-al-Khayyam was edited and translated into French by F. Woepeke in Paris in 1857.

A great astronomer Al-Zarqani (Latin Arzachel) explained the construction of the trigonometrical tables. Jabir ibn Aflah, in his book on astronomy named *Kitab-al-Haiah* or *Islah-al-Majisti* wrote an important introduction on trigonometry. He gave the equivalent of the formula:

$\cos B = \cos a . \sin B$ for a spherical triangle rectangular in C.

Ibn-al-Yasmini wrote a short poem on algebra, and Muhammad-al-Hassar, who flourished in the 12th or 13th century, wrote a treatise on arithmetic and algebra, which was translated into Hebrew in 1271.

'Abd-al-Malik-al-Shirazi abbreviated Apollonios' treatise, and Fakhr-al-Din-al-Razi, scholar and philosopher, wrote on Euclid's Postulates.

Muhammad Abd Allah Ibn-al-Hassar composed, with the help of Ibn Yunus a treatise entitled *Risalah-al-Birkar-al-Tamam* (the treatise on the perfect compass). The 'perfect compass' is an instrument by which every conic could be drawn.

The Hispano-Muslim mathematician, Ibn Badr, composed a compendium of algebra, called *Ikhtisar-al-Jabr wal-Muqabalah.* This compendium includes the theory as well as numerical examples. It deals with quadratic equations, surds, multiplication of polynomials, arithmetical theory of proportion, linear Diaphantine equations and similar problems.

The encyclopaedist Karnal-al-Din Ibn Yunus (d. 1242) wrote a treatise on arithmetic, algebra, square numbers, and regular heptagon and similar topics. He solved one of the questions asked by the Emperor Frederick II, which were submitted to him by the Ayyubi-al-Kamil, (the ruler of Egypt from 1218 to 1238 and of Damascus from 1234 to 1235). The question he solved was how to construct a square equivalent to a circular segment. The proof of the solution was given by one of his pupils, Al-Mufaddal Ibn Umar-al-Abhari, who wrote an essay on it.

The Moroccan astronomer, mathematician and geographer Al-Hasan-al-Marakashi, who flourished until c. 1262, wrote various works on astronomy. His main work named *Jami'-al-Mabadi wal-Ghayat* (The uniter of the beginnings and the ends; i.e., principles and results) is a good compilation of practical knowledge on astronomical instruments and methods, trigonometry and gnomonics. In this work he mentions not only the sine and versed sine (*sahm arrow*), but also what he called complementary sine *(Jaib tamani)* sin (90° – a) = cos a and exceeding sin *(Jaibfadl)*, sin (a – 90°) = – cos a. He compiled a table of sines for each half degree and the tables of versed sines and arc sines.

Another Moroccan mathematician and astronomer of the 13th century, Abul-Abbas Ahmad Ibn Muhammad was a very popular Muslim writer. He is the author of about 74 works, most of which are on mathematics and astronomy. The most popular of his works is the book *Al-Talkhis 'an-al-Hisab.* This book was studied for at least two centuries, and many commentaries were written on it. It was highly admired by Ibn Khaldun. A french translation of it appeared in 1864. It is an arithmetical summary which contains many interesting features; improved treatment of fractions; constant use of Hindi numerals, in their western form of course *(ghubar)*. It also contains the summation of squares and cubes; casting out of nines, eights, and sevens; rule of double false position.

$$\sqrt{(a^2 + r)} = a + \frac{r}{2a}, \text{ if } r \leq a$$

$$\approx a + \frac{r}{2a+1}, \text{ if } r > a$$

Beside *Talkhis,* the author composed four treatises on calculations which deal respectively with integers, fractions, roots and proportions. He also wrote a treatise on binomials and apitomes i.e., quantities of the form a ± √b or √a ± √b; on inheritance problems, and on geometry. He wrote an introduction to Euclid and a treatise on the measurement of surfaces. A book on algebra is also ascribed to him.

Now we come to the mathematical work of Nasir-al-Din Al-Tusi who was a Persian philosopher, mathematician, astronomer, physician and scientist. He wrote in Arabic and Persian. He was one of the greatest Muslim mathematicians and scientists. He was born in 1201 in Tus, Khurasan. After the end of the Abbasi Caliphate in 1258, he became minister to Hulagu. Sixty-four writings on many subjects are ascribed to him. He wrote a number of treatises or commentaries on geometry and a treatise on algebra. Some arithmetical works are also ascribed to him. He wrote on inheritance problems and a treatise on the proof that the sum of two odd squares cannot be a square. He proved that if a circle internally touches another circle of double diameter and if the two circles turn or roll uniformly in opposite direction, remaining tangents and the speed of the smaller being twice greater than that of the other, then the original point of contact of the smaller circle will move along a diameter of the greater circle.

Nasir-al-Din is well-known mostly for his high achievements in trigonometry. He made a translation of Menelaos's spherics, and himself wrote on the subject a separate treatise called *Shakl-al-qatta'* which means the figure of sector. This phrase refers to Menelaos' theorem about the triangle cut by a transversal; the Latin words *cata* or *catta* in the Latin phrases *figura cata* or *regula catta* for *Shakl-al-Qatta"* is the corruption of the Arabic word *Al-Qatta'*. Out of the five books of the *Shakl-al-Qatta'* the books 3 and 4 are devoted to plane and spherical trigonometry respectively. It was the first book wherein trigonometry was treated as a separate branch of science and independently from astronomy. It was the greatest work of its kind in the Middle Ages. It contains the first explicit formulation of the sine law relative to plane triangles with two proofs of it. It also contains the six fundamental formulae for the solution of spherical right angled triangles. It also gives the method for the solution of other triangles replacing, if necessary, the consideration of angles by that of sides and *vice versa* by means of polar triangles.

After the *Shakl-al-qatta"* of Nasir-al-Din, a book bearing the same title was written by Muhiyy-al-Din-al-Maghribi who was a Hispano-Muslim mathematician and astronomer. The latter is partly based on the former, yet it contains important original developments, for example, it gives two proofs of the sine theorem for right angled spherical triangles. One of the proofs is different from those given by Nasir-al-Din. This theorem is then generalized for other triangles. The author has also produced editions of Greek classics as *Euclid's Elements, Apollonios's conics,* with a brief preface, the *Odosios and Menelaos' Spherics* and other works.

Physics

The Muslim scientists studied deeply the fundamental questions of physics. For instance, Ibn Sina made a profound study of such phenomena as force, motion, light, heat, vacuum, etc. A great progress was made in theoretical and applied mechanics. Useful work was done in the field of mechanics on the wheel, axle, lever, pulley, inclined plane, windmill, water-wheel, toothed wheel, etc. The physicist and astronomer Al-Khazini wrote a book on mechanics, hydrostatics and physics, named *Kitab Mizan-al-Hikmah* (Book of the balance of wisdom) which is the most remarkable medieval work on these subjects. It gives a theory of the force of the attraction of the earth (gravity), according to which the universal force is directed towards the centre of the universe, which was supposed at that time to be the centre of the earth. It includes the tables of specific gravity of many liquids and solids (based on the work of Al-Beruni), and a history of the subject; the gravity of air; observations on capillarity; the use of areometer for the measurement of densities and the appreciation of the temperature of liquids; the theory of lever; the application of balance to levelling and to the measurement of time. The analysis and extracts of this book have been published in Arabic and English.

In another book on balance Al-Khazini stresses the need to remove, as far as possible, the influences of temperature variation during weighing. When Al-Khazini's other studies are considered, he seems to be a precursor of Galileo.

Al-Khazini's full name was Abul-Fath Abd-al-Rahman-al-Mansur-al-Khazini (or Al-Khazin). He flourished about 1115-1121. He was a Greek *(Rumi)* slave. His master Ali-al-Khazin-al-Marwazi arranged for his good scientific and philosophical education in Marw. Al-Khazin compiled the astronomical tables called *Al-Zij-al-Mutabar-al-Sinjari (The* esteemed Sinjaric Tables) which were named after Sinjar Ibn Malikshah Ibn Alp Arsalan, governor and later Sultan of Khurasan (1097-98 to 1157-58). They give the position of the stars for the year 1115-1116.

Before Al-Khazini, Umar-al-Khayyam did the greatest work on the balance. Ibn Sina and Al-Razi contributed to the theory of the balance. Banu Musa (the sons of Musa), who flourished during the reign of the Caliph Al-Mamun, wrote many mechanical works. An important work on the balance called *Farastun* or *'Qarastun* is ascribed to them. Al-Razi (d. 923-24) made investigations on specific gravity by using the hydrostatic balance. This balance was called *Al-Mizan-al-Tabii* (the physical balance).

Muhammad Ibn Ali Ibn Rustam-al-Khurasani was a famous constructor of clocks and, therefore, he was called Al-Saati (the clock maker). Between 1146 and 1169, he constructed a clock placed in the *Bab-e-Jairun* (often called *'Bab-al-Saah,* the door of the clock). Al-Saati remained incharge of his clock until his death in 1184-85.

Another Muslim mechanician of the 13th century was Abul-Isa Ismail Ibn Razzaz (the son of rice-merchant) Badial-Zaman-al-Jazari. He was patronized from 577-578 to 601-602 A.H., 1181-1182 to 1205-1206 A.C, by the Urtuqid rulers of Diyar Bakr, a district of Al-Jazirah. He wrote a treatise on the knowledge of the geometrical mechanical contrivances entitled *Kitab fi Marifat-al-Hiyal-al-Handsiyyah,* which was dedicated to the Urtuqid Nasir-al-Din Mahmud (ruled from 1200 to 1222). It deals mainly with hydraulic apparatus (elepsydras, fountains, etc.). This important work is interesting from the technical point of view, and represents the best Arabic work on applied mechanics. It is divided into six parts. The first part which deals with the various types of the elepsydras indicating either equal or temporal hours is the most important. Muslims divided the day into twenty-four equal hours. But they adopted another type of division. They divided the day and night each into twelve hours of varying length according to the season. Such type of hours were also used by the Christians in Europe e.g., Italy, until the middle of the 18th century.

The book was translated into German, and commentaries on it were also written.

Al-Saati's son Ridwan repaired and improved the clock, and also wrote a book to describe its construction and use. This book is an important source of the study of early Muslim clocks. Ridwan was a mechanician, physician and poet, and had knowledge of literature and music. He played the flute. Originally he belonged to Khurasan. He was appointed as *Wazir* by the Ayyubi prince Al-Faiz Ibrahim and his brother Al-Muazzam Isa. Ridwan also wrote a supplement to Ibn Sina's treatise on grapes, and a commentary on his *Qanun* (Canon).

Qasar Ibn Abil-Qasim, the Egyptian mathematician, astronomer (d. 1251 A.C.) made a celestial globe. He probably made improvements on the water-wheels or water-mills. Such improved types of water-wheels are still seen on the Orontes, and are among the glories of Hama. He constructed these water-wheels *(naura)* for Al-Muzaffar-al-Taqi-al-Din Mahmud, the ruler of Hama from 1229 to 1244 A.C.

The philosopher Abu Nasr-al-Farabi refuted the existence of a vacuum. He wrote a remarkable essay on the elasticity of the air. It is an original piece of research. The Muslim scientists took interest in the determination of the specific gravity of various substances. Sanad Ibn Ali, a scientist of the ninth century made investigations on specific gravity. Al-Beruni determined the specific gravity of 18 precious stones and metals. Ibn Sina and Al-Razi also made research on this subject.

Ibn Yunus (d. 1009 A.C.) applied the pendulum to the measurement of time. Al-Beruni devised a time-machine based on the Roman calendar. He constructed it for use in the mosque of Ghazna. But the Imam of the mosque rejected it saying that it was based on a non-Muslim work. At this Al-Beruni was very much annoyed. He said that the determination of time is a purely secular matter. It is, therefore, of little value whether it is based on a Muslim calendar or a non-Muslim one. Only convenience should be taken into consideration.

Al-Beruni made reference to a certain kind of wells which are obtained by boring the earth to that level of water which is submitted to the hydrostatic pressure in which case due to the pressure water is driven upward as in the natural springs. He correctly explains the action of such wells by the principle of communicating vessels.

Development of Techniques : The Muslims developed the techniques of bathing. They constructed the hot steam-bath called *Hammam* (from the Arabic root *Hamm* meaning to heat). When the European Crusaders came to the East and experienced the comforts of these baths, they introduced them into their own countries.

The Muslims were the first to apply the directive property of the magnetic needle to the determination of the direction of their journey while travelling on sea. The Chinese were the first to discover this property. The maritime trade between the Muslims gave much importance to the southern end of the needle than the northern one as it is done these days. This was probably because in some places like Syria and Asia Minor the southern end pointed roughly towards Mecca. Thus this end of the needle gave the general direction of the *Qibla*. In the West the compass was first of all used by the Italian sailors. Some Muslims have referred to the compass in their writings. For instance. Bailak-al-Qabajaqi in his book entitled *Kanz-al-Ahjar* described the use of a floating compass witnessed by him in 1242-43.

The Muslims were also the first to invent guns and cannons and use explosive material in them. The purpose of this invention was to throw bullets at the enemy from a long distance. The Chinese used sodium nitrate only. But the penetrating power of explosives was discovered and made use of only by Muslims. The historians generally write that first of all guns were used in the war of Cressi, but from the writings of many Muslims it is revealed that guns had been used a long time ago. In one of these writings there is a story that some ruler named Yaqub besieged in 602 A.H. (1205 A.C.) an African town Mehdra which was under the control of his chief rebel, and attacked the walls with the help of sounding guns and machines. From every machine there came out a number of showers of big stones and fire balls.

The statement given by Ibn Khaldun in his 'History of Berbers' also proves the use of the guns at the time of war. He writes "Abu Yusuf, the Sultan of Morocco besieged in 672 A.H. (1273 A.C.) the city of Sijilmasa. He installed the instruments for besiege in front of the city. These instruments consisted of *Manjneeq, Urawe* and *Handam* with which the bits of iron were thrown. These bits were filled in the box of *Handam,* and the explosives kept behind them were set on fire. Its effect was strange and its results could be called an act of Allah. One day with the help of a stone thrown by *Manjneeq,* part of the wall fell, and from there the attack was made on the city"

Science of Optics : The Muslims developed the science of optics. Ibn-al-Haitham (Latin Alhazen) made a remarkable contribution towards this science. Indeed modern optics began with him. Before Ibn-al-Haitham it was generally thought by the Greek, Roman and Muslim scientists that rays are emitted from the eyes towards the objects seen. Plato suggested that there was another set of rays which emanated from the object seen. Alexandarians believed that the vision lies in the lens of the eye. Ibn Sina and Al-Beruni also believed that the ray went from the object to the eye. Aristotle's ideas were very near to modern conception. The atomists put forward an atomical theory. Hunain Ibn Ishaq in his work entitled "*Questions on the eye*" put forward a theory which was somewhat like that of Plato. In his opinion the lens was the central organ of vision. Both the visual force coming from the brain and the image of the object coming from without were received in the lens. Al-Razi, too, in his monograph on the nature of vision showed that the eyes do not radiate light.

Ibn-al-Haitham changed the traditional view by putting forward the theory that the objects are seen by rays passing from them towards the eye and not by the opposite process. Most of his successors did not agree with his view, but Al-Beruni and Ibn Sina independently and fully agreed with him. Ibn-al-Haitham solved a number of optical problems on the basis of the mathematical knowledge of his day.

Ibn-al-Haitham dealt with such a medley of topics as the structure of the eye, optical illusion, perspective, binocular vision, vision of outlines, shadows and colours, the ancient catoptrics and dioptrics with new developments, *camera obscura,* Alhazen's problem, mirages, comets, the Milky Way, rainbows, halos, etc.

Ibn-al-Haitham conducted research on catoptrics which contains the problem known as Alhazen's problem. It is as follows:

> 'From two points in the plane of a circle to draw lines meeting at a point of the circumference and making equal angles with the normal at that point'. This leads to an equation of the fourth degree. Ibn-al-Haitham solved it by the help of an hyperbola intersecting a circle. He also solved the so-called Al-Mahani's cubic equation.

Ibn-al-Haitham showed a marked progress in experimental techniques. He made research on spherical and parabolic mirrors; spherical aberration and dioptrics. He noticed that the ratio between the angles of incidence and reflection does not remain constant. He described the magnifying power of a lens' and studied atmospheric refraction. He stated that the twilight only ceases or begins when the Sun is 19° below the horizon, and tried to measure the height of the atmosphere on that basis. He gave a better description of the eye and vision. He tried to explain binocular vision, and gave a correct explanation of the apparent increase in the size of the sun and the moon near the horizon. He gave the first mathematical treatment of the 'camera obscura'.

Thus, he deals with the problems which now come under at least seven subjects including anatomy, physiology, psychology, mathematics, astronomy, physics and meteorology.

The full name of Ibn-al-Haitham is Abu Ali Muhammad Ibn-al-Hasan Ibn-al-Haitham. He was a native of Basra and was born in 354 A.H. (965 A.C). He migrated to Egypt where he lived till his death. He was a noble person and a genius who had the knowledge of many sciences. He was the greatest mathematician of his age and one of the greatest opticians in history. He was also well-versed in medicine and Arabic language. When the Caliph Al-Hakim bi-Amrillah, who was very fond of philosophy, heard about Ibn-al-Haitham, he had a great desire to see him. Al-Hakim was informed that Ibn-al-Haitham had disclosed that if he had been in Egypt, he might have done something in connection with the river Nile, so that it would become beneficial in every case, whether the level of water was high or low.

According to Ibn-al-Haitham, the river water fell from a high place lying in the territory of Egypt. Hearing this report Al-Hakim became more fond of meeting Ibn-al-Haitham. Al-Hakim sent a great amount of money to him, and persuaded him to come to his court. Ibn-al-Haitham left for Egypt. When he reached near Cairo, Al-Hakim went to receive him. They met in a village near Bab-al-Qahirah (the gate of Cairo). Al-Hakim honoured him, provided him with all the facilities, and asked him to fulfil his promise regarding the river Nile. A group of workers was provided to help him in executing his plan. When Ibn-al-Haitham made the survey of the site and came to a place called 'Janadil' (now called Shalal), which lies near Aswan on an elevated ground, he realised the difficulties involved. Finding himself unable to fulfil his promise, he became very ashamed. Now he feared Al-Hakim and to get rid of him he acted as a mad man and remained in the condition of madness until the death of Al-Hakim. Then he came to his senses and settled in Qubbah near the gate of Jamiah-al-Azhar, and engaged himself in writing books. He died in 1038.

Ibn-al-Haitham is the author of many works. He summarised Aristotle's works, and wrote commentaries on them. He also summarised many medical works of Galen. His writings on mathematics and physics are 15 and on metaphysics and physics are 44 in number. His books include the one on plants and one on the properties of simple and compound drugs.

His *Kitab-al-Manazir* (the optical thesaurus), is one of the leading classics which influenced scientific thought for more than six centuries. The Latin, Muslim and Hebrew writers such as Roger Bacon, John Peckham, Witelo, Ahmad Ibn Idris-al-Qarafi, Qutb-al-Din-al-Shirazi, Levi Ben Gerson based their works on this great book.

Ibn Sina made a deep study of light. He observed that if light is emitted due to the ejection of some sort of particles by the luminous source, the speed of light must be finite. Al-Beruni noticed that the speed of light is immensely greater than that of the sound.

Nasir-al-Din-al-Tusi wrote two books on Optics. One of them, is entitled *'Al-Mabahith fi Inikas-al-Shuaat wa Initafiha'* (Research on the reflection and refraction of rays), contains a proof of the equality of the angles of incidence and reflection.

The other is entitled *'Tahrir Kitab-al-Manazir'*. In the preface, the author remarks that one perceives objects because of the light rays emanating from them, but that everything happens as if the rays emanated from our eyes. Qutb-al-Din-al-Shirazi, (d. 1311) who was one of the greatest scientist of all times presented his views on Optics in his astronomical works. In one of such works, entitled *'Nihayat-al-Idrak fi Dirayat-al-Aflak'* (Highest understanding of the knowledge of the Spheres), he discusses questions of geometrical optics, the nature of vision, and finally the rainbow. He was the first to give a satisfactory account of the rainbow. His explanation of the rainbow is based on his study of the passage of a ray of light through a transparent sphere (drop of water). He discovered that the rainbow is formed when the rays are refracted twice and reflected once (or tunice in the case of the secondary rainbow) in the humid atmosphere.

Another important physicist and mathematician of the 14th century, was Karnal-al-Din Abul-Hasan-al-Farisi. He wrote a book entitled *'Tanqih-al-Manazir'* (Correction of optics) which is an elaborate and original commentary on Ibn-al-Haitham's *Kitab-al-Manazir* (the book of optics). It covers not only physical and physiological optics, but also meteorology, perspective and many other subjects. It includes remarks on aerial perspective, colour effects, etc.

Karnal-al-Din suggested the use of hyperbolical lenses in order to avoid spherical aberration. He gave an account of the refraction of light. According to George Sarton, this account implies the following facts; the speed of light is finite but very great; the speed of light in different media is inversely proportional to the optical density (not the same as the material density). The second of these facts seems to be an adumbration of the wave theory of light as against the corpuscular theory.

Karnal-al-Din performed a number of experiments on *camera obscura* and improved its use initiated by Ibn-al-Haitham. He showed that the images obtained on a screen in a dark room by means of the rays of light passing through a narrow hole, are independent of the shape of the hole, and that the smaller the hole, the sharper the images. It was also proved that the images of many objects are formed separately on the screen, but the images and the directions were reversed. With the help of the camera he observed eclipses and the movements of the clouds and birds.

Al-Hasan-al-Rammah (the lancer) Najm-al-Din-al-Ahadab (the hunchback) wrote on military subjects. He flourished in Syria. He wrote two treatises on horsemanship and the art of war, (1) *Kitab-al-Furusiyah wal Munasab-al-Harbiyah* (Horsemanship and war stratagems), (2) *Nihayat-al-Suul wal Umniya fi Ta 'allum-al-Amal-al-Furusiyah.*

The first treatise deals with the military matters such as the military operation, means of using lances, bows, siege engines, and the method of fighting at sea and the communication of fire etc. It contains various pyrotechnic recipes. Al-Hasan considered saltpeter the fundamental substance of pyrotechnics. He explained the methods of preparing and purifying it by means of potash and of repeated crystallizations.

In the opinion of George Sarton, that is more important than it may seem, for the impurities of saltpeter are hygroscopic, and thus tend to destroy its value. To discover saltpeter and its uses was one thing, to purify it was another.

The Muslims improved the art of shipbuilding, taught Mediterranean seamen to construct lighter sailing-ships or caravels *(garaf),* to caulk their boats with tarstill known in romance languages by the Arabic name of *gatran* (Fr. *goudron,* It. *caltrame)* to handle sails and cables (Ar. *habl).*

Chemistry

Chemistry deals with the composition and properties of substances and the changes of composition they undergo. It has been divided into Inorganic and Organic. The conception of this division in modern Chemistry came from Al-Razi's classification of chemical substances into mineral, vegetable and animal. Inorganic Chemistry, which deals with the preparation and properties of the elements and their compounds, originally arose from the study of minerals and metals, whereas Organic Chemistry, which deals with carbon compounds, developed through the investigation of animal and plant products.

Prior to 1828 it was not possible to synthesize organic substances from their elements and, therefore, it was supposed that there existed a fundamental difference between Organic and Inorganic Chemistry. In 1828, F. Wohler synthetically prepared urea, an organic substance; thereby revealing that there was no fundamental difference between these two branches of Chemistry. Since carbon compounds were numerous, their study was separately made under Organic Chemistry, and the study of elements and non-carbon compounds was included in Inorganic Chemistry.

The earliest discoveries in Inorganic Chemistry were made in metallurgy, *Materia Medica,* painting, enamelling, glazing, glass-making, chemical arts, etc. These arts, and many metals, metallic compounds and alloys were known to the ancients. Similarly, the discoveries in Organic Chemistry were made in the arts of dyeing, tanning, in the manufacture of paper, in the study of oils, fats, both of plant and animal origin, in medicine, etc. Thus, Chemistry had its sources in phototechniques, minerology, metallurgy, *Materia Medica* and decorative arts. It is the product of the art of transmutation of baser metals into gold, and philosophical thoughts of practical or theoretical interest. Finally, it is the result of the study of the properties of the substances.

A Greek philosopher, Empedocles, held the view that all the four elements, air, water, earth and fire, were the primal elements, and that the various substances were made by their intermixing. He regarded them to be distinct and unchangeable. Aristotle considered these elements to be changeable i.e., one kind of matter could be changed into another kind.

Jabir ibn Hayyan (Latinized as Geber), a great Muslim Chemist of the 8th century A.C, modified the Aristotelean doctrine of the four elements, and presented the so-called sulphur-mercury theory of metals .According to this theory, metals differ essentially because of different proportions of sulphur and mercury in them. He also formulated the theory of geologic formation of metals.

Unlike his Greek predecessors, he did not merely speculate, but performed experiments to reach certain conclusions. He recognised and stated the importance of experimentation in Chemistry. He combined the theoretical knowledge of the Greeks and practical knowledge of the craftsmen, and himself made noteworthy advance both in the theory and practice of Chemistry.

Jabir's contribution to Chemistry is very great. He gave a scientific description of two principle operations of Chemistry. One of them is calcination which is employed in the extraction of metals from their ores. The other is reduction which is employed in numerous chemical treatments. He improved upon the methods of evaporation, melting, distillation, sublimation and crystallization. These are the fundamental methods employed for the purification of chemical substances, enabling the chemist to study their properties and uses, and to prepare them. The process of distillation is particularly applied for taking extract of plant material.

In the opinion of Jabir, the cultivation of gold was not the only object of a chemist. The preparation of new chemical substances was also regarded by him as the chief object of Chemistry. We owe to him the first preparation of such substances as arsenic and antimony from their sulphides, and basic lead carbonate. He also did important work in the preparation of steel, and the refinement of metals. Jabir also deals with such applications as the use of manganese dioxide in glass-making, varnishes to water-proof cloth and protect iron, use of iron pyrites for writing in gold and distillation of vinegar to concentrate acetic acid.

Significant Discovery: The most important discovery made by Jabir was the preparation of sulphuric acid. The importance of this discovery can be realised by the fact that in this modern age the extent of the industrial progress of a country is mostly judged by the amount of sulphuric acid consumed in that country. Another important acid prepared by him was nitric acid which he obtained by distilling a mixture of alum (of Yemen) and copper sulphate (of Cyprus). Then by dissolving ammonium chloride into this acid, he prepared *aqua regia* which, unlike acids, could dissolve gold in it.

Jabir classified chemical substances, on the basis of some distinctive features, into bodies (gold, silver, etc.) and souls (mercury, sulphur, etc.) to make the study of their properties easier.

Jabir is the author of a large number of books on Chemistry and a book on astrolabe. About one hundred chemical works ascribed to him are extant. His fame chiefly rests on his chemical books preserved in Arabic.

We find that the author recognised and stated clearly the importance of experimentation more clearly than any other early chemist. He gave remarkably sound views on methods of chemical research. It is impossible to reach definite conclusions regarding the extent of his contributions until all the Arabic writings ascribed to him have been properly edited and studied. But on the basis of our present knowledge, Jabir appears to be one of the greatest scientists whose influence can be traced throughout the whole period of the historical development of the Muslim and European Chemistry. In the light of these facts it would not be improper to call Jabir as the father of Chemistry.

Some of the chemical writings to which Jabir's name is attached were translated into Latin. The first such version, the *Book of the Composition of Alchemy* was made by Robert of Chester in 1144. The *Kitab-al-Sabin* (the book of the seventy) was translated by Gerard of Cremona in the 12th century. The translation of the *Sum of Perfection* was made by Richard Russell. One of his books has been translated into French by Berthelot.

Several technical terms have passed from Jabir's Arabic writings through Latin into the European languages. Among these are realgar (red sulphide of arsenic), tutia (zinc oxide), alkali, antimony, and alembic for distillation vessel. The Arabic equivalents for the last three words are *'alqali, ithmad,* and *Al-anbiq* respectively.

Before Jabir Ibn Hayyan, the Umayyad prince Khalid Ibn Yazid, who was a philosopher, poet and chemist, encouraged Greek philosophers in Egypt to translate Greek scientific works into Arabic. These were among the earliest translations in Arabic from other languages. He was himself deeply interested in medicine, astrology and chemistry. Many chemical works are ascribed to him. One of them is entitled *Firdaus-al-Hikmah fi Ilm-al-Kimiya*. This work was in verse, and contained 2,315 couplets.

An encyclopaedic scientist, and philosopher, Abu Yusuf Yaqub-al-Kindi considered the art of transformation of one metal into the other as an imposture. A few of his numerous works dealing with many sciences are extant. One of his works is on pharmacy, a branch of applied chemistry.

Chemistry was usually mixed up with minerology and geology. The oldest Muslim lapidary which may serve as an important source of chemistry was written by Utarid Ibn Muhammad-al-Hasib who flourished in the ninth century. It deals with the properties of precious stones.

In the same century, Jabir's work was further advanced by Al-Razi who wrote many chemical treatises, and described a number of chemical instruments. One of his treatises consists of 25 pieces of chemical apparatus. He made investigations on specific gravity. One of his important works is on the art of transformation of baser metals into the noble ones. He applied his chemical knowledge for medical purposes, thus laying the foundation of Iatrochemistry.

Other important chemists of this century were Dhul-Nun and Al-Jahiz. The former mostly dealt with the art of transmutation of metals. The latter prepared ammonia from animal offals by dry distillation.

In the tenth century, Ibn Wahshiyah wrote on chemistry. His work may help to understand chemical symbolism. Maslamah Ibn Ahmad, an astronomer, mathematician and oculist of this century wrote two chemical works entitled, *Rutbat-al-Hakim* and *Ghayat-al-Hakim*. The second is well known in the Latin translation made in 1252 by the order of King Alfonso under the title *Picatrix*.

A Persian pharmacologist Abu Mansur Muwaffaq Ibn Ali-al-Harawi who flourished in Herat in the tenth century, was apparently the first to think of compiling a treatise on *Materia Medica* in Persian. He travelled extensively in Persia and India to obtain necessary information. He wrote, between 968 and

977, a book entitled *Kitab-al-Abniyahan Haqaiq-al-Adwiyah.* It contains Greek, Syriac, Arabian, Persian, and Indian knowledge. It deals with 585 remedies (of which 466 are derived from plants, 75 from minerals, and 44 from animals). He classified them into four groups according to their action, and gave the outline of a general pharmacological theory.

Abu Mansur distinguished between sodium carbonate (natrum) and potassium carbonate *(qali).* He had some knowledge of arsenious oxide, cupric oxide, silicic acid, antimony and so on. He knew the toxicological effects of copper and lead compounds, the depilatory virtue of quicklime, the composition of plaster of Paris and its surgical use.

Greatest Surgeon : The greatest Muslim surgeon, Khalaf Ibn Abbas-al-Zohrawi (d. 1013) wrote a great medical encyclopaedia, *Al-Tasrif* in 30 sections, which contains interesting methods of preparing drugs by sublimation and distillation, but its most important part is the surgical one.

Abu Rayhan Muhammad-al-Beruni (973-1048) took a great interest in the determination of the specific gravity of eighteen precious stones and metals. A voluminous unedited lapidary by Al-Beruni is extant in unique manuscript in the Escorial Library. It contains a description of a great number of stones and metals from the natural, commercial, and medical point of view. Moreover, he composed a pharmacology *(saydalah).* Important information could certainly be obtained from his unedited works, on the origin of Indian and Chinese stones and drugs, which appeared in early Arabic scientific works.

Ibn Sina wrote a treatise on minerals, which was very important and one of the main sources of geological knowledge, also a source of chemistry in Western Europe until the Renaissance.

As we mentioned before, minerology stood in close relation to chemistry. Nearly fifty Arabic lapidaries have been named. The best known of them is the 'flowers of Knowledge of Stones', by Shihab-al-Din-al-Tifashi (died in Cairo in 1154). It gives in 25 chapters extensive information on the subject of the same number of precious stones, their origin, geography, examination, purity, price, application for medicinal and magical purposes, and so on. Except for Pliny and the superior Aristotelean lapidary, he quotes only Arabic authors.

The output of the books on Chemistry was very great after the eleventh century. Thus, there are known books of about forty Arabic and Persian chemists. Ibn Khaldun, (d. 1406) the talented Arabian philosopher of history and the greatest intellect of his century, was a violent opponent of the idea of transmutation of metals by chemical means.

Some chemists thought that one metal can be transformed into another by artificial methods. For such transformation they followed different procedures depending on the character and form of the chemical treatment and the substance chosen for this purpose; the substance being called the 'Noble Stone' or 'Philosopher's Stone'. This may be excrements, or blood, or hair, or eggs, or anything else. After the substance has been specified, it is treated along certain lines mentioned in their books. The result is an earthen or fluid substance which is called *Elixir*. These chemists think that if *Elixir* is added to silver which has been heated in a fire, the silver turns into gold. If added to copper which had been heated in a fire, the copper turns into silver.

The question arises whether the metals are of specific differences, each constituting a distinct species, or whether they differ in certain properties and qualities and constitute different kinds of one and the same species?

Abu Nasr-al-Farabi and his followers held the opinion that the difference in metals is caused by certain conditions such as humidity and dryness, softness and hardness, and colours such as yellow, white and black. According to him the metals are different kinds of one and the same species.

On the other hand, Ibn Sina and his followers believed that metals have specific differences and belong to different species, each of which has its own differential and genus, like all other species.

According to Abu Nasr-al-Farabi, it is possible to transform one metal into another, because it is possible to change their conditions.

"Ibn Sina thought that such transformation was impossible. His assumption is based on the fact that specific differences in metals cannot be changed by artificial means. He believed that since the metals are created by the Creator and Determiner of things, God Almighty, and the mystery of their real character was utterly unknown and could not be perceived, any attempt for transformation would be meaningless".

Art of Transformation : Muslims' art of transformation of metals was based upon Hellenistic and Iranian traditions, but apparently the main principles and the main operations were already established long before the 12th century. Before this century the Muslims had not only made many experiments, and produced several works on this art, but they had begun to doubt and criticise the most advanced theories concerning it. This proves that the standard of their chemical thinking was advanced.

The 12th and 13th centuries added very little to their knowledge about the transformation of metals, but their research continued in various fields. The main chemical writer of this age was Abul-Qasim Muhammad-al-Iraqi who flourished in the second half of the 13th century. He was an experimenter and a theorist. His works represent the full development of the Arabic doctrine.

The 14th century was an enlightened period when a group of intelligent writers began to reject the idea of transformation of metals by chemical means. One of such persons was a historian, Rashid-al-Din who described such chemical practice in Mongol Persia and expressed his distrust of such chemists. The large encyclopaedic work Nukhbat-al-Dahr of-al-Dimashqi contains, in part second, much information on metals, their properties, and influences. As usual in Arabic treatises, chemistry is mixed up with minerology and geology. Even in their purely chemical researches on transformation of metals, the Muslim chemists achieved by no means unimportant results. In their efforts to discover *Elixir* they often discovered new chemical processes, and hit upon the catalytic properties of various substances. The pains, which they took in the search of gold, ultimately resulted in their great contribution to the development of modern chemistry.

The last important chemist of the 14th century was Izz-al-Din Ali Ibn-al-Jildaki. Some twenty treatises are ascribed to him. The list shows-al-Jildaki's great activity as a chemical writer. A complete study of his vast writings is necessary to know what he actually tried to establish. To some extent, this study was made by Ruska, Stapleton, Holmyard, and their disciples.

One of Al-Jildaki's important books entitled *Nihayat-al-Talab fi Shark-al-Muktasab* contains many quotations from the earlier works, and some novelties, as the use of nitric acid to extract silver out of the gold-silver alloy. Al-Jildaki remarked that the substances do not react except by definite weights. This is one of the four fundamental laws of modern chemistry.

The Muslim chemists applied their chemical knowledge to a large number of industrial arts. Only three such arts are mentioned here, which will enable the readers to estimate the extent of their knowledge of Applied Chemistry.

Paper : Paper was invented by the Chinese who prepared it from the cocoon of the silk-worm. Some specimens of Chinese paper extant date back to the second century A.C. The first manufacture of the paper outside China occurred in Samarqand (757). When Samarqand was captured by Muslims the manufacture of paper spread over the whole Muslim world including the Maghrib. (Tunis, Morocco, Algiers).

By the end of the 12th century there were four hundred paper mills in Fas alone. In Spain, the main centre of manufacture of paper was Shatiba which remained a Muslim city until 1239. Cordova was the centre of the business of paper in Spain.

The Muslims developed this art. They prepared paper not only from silk, but also from cotton, rags and wood. In the middle of the 10th century the paper-industry was introduced in Spain. In Khurasan, paper was made of linen.

There is an early treatise dealing with paper-making, the *Umdat-al-Kuttab wa Uddatu dhawil-Albab* which is ascribed to the Amir-al-Muizz Ibn Badis, a ruler of the Zayri dynasty (1015-61) in Tunis. The 11th chapter of this treatise, dealing with paper, has been edited, translated and elaborately discussed by the foremost student of Arabic paper, Josef Karabacek. This work explains how to prepare the pulp, make the sheets, wash and clean them, colour, polish and paste them, and give them an antique appearance. No text comparable to this in any other language of so early a date is known.

The preparation of pulp involves a large number of complicated chemical processes, which shows the advancement of the chemical knowledge of the Muslims at that time.

The manufacture of writing-paper in Spain is one of the most beneficial contributions of Muslims to Europe. Without paper the scale on which popular education in Europe developed would have not been possible. The preparation of paper from silk would have been impossible in Europe due to the lack of silk production there. The Muslim method of producing paper from cotton could only be useful for the Europeans. After Spain the art of paper-making was established in Italy (1268-76). France owed its first paper mills to Muslim Spain. From these countries the industry spread throughout Europe.

Another type of paper, marbled paper, which was common upon end-papers, paper covers and edges of books, was prepared in the East, and exported to the West. About the preparation of marbled paper Roger Bacon tells us: "The Turks have a pretty art of chamoletting of paper, which is not with us in use. They take diverse colours, and put them severally (in drops) upon water; and stirr the water lightly and then wet their paper (being of some thickness) with it, and the paper will be waved, and veined, like Chamolet or Marble".

Books bound in the West towards the end of the 16th century are found with end-papers brought from the East, but it was not until about a century later that European binders began to make them themselves. Hand-made marbled papers are now rarely used, but more or less clumsily reproduced imitations still serve various purposes.

There is an Arabic word *'rizma'* meaning a bundle of merchandise, which had been adopted in almost every Western language with slight variations to mean a bundle of paper (English: ream). This also testifies to the Arabic origin of that business in the West.

Tiles : The industry of tile-making which involves a large number of complex technical and chemical processes, was highly developed by Muslims. The earliest treatise, a Persian text, dealing with the manufacture of faience, was unique of its kind in world literature until the 16th century. It has been written by Abd Allah Ibn Ali Kashani in the 13th century. This book entitled *Jawahir-al-Arais Wa Ajaib-al-Nafais* was written on precious stones and perfumes. It explains the manufacture of Faience, the ingredients (as clay, borax, feldspar, cobalt, lapis lazuli, lead, manganese, tin etc.), their mixtures the kiln processes and implements, the methods of glazing and decorating. This treatise is similar to the various other treatises on precious stones written in Arabic and Persian. The final chapter deals with the art of enamelled pottery. This account is specially valuable because it is based on actual and traditional practice.

The maker of the beautiful lustre 'mihrab' (arch) of the tomb of Imam Yahya (now in the Hermitage, Leningrad), dated 1305 A.C, Yusuf Ibn Ali Ibn Muhammad, was possibly a brother of the author.

Ceramics : The early history of Muslim ceramics has not so far been written. Many interesting specimens have been discovered in recent years which throw much light on the development of this industry in the Muslim world. The centres of this industry were situated in Persia, Mesopotamia, Syria, Egypt and Valencia from where various types spread rapidly throughout the Islamic Caliphate.

Under Muslim influence the potters in these Centers revived old technical processes, developed new ones and began to experiment with decorative and ornamental schemes. The Muslim potters readily absorbed progressive ideas but at the same time maintained great originality. Two types of pottery were in common use; enamelled and lustered. In enamelled pottery (the glazed earthenware) the Muslims, from an early period, were expert masters. In lustered pottery also they made great progress. "In this the design is painted in a metallic salt on a glazed surface and fixed by firing in smoke in a way that gives it a metallic gleam, which varies in different specimens from a bright copper-red to a greenish-yellow tint, and in some cases throws off brilliant iridescent reflections.

In the last chapter of the Persian text *Kitab-ai-Jawahir-al-Arais wa Ajaib-al-Nafais,* the author describes the techniques of glazing with two fires (lustres), leaf building, overglaze decoration fired in a muffle kiln (i.e., separated from the flame, the source of heat being outside), *haft rang,* a Persian term referring to the seven colours of the planets. There may be a reference to the polychrome overglaze technique, the so-called *minai* ware. (Another Persian term; *mind-wash* means lustre; *mind* coloured). The author indicates differences between the art as practised in Kashan, Baghdad and Tabriz. In Baghdad and Tabriz other kinds of firewood and potash were used.

In the 15th century, the Muslim ceramic art was followed by Italian potters, who obtained much of the mature technical knowledge from Muslim sources. This technical knowledge proved to be helpful in the revival of ceramic art during the Renaissance.

Geography

The Muslims had to travel to distant lands across plains and cities, deserts and mountains, rivers and seas in connection with trade, *jihad* and the administration of their vast empire and other purposes. Within one hundred years after the advent of Islam, their empire stretched from Arabia to India in the East, Morocco and Spain in the West and the River Oxus in the North. In the 10th century, the Muslim empire comprised the following territories: Arabia, Egypt with the entire Northern coast of Africa, (including the Atlantic coast as far as Anti-Atlas), nearly the whole of Spain, the islands of Sicily, Greece, some Italian towns, Syria, Armenia, the South-East of the Caucasus, Mesopotamia including Iraq, the whole of modern Persia, Afghanistan, Transoxania including the delta region of Khawarizm, the valley and the mountains of Farghana and the territories of the lower course of the Indus with Sind. Travels in these vast lands and their administration necessitated the accumulation of information on them.

The science of geography is somewhat allied to astronomy. Therefore, the study of geography was also motivated by the same incentive with which the study of astronomy was made. That incentive was the need for the determination of the direction of the Kaaba for the orientation of the mosque and for turning faces towards it at the time of the prayer. This determination depended on the knowledge of the latitudes and longitudes of the places where the Muslims lived.

A great factor in the promotion of the geographical study was the *Hajj*, (the pilgrimage to Mecca). Before leaving for *Hajj*, the *Hajjaj* (pilgrims) generally collected information on the territories which lay on the way to Mecca. To provide such information many itineraries were compiled, in which stations and the stages of the roads leading from different countries to Mecca were shown. In the early days of Islam, information on various lands and the peoples was supplied chiefly by the traders and travellers. Muslim traders were very active in those days. They reached as far as China, Russia, Zanjibar and the southern tip of Africa.

At the time of the *Hajj,* the Muslims of different countries have a chance of meeting one another, discussing their mutual needs and problems, and getting knowledge of one another's territories. Thus, the *Hajj* is an important factor in disseminating knowledge of the world among Muslims, promoting Muslim unity and strengthening the ties of commerce and trade among them.

The Muslims used to travel to far off lands in order to seek scholars and books for acquiring knowledge. They also developed a taste for travel in order to gain the knowledge of the world through direct experience. With their keen sense of observation and passionate curiosity they made a study of the religious, social, political, historical, geographical, economic and agricultural conditions of the lands they passed through, and recorded their observations in their travelogues, in which they also supplied information on the scholars of their time.

A large number of books on geography were produced by Muslim geographers and travellers, which were widely studied. The translation of these books was made into many European languages, and for centuries the Europeans acquired the knowledge of the world through these books. Until modern times they depended for their knowledge of Africa on the work of the Moroccan Hasan-al-Wazzari (Leo Africanos) who wrote an account of his travels at the end of the 16th century. For two centuries this work was occasionally published in many European languages.

The idea of the sphericity of the earth, denied and opposed by Christian theologians, had been transmitted long before Christopher Columbus to Europe through the works of Muslim astronomers and geographers. On the basis of this idea, Columbus thought that by sailing towards the West he could reach the East. The Ephemerides which had made the voyage of Columbus possible were constructed by Regiomontanus from Al-Battani's tables. This ultimately led to the discovery of America.

Vasco Da Gama's sea journey to India was made with the help of a Muslim Arab pilot, Shihab-al-Din Ahmad Ibn Majid who was called 'The Lion of the Sea'. This pilot indicated to Vasco De Gama the way to India, and even took him there from the east coast of Africa. Ibn Majid is the author of several manuals on navigation and oceanography.

Prince Henry of Portugal set up under Muslim and Jewish teachers (trained in Muslim lands) his great nautical academy at Cape St. Vincent, which prepared the way for Vasco Da Gama, and for the expansion of Europe to the uttermost ends of the earth.

Route to India : The Muslims opened up the land-routes to India, to China, Malacca, and Timbuctoo, the emporium of Central African trade; and sent their carvans to the rich lands beyond the Sahara long before the Portuguese doubled Cape Verde. They held the monopoly of the sea-routes to India, and the Emosaids founded along the eastern coast of Africa a line of trading colonies from the Sudan coast and Socotra to Mombaza, Mozambique, Zanzibar and Madagascar.

The seventh Abbasi Caliph Al-Mamun took a keen interest in geography. He appointed seventy scholars to draw a large map of the world. One of these scholars was Muhammad Ibn Musa-al-Khwarizmi. He compiled a geographical work called *Rasm-al-Mamur min-al-Bilad* (the description of the inhabited lands) which contains the results of the researches of these scholars. He made improvement on Ptolemy's geographical work, both in the text and in the maps. He followed Ptolemy in giving the latitudes and longitudes of various places. He also gave the geographical positions of the places which originated after the rise of Islam.

In 851 A.C. appeared the narrative of a Muslim merchant named Sulaiman who undertook travels to China and to many coast lands of the Indian Ocean. It is the first description of these lands in Arabic. It throws light on the commercial relations between the Chinese and Muslims in the first half of the tenth century. Another description of such a journey was written by Abu Zaid. This journey was made to China by Ibn Wahab in 870.

In the ninth century A.C. several descriptions of roads and countries came into existence. One such description entitled the *Kitab-al-Masalik wal-Mamalik* was composed by Ibn Khurdadhbih, a geographer of Persian origin, who was the director of posts. The book, which is the author's main work, also contains brief narrations of journeys in distant lands. It is an important source for the study of the topography of the Muslim empire. It was translated into French. The author of this work was born in about 825 and died in 912.

Another such description of the same period entitled *Kitab-al-Masalik wal-Mamalik* was written in 891-92 by Ahmad Ibn Abi Yaqub. A historian and geographer, usually known as Al-Yaqubi. This book is the masterpiece of the author. The author himself travelled in various lands in the East and West. He visited Persia, India, Arabia, Syria, Maghrib (Tunis, Algiers and Morocco) and Spain. He collected information on the habits, customs, the governments of the inhabitants of these lands, and the distances between various places in their countries. He also described whatever he knew about the conquest of lands by the caliphs and other rulers, and mentioned the amount of *Khiraj* (land tax) collected by the governments. This book is one of the earliest and authentic sources of geographical knowledge. The description of Baghdad is particularly interesting."

An important geographer and traveller of the tenth century was Abu Ishaq Ibrahim Ibn Muhammad-al-Istakhri. He travelled in Arabia and some of the Indian territories, and reached the Atlantic regions. He wrote two geographical works. One of them is the *Suwar-al-Aqalim* (figures of climates) which is a revision of Al-Balkhi's work bearing the same title. The other is the *Masalik-al-Mamalik.* It contains a coloured map for each country. Both of these works or one of them was utilized by Al-Yaqut in his *Mujam-al-Buldan* (dictionary of the countries).

Another traveller and geographer of this time was Abul Qasim Muhammad Ibn Hawqal. He was a merchant by profession. He began his journey from Baghdad in 943, and came to Maghrib and Sicily. He also travelled in Spain and other countries. He revised the maps and the text of his geographical work at the request of the geographer Al-Istakhri. Then he wrote a work of his own called *Kitab-al-Masalik wal Mamalik* which contains a map for each country.

Another well-known Muslim geographer and traveller was Muhammad Ibn Ahmad Ibn Abu Bakr-al-Maqdisi who at first travelled extensively in connection with business. The travels provided him detailed information of various lands. Later, he gave up the profession of business, and began to travel just to gain the knowledge of the world. These travels offered him the opportunity of making close and intimate observations, and provided him detailed knowledge of various lands. Al-Maqdisi of making close and intimate observations, and provided him detailed knowledge of various lands. Al-Maqdisi wrote his travelogue entitled *Ahsan-al-Taqasim fi-Marifat-al-Aqalim* (best divisions for knowledge of the climates). It contains much original information, and has been translated into English. The part of the book dealing with Syria and Palestine has been translated into German. The author spent some time in India, wrote a number of geographical works, and discussed the question of the rotation of the earth round its axis. He regarded the Indus Valley to be originally a sea basin which was then filled with alluvial soil. He determined accurately the latitudes and longitudes, and made geodetic measurements.

Another important geographer of the 11th century was Abd Allah Ibn Abd-al-Aziz-al-Bikri. He was also a botanist, lexicographer and historian. He was well-versed in literature and genealogy. He was born in Saltes, and migrated to Cordova where he died at a very old age in 1094. He wrote valuable books on many subjects. The Kings of the Spanish territories used to send his books to one another as a gift. One of these books is geographical work called *Kitab-al-Masalik wal Mamalik.* It is in the form of an itinerary. It also contains historical and ethnographical information. He also composed a geographical dictionary, chiefly, of Arabia.

Another traveller of the 11th century was Nasir Khusrau who was also a philosopher and a poet. He was born in 1003, and died in 1088. He travelled from 1045 to 1052 in Arabia, Syria, Egypt, Palestine and Persia, and gave an account of his travels in a book written in Persian. It is entitled *Safarnamah.* It contains geographical, ethnographical and archaeological information.

A geographer of the 12th century who also wrote in Persian was known as Ibn-al-Balkhi. In the beginning of the 12th century Ibn-al-Balkhi wrote in Persian a description of the province of Fars which corresponds to the south-west part of modern Persia along the Persian Gulf. This description is entitled *Farsnamah.* It has been translated into English.

One of the travellers, geographers and cartographers of the same period was Abu Abd Allah Ibn Abd-al-Rahim-al-Gharnati who was born in 1080, in Granada, and died in 1169 in Damascus. He travelled from Spain towards the East. In 1117, he sailed from Spain to Egypt, via Sardinia and Sicily. He went to Baghdad, Abhar, Jibal, Sakhsin (or Saqain) on the upper Volga. In the latter region he spent many years. He also travelled in Balghar (near Kazan on the Volga), Bashgird, Hungary. In 1160 he was in Baghdad. Later, he lived at various places in Khurasan and Syria. He is the author of many geographical works. His descriptions of the foreign countries are largely anecdotic.

A Great Book : One of his works is entitled *Tuhfat-al-Albab wa Nukhbat-al-Ajaib.* It is divided into many sections as follows:

> Introduction (1); General description of the world and its inhabitants including *Jinn* (2); Singularities of various countries (3); Seas, islands, and the strange animals living in them (4); Caravans, fossils, etc.

Al-Gharnati gives an account of the fossil bones. In 1136, while he was in Bulghar, he found that trade in bones was being carried out there. They were exported as far as Khwarizm.

Another illustrious scholar of this age and the greatest geographer of the Middle Ages was Abu Abd Allah Muhammad Ibn Muhammad Ibn Abd Allah, usually called Al-Sharif-al-Idrisi. He was also a historian, botanist, traveller, literator and poet. He was born in 1099. He was brought up at Cordova where he received his education. Then he undertook long travels in the Mediterranean region until at last he reached Sicily. He settled down in Palermo where he became the courtier of Roger II, the Norman King of Sicily. For this reason he is also called Al-Siqali.

At Palermo, Al-Idrisi began to compile his monumental work on world geography entitled *Nuzhat-al-Mushtaqfi Ikhtiraq-al-Afaq* or *Kitab-al-Rujuri* which was completed in 1154. It is the most comprehensive work ever written on medieval history and geography. It is the best Arabic work on the description of Europe. The later Muslim geographers derived information on Europe from this celebrated work.

Nuzhat-al-Mushtaq contains seventy one maps. Of these, a round world map is given in the beginning of the book, and the remaining seventy in the middle of it. Each map represents a tenth part of one of the seven climes in which the world was divided by Ptolemy. These climes are the latitudinal lands which lie to the north of the Equator, and are divided by lines of longitude into ten parts. In his text Al-Idrisi gathers, in an orderly fashion, the historical, geographical and miscellaneous material relating to the areas covered by these maps. Each section of the book is devoted to the description of one of these seventy maps. Al-Idrisi got a map engraved by the artisans on a round base made of silver. It was the result of the cooperative efforts of the scholars who worked for about fifteen years on collecting material on the then known world. This material was collected from the envoys of the king, from all the available geographical treatises, and from other sources of information.

The maps given in the book show that the author accepted the sphericity of the earth. Among the remarkable features of these maps is the location of the exact sources of the Nile, which is wrongly considered to be a discovery of the 19th century.

The whole Arabic text of Al-Idrisi's work has not been critically studied as yet. It has never been published in full. Many scholars undertook the task of editing it, but due to the difficulties involved they either gave up this task or remained contented with the editing of one or two sections only. The section dealing with India and the neighbouring territories was published in India in 1954. The book was translated into Latin, English, French and German.

A famous scholar, traveller and geographer of this century was Muhammad Ibn Ahmad Ibn Zubayr-al-Kanani-al-Andalusi. He was born in 1144 in Valencia or in Shatiba, lived in Granada and died in 1217 in Alexandria. He had knowledge of literature, poetry, *Fiqh* and *Hadith*. He received his education from a number of teachers living in different lands.

Ibn Zubayr's writings were based on his travelogue and poetry. He composed some of the verses mourning the death of his wife, and some others as a satire on the age he lived in. Ibn Zubayr made travels to the East thrice, starting each travel from Spain and performing the *Hajj* each time.

He started his first travel from Granada in 1182 after which he wrote his famous travelogue. He went on his second journey on hearing the news of the conquest of Jerusalem. He left for that city from Granada in 1189, and returned in 1197. On return he first lived in Granada, then in Malaga and later in Sabta, and finally in Fas devoting himself to lecturing on Hadith and Sufism and reporting the Hadith he knew. He started his third travel after the death of his wife. First of all he went to Mecca where he stayed for a long time. From there he went to Jerusalem and from there to Egypt and Alexandria where he engaged himself in reporting the Hadith until his death.

Ibn Zubayr's first travel continued for two years and three and a half months. It was begun in 1182, and ended in 1185. In the course of this travel he visited Egypt, Arabia, Iraq, Syria and Sicily. At the end of this travel he wrote a travelogue in which he gave an account of the places where he stayed or through which he passed. He gave particular emphasis on the description of the mosques, the graves of the Prophet's Companions and of other well-known people, hospitals and famous monuments. He mentioned particularly some of the social and economic aspects of Egypt, religious aspects of the Arab cities, the activities of the religious preachers in Iraq, the political and economic conditions of Syria, the wars between the Muslims and the Crusaders, and the state of Muslims of Sicily, living under the suzerainty of King Guillaume. Giving an account of various places he attached importance to the things for which those places were well-known, such as the Light House of Alexandria, the Pyramids and Sphinx of Cairo, the size of the Rhodes Island, the Temple of Dandara, the holy Islamic places of Mecca, the Prophet's Mosque in Medina, the mosque of Kufa, the inflammable oil of Mosul, the fort of Aleppo, and the Umayyad mosque in Damascus.

Ibn Zubayr's travelogue contains some information which is indispensable for geographers, historians and litterateurs interested in this important period of Islamic history. The author depicts Salah-al-Din-al-Ayyubi as a great personality, and gives an account of the high position that this hero had got in the hearts of the Muslims of his age. The author also gives a description of the relations between Muslims and Crusaders in war and peace, which is not available in most of the books on history. He fully describes the conditions of Muslims living in Sicily and in the territories where the Crusaders reached from Syria. He also makes some references to the life and manners of the Easterners, most of which can still be seen.

This travelogue is very important and interesting. Many Orientalists took a keen interest in its study, and wrote useful commentaries on it. The part of the travelogue concerning Sicily was translated into French and Italian.

An important Muslim traveller and geographer of the early 13th century was Abu Abd Allah Yaqut ibn Abd Allah Shihab-al-Din-al-Hamawi-al-Rumi. He was also a reliable historian, lexicographer and philologist. He was born in a Greek family in 1179, and died in 1229. He started his travel when he was still young. He was enslaved in Baghdad by a merchant who patronised him, helped him to be educated, and employed him to carry on his business. Then, he was set free. Yaqut earned his livelihood by copying books. He remained with his master until the latter's death. Then, he carried on his trade independently. He travelled extensively until he reached Marw (Khurasan), and carried on his trade there. He also travelled to Syria and Egypt. His journeys were full of adventures.

Yaqut wrote a geographical dictionary called *Mujam-al-Buldan*. It is the author's main work, and is one of the most important works of Arabic literature. It is a mine of information on geography and other subjects like history, ethnography and natural history. It is arranged in alphabetical order. The introduction deals with mathematical, physical and political geography, the seven climes, the size of the earth and similar topics. The dictionary gives information on the structure and proper pronunciation of the names of the places mentioned therein. It also contains a great deal of historical notes, biographical sketches of learned people, discussions on grammar and so on.

Yaqut is the author of various other works including biographical dictionaries of the poets and literati.

A Muslim geographer of the 13th century was Abul-Hasan Ali Ibn Musa Ibn Muhammad-al-Maghribi. He was also a historian and poet, and had a good knowledge of the Arabic literature. He was born in 1208 near Granada and died in 1274 or in 1286. He travelled extensively and visited Egypt, Syria and Iraq. He was the guest of Hulagu, (Il-Khan of Persia from 1256 to 1265).

In 1251, during his stay at Baghdad Ali Ibn Musa visited 36 libraries in that city. He had the knowledge of the mouth of the river Senegal. He gave an account of the northern countries of Europe where white bears are found. He mentioned that Iceland is called the island of white falcons and that the true falcons are found in Denmark.

Ali Ibn Musa is the author of many works on different subjects. His main work is a geographical treatise entitled *Kitab Bast-al-Arafil-Tul wal-Ard.* It is also called *Kitab-al-jughrafiyah.* It is based on the geographical works of Ptolemy and Al-Idrisi, but also gives information on the facts discovered after the latter's time. It also contains the geographical coordinates of every important place, which were not mentioned by Al-Idrisi. He also wrote a history of pre-Islamic Arabia and two other works, one dealing with the West and the other with the East."

A traveller of the late 13th century was Abu Muhammad. Muhammad Ibn Muhammad Ibn Ali, Al-Abdari. He is called Al-Abdari because he was the descendant of Abd-al-Dar. He was born at a village in Valencia. This village contained hot mineral waters in it. In 1289, he left for Mecca for the performance of the *Hajj*. He made his journey both ways by land. In the course of his journey he visited Baja, Tunis and Qairawan, and passed through Alexandria. Thus, he crossed the whole of North Africa twice. He wrote a travelogue in which he gave a description of the North African countries. This travelogue contains topographical data, and throws light on the Muslim life and the scholarship of that time.

Another traveller of the same city who belongs to the eastern Muslim empire was Ali Ibn Abi Bakr Ibn Ali-al-Harawi. He was a historian as well. He was born in Mosul, and died in 1214 in Aleppo where he had a stable. He travelled in many lands. In 1173-74, he visited Jerusalem which was then under Christian control. He witnessed an eruption of Etna. He was in contact with Manuel I Comnenos (Emperor from 1143 to 1180) in Constantinople. In 1191, he was caught at sea by the fleet which was carrying Richard, *Coeur-de-Lion* to the siege of Acre. He wrote a book which served as a guide for pilgrims. This guide book is called *Kitab fi Marifat-al-Ziyarat.* In this book he deals with Syria, Palestine, Egypt, the Byzantine empire, Mesopotamia, India, Arabia, the Maghrib, and Abyssinia, giving brief but first-hand information about all these countries excluding the last two. He also wrote a travelogue and several other works on different subjects. It is said that he used to write on the walls of nearly every famous place he passed through. Some sea warrior chiefs state that while travelling on sea they found a piece of land having a wall on which there was his writing.

Under Tughril II who was the last Saljuq ruler of Iraq and Kurdistan (1177-1194) there flourished a Persian cosmographer, Muhammad Ibn Mahmud Ibn Ahmad-al-Tusi-al-Salmani who wrote in Persian a cosmograph entitled *Ajaib-al-Makhluqat.* It contains at the beginning six maps which represent the Caspian sea, the Mediterranean sea, Jibal, Sind, the Arabian sea and Arabia.

Astronomy

Astronomy *(Ilm-al-Hayah)* or the science of formation (i.e. of the heavens) deals with such things as the structure of the heavens, the number and configuration of the stars, the signs of the zodiac, the distances of the stars, their size and their motions. It also deals with the compilation of planetary tables, the catalogue of stars for the making of calendars and similar tasks.

The Arabs took a keen interest in the study of heavens. They developed this interest firstly, because they had once worshipped heavenly bodies, and secondly, because the dwellers of the desert who usually travelled at night in connection with trade, war and migration from one place to another, found the direction of their journey with the help of the stars. The clear sky of the desert gave them a chance of making precise observations. Thus, there was some locally acquired knowledge of the fixed stars, the movements of the planets and the changes of the weather.

After the advent of Islam, the Muslims had to determine the time of the prayers and the direction of the Kaaba to turn their faces towards it at the time of prayers. For this purpose it was necessary to know the altitude of the sun and the latitudes and longitudes of all the places where the Muslims lived. The same need arose for the orientation of the mosque. This gave a religious impetus to the study of astronomy and the allied subjects such as astronomical geography and mathematics. On the other hand, the Muslims, who once carried on flourishing trade all over the world and occasionally launched *Jihad,* had to travel on the land and the sea. As an aid to travel, navigation and meteorology, a by-product of navigation, they needed star maps. The necessity of such maps was also a cause of their interest in astronomy.

There was a group of astronomers who believed in the influence of heavenly bodies on the terrestrial affairs, and the fate and future of human beings. According to them, the prognostication of sub-lunar events from the revolution of the heavens, the signs of the zodiac in the ascendant and the motion of the planets was possible. The science dealing with such influences was termed as Astrology (*Ilm-Ahkam-al-Nujum*). Astrology, as a part of astronomy, was studied and developed by ancient Babylonians.

The study of this art or science was then made in Greece and Rome, a few centuries before the opening of the Christian era. It was also cultivated in India, China and Egypt. From the 7th to the 13th century it was further developed by the Muslims and later on by the Europeans. In the 14th and the 15th centuries, the astrologers had great influence on the kings of the European countries. The orthodox Muslims did not believe in the influence of the heavenly bodies on fate or the future of human beings.

The regular study of astronomy and mathematics was begun at Baghdad in the second half of the 8th century during the reign of the second Abbasi Caliph Al-Mansur. After that the patronage and generosity of other Muslim rulers, particularly of the seventh Abbasi Caliph Al-Mamun, provided stimulation to the astronomical and mathematical researches of every kind. Indian, Persian and Greek astronomical works were translated into Arabic, and for making the astronomical observations the observatories were established by the caliphs and private persons at various places in the Muslim world.

Astronomy was studied with great interest with the result that the number of Muslim astronomers rose surprisingly in a short period of time, and by the end of the 10th century, a large number of eminent Muslim astronomers gathered in Baghdad. In the 11th and the 12th centuries astronomy flourished in

Muslim Spain where a good deal of creative and original work on this branch of science was done.

The Muslim scientists attached utmost importance to accuracy in observations and calculations, without caring for the length of time needed for it. Thus, sometimes their astronomical researches extended for more than forty years. Due to this desire of accuracy the Muslims did not accept as such the astronomical tables or measurements of Ptolemy, a great Greek astronomer and mathematician. They only accepted his planetary theory just to provide a basis for astronomical research. They themselves conducted astronomical researches in Baghdad, Samarqand, Nishapur, Cordova, Damascus and Ray, and after making a careful study of the heavens they not only corrected and amplified Ptolemy's astronomical tables, but also compiled a number of new ones and drew up new star catalogues. On the basis of fresh observations, the Ptolemaic system was repeatedly criticised by the Muslim astronomers, particularly those of Spain.

The investigations on astronomy were continued, and till the end of the 11th century, nearly all the original and creative work was done by Muslims, and even the works of non-Muslims were written in Arabic. Astronomy reached its highest in the 13th and 14th centuries. In the 12th century, the Christians and Jews started the work of translation from Arabic into Latin and Hebrew, and began to conduct research in this field. But until the end of the 13th century, no mathematical and astronomical work comparable to that of the Muslims could be produced by the Christians or Jews. It is interesting to note that in the 12th century, while Ptolemy's astronomical work, *Almagest*, after a thorough study and research, was subjected to severe criticism by Muslims particularly those of Spain, the study of this work was begun in the Latin world.

Beside compiling the astronomical tables, the Muslims prepared celestial globes on which the positions and magnitudes of the stars were represented. The globe is of Greek origin, but since Ptolemy's time there has been a continuous improvement on it. The Muslim scientists also wrote comprehensive books on astronomy and mathematics, and also composed treatises on various branches of this science.

Star Maps : The Muslim astronomers also prepared the star maps to preserve the old astronomical knowledge, and to use them as an aid to travel, navigation and meteorology.

A great incentive for the study of astronomy came from an Indian astronomical work called *Siddhanta* which was brought to the court of Baghdad by a Hindu named Kanka. Kanka met Yaqub Ibn Tariq in 767 who was one of the greatest astronomers of his time. Yaqub Ibn Tariq introduced him to the Caliph Al-Mansur. Kanka showed the book to the Caliph who ordered Muhammad Ibn Ibrahim Al-Fazari to translate it into Arabic. He also ordered that a work based on *Siddhanta* should be composed, which could serve as a reference book for the Arabs. Muhammad Ibn Ibrahim took this responsibility and prepared a book which was called by the astronomers as *Sind Hind-al-Kabir* (the great *Siddhanta*). It was used until the time of the Caliph Al-Mamun. Then Al-Khwarizmi, who was one of the greatest scientists, prepared a summary of this book. He also compiled astronomical and trigonometrical tables according to the combined methods of Indians, Persians and Greeks. These tables were revised by Maslamah-al-Majriti (c. the second half of the 10th century). They gained so much popularity that they were used even in China. In the 12th century, the translation of these tables was made into Latin. Al-Khwarizmi glimpsed in his works on astral motion and the force of attraction, the law of universal gravitation.

The astronomer Ibrahim Ibn Habib-al-Fazari was the first Muslim who constructed astrolabes. He composed a poem on astrology, and compiled a *Zij* (calendar) according to the Arab method. He also wrote on the use of astrolabes and on the armillary spheres.

In 762-63 the Persian astronomer and engineer, Naubakht, together with Masha' Allah (Latin Macellama, Macelarama, Messahala), made a survey before the building of Baghdad. Masha' Allah (d. 815 or 820) was one of the earliest astronomers and astrologers, who flourished under the Caliph Al-Mansur. Naubakht (d. 776-77) was the author of a book on astrological judgements entitled *Kitab-al-Ahkam).*

During the reign of the Caliph Al-Mamun, the important work of translation of Ptolemy's *Almagest* from Greek into Arabic was completed. The Caliph was very anxious to get it translated correctly. It was translated several times. Many commentaries on it were written. Its summaries were also made. The Minister Yahya Ibn Khalid Barmaki was the first to get it translated. A group of scholars wrote for him a commentary on this book, but he did not like it. He appointed Abu Hasan and Salman who were attached to the scientific academy called *Bait-al-Hikmah* (The house of wisdom) to write a commentary on it. The *Almagest* represents the best example of Greek classical works on astronomy. It served as a basis for the later astronomical works. Al-Hajjaj Ibn-Yusuf was one of the first translators of the *Almagest.* He made this translation on the basis of a Syriac version.

The Caliph Al-Mamun (169-218/786-833) was very fond of philosophy and science. The more he got acquainted with the interesting problems of science, the more his interest grew in the practical work. He built an observatory at Baghdad in his *Bait-al-Hikmah* and another in the plain of Tadmor (Palmyra). In these observatories the fundamental elements of the *Almagest* like the inclination of the ecliptic, the length of the solar year, and the precession of the equinoxes were verified. Observations on the celestial motions were carried out and geodetic measurements were made."

Al-Mamun ordered Ahmad, Muhammad and Hasan, who were eminent scientists and his courtiers, to measure in collaboration with other court scientists the length of the terrestrial degree and the circumference of the earth in some vast planes. The planes of Sinjar and Tadmor were selected for this purpose. The astronomers stayed at a place and noted with the help of instruments the altitude of the North Pole, and pitched a nail there. Then tying a long rope with the nail, they carried the rope in the direction of the North. Where the rope ended they pitched another nail and tied another rope with it, and proceeded in the same direction. They continued this process as well as observations on the altitude of the North Pole, until on reaching a particular spot they noticed that the altitude of this Pole had increased by one degree. The distance they covered was also measured, which was found to be $56\frac{2}{3}$ miles. From these observations it was inferred that for each terrestrial degree the distance covered on the earth amounts to $56\frac{2}{3}$ miles. The same operation was repeated in the direction of the South where at one spot they noticed that the altitude had decreased by one degree. The distance covered was the same as in the first case. Now on multiplying this distance by 360 which is the total number of terrestrial degrees, the circumference of the earth was found to be equal to 20,400 miles, and the diameter equal to 6,500 miles.

The chief of astronomers who carried observations under Al-Mamun was Sanad Ibn Ali. He was a Jewish convert to Islam. He constructed an observatory (Kanisah) at the back of the Shamasiah Gate at the palace of Muizz-al-Dawlah in Baghdad. An astronomical table and some writings on astronomy and mathematics, including a book on Arabic numerals, are ascribed to him.

Ali Ibn Isa-al-Asturlabi who flourished in Baghdad and Damscus in the first half of the 9th century, took part in the measurement of the length of the terrestrial degree ordered by Al-Mamun. He made astronomical observations at Baghdad and Damascus from 829 to 833. He was the famous constructor of astrolabes; hence the nickname Al-Asturlabi (maker of astrolabe). He wrote a treatise on astrolabes, which is one of the earliest works on this instrument.

Yahya Ibn Abi Mansur also took part in the observations made at Baghdad in 829-30, and compiled the astronomical tables called *Mamunic* tables. Like the tables of Habash these, too, are a collective work of various astronomers. Al-Marwarudhi, who also flourished under Al-Mamun, made solar observations.

In the 9th century astronomy flourished in the East. Astronomical researches were conducted in the observatories of Baghdad, Damascus and other places. More original and improved work was done in the second half of the 10th century. The elaboration of trigonometry, which was considered to be a branch of astronomy at that time, was also continued. A great attention was paid to the construction of good astronomical instruments, specially to the spherical astrolabe which was newly introduced at that time. Hamid Ibn Ali was a famous constructor of spherical astrolabes. Jabir Ibn Sinan was also a maker of this as well as of other astronomical instruments. According to Al-Beruni he was the first to make a spherical astrolabe. Al-Nairizi wrote on this instrument an elaborate treatise which represents the best Arabic work on this topic. In this treatise the author, after giving the introduction, describes the instrument, and gives its applications. Beside this work, Al-Nairizi compiled astronomical tables. A great scientist Al-Mahani made for 33 years (833-866), a series of observations on lunar and solar eclipses and planetary conjunctions. Another astronomer of this time Ahmad-al-Nahawandi, who flourished at the time of Yahya Ibn Khalid Ibn Barmaki, made astronomical observations at Jundishapur and compiled tables called *Mushtamil*.

After carrying out astronomical observations for ten years (825 to 835) Habash-al-Hasib compiled three astronomical tables. The first were according to the Hindu method (based on

Siddhanta). The second called *Al-Zij-al-Mumtahan* (the "tested Tables") were according to the Arab method. They were very important and were probably due to the cooperative efforts of Al-Mamun's astronomers. The third called *Al-Zij Al-Saghir* (the small tables) were commonly known as the *Tables of Shah.* Habash-al-Hasib determined the time of the solar eclipse of the year 829. He was the first to determine time by an altitude (in this case, of the sun). This method was generally accepted and adopted by Muslim astronomers.

The most illustrious scholar of this age, and one of the greatest astronomers of Islam, was Abd Allah Muhammad Ibn Jabir Ibn Sinan-al-Battani (Latin; Albategnius, Albatenius). His ancestors were Sabeans of Harran, but he himself was a Muslim. He carried out astronomical observations of a wide range and with remarkable accuracy for about 41 years (877-918). He determined many astronomical co-efficients, like the precession 54.5", a year, inclination of the ecliptic 23° 35′, with great accuracy. He noticed an increase of 6° 47' in the longitude of the sun's apogee since Ptolemy's time. This led to the discovery of the motion of the solar upsides and of slow variation in the equation of time. Al-Battani proved the possibility of the annular eclipses of the sun. He also wrote many astrological works. His main work is a large astronomical treatise including the astronomical tables. His tables contain a catalogue of fixed stars for the year 880-81. His work is an advance on that of Al-Khwarizmi, and shows more divergence from Indian methods. Observations regarding the first appearance of the new moon, the length of the tropic and sidereal year, the obliquity of the ecliptic, the lunar anomalies, the parallaxes, etc., are more complicated and more accurately made by Al-Battani than by Al-Khwarizmi.

Al-Battani's astronomical treatise was translated into Latin and Spanish in the 12th and 13th centuries respectively. It exerted great influence on the European scholars of the Middle Ages and Renaissance.

Thabit Ibn Qurrah (d. 901) who was a physician, mathematician, astronomer and translator from Greek and Syriac into Arabic, published his solar observations made at Baghdad. He particularly determined the altitude of the sun and the length of the solar year.

The astronomer and mathematician Wijan Ibn Rustam-al-Kuhi wrote many astronomical and mathematical works, including a treatise on the construction of the astrolabe. He was the head of the astronomers working in 988 at the Buwayhid Sharaf-al-Dawlah's observatory. His co-worker Ahmad Ibn Muhammad-al-Saghani was the inventor and maker of astronomical instruments. Abul-Wafa is said to be the discoverer of the variation, the third inequality of the moon; a discovery which was later ascribed to Tycho Brahe.

Ali Ibn-al-Hussain-al-Alawi (d. 985) showed a remarkable accuracy in observations. He compiled astronomical tables which remained very popular for at least two centuries.

Eminent Astronomer: Now we come to a famous astronomer of the 10th century, named Abul-Hussain Abd-al-Rahman-al-Sufi. He was born in Ray (Persia) in 903, and died in 966. He was a prominent astronomer of the medieval times. His knowledge of both the Islamic and Greek astronomy, particularly urinometry, was comprehensive. He was the first to observe the change of the colour of stars, the change in the magnitude of stars, the proper motion of stars, the long period variable stars and the Southern constellations which have been wrongly ascribed by modern astronomers to some later ones.

Abd-al-Rahman-al-Sufi was patronized by the Buwayhid ruler Adud-al-Dawlah (949-982) who was a great patron of astronomy, and had built an observatory at Shiraz. Al-Sufi wrote for the ruler a book on urinometry, entitled *Suwar-al-Kawakib* (The book of the fixed stars). In this book he gives a complete description of the constellations of the heavens. He also gives the position of each star of the constellations, illustrating with pictures. The book contains 55 astronomical tables along with illustrations of 48 constellations in 96 diagrams as seen in the heavens. The artistic value of the pictorial illustrations in this work is very great, and represents one of the best examples of the Persian miniature paintings. Al-Sufi has not only corrected the errors of observations in the work of his predecessors like Al-Battani, but also pointed out many faulty observations found in Ptolemy's *Almagest*. He defined carefully the boundaries of each constellation, and recorded the magnitudes and positions of stars after making new observations.

The *Suwar-al-Kawakib* is one of the three masterpieces of observational astronomy of the medieval times; the other two being the catalogues of Ibn Yunus and Ulugh Beg prepared in the 12th and 15 centuries respectively. It is an addition to the Muslims' knowledge on urinometry. The later astronomers, like Al-Beruni, Alfonso, Prince of Castile, Khwajah Nasir-al-Din Tusi, Prince Ulugh Beg and Jai Singh II, based their catalogues of stars on this authentic catalogue. This work was translated into Latin, French and Persian, and a commentary on it was written in Spanish.

It served as a basis for later works in Western Europe. The modern astronomers like Hauber, Down, Argelander, Ideler, Schellerup and Knobel had made an extensive use of it.

Al-Sufi prepared a fine celestial globe. Several celestial globes which cover the period from the 11th to the 18th century show the star positions and magnitudes according to Al-Sufi. He showed a remarkable accuracy in the design of the astrolabes. He wrote a treatise on this instrument. In this treatise he throws light on the astronomical techniques as practised at that time.

Another great astronomer and one of the greatest Muslim astronomers was Abul-Hasan Ali Ibn Abi Said Abd-al-Rahman Ibn Ahmad ibn Yunus-al-Sadafi, generally known as Ibn Yunus.

He was well versed in Arabic literature, poetry and history, and had a knowledge of many other subjects. He belonged to Egypt where he died in 1009. He was a courtier of the Fatimi Caliph Al-Aziz Billah (975-996). He got a chance of working in a well-equipped observatory which was part of a Muslim academy of science, named *Dar-al-Hikmah* (the house of wisdom) founded in Cairo by the Fatimi rulers. He made astronomical observations, and by the order of the Caliph Al-Aziz he compiled the astronomical tables.

The work of compilation of these tables was begun in 990 during the life-time of the Caliph, but it was completed after his death under his son Al-Hakim (966-1020). Hence, they were named after him *Al-Zij-al-Kabir-al-Hakimi.* In these tables he entered his observations about the eclipses and conjunctions, old and new, improved values of astronomical constants (inclination of the ecliptic, 23° 35'; longitude of the sun's apogee, 86° 10'; solar parallax reduced from 3' to 2'; precession, 51.2' a year). He gave an account of the geodetic measurements which were carried on by the order of the Caliph Al-Mamun in the ninth century.

Ibn Yunus in his astronomical tables (written in 4 volumes) corrected the errors of observations in the astronomical tables of his predecessors. The people of Egypt relied on these tables. It is said that after their compilation the use of all the previous tables in the world was given up. Even the astronomers of China extensively utilized them. The translation of a large part of the tables, except the chronological section, has been made in French in 1804.

Beside these tables, Ibn Yunus has composed many books. One of these is *Jaddwil-al-Samt Jaddwil-al-Shams wa 'l-Qamar* (the tables of the sun and the moon).

A famous astronomer of the 11th century, who belonged to Cordova (Spain), was Abu Ishaq Ibrahim Ibn Yahya-al-Naqqash, commonly known as Ibn-al-Zarqala or Al-Zarqali

(Latin: Arzachel). He was also an eminent astronomer of this century. He lived from 1029 to 1087. He was the best observer of his time, who made astronomical observations for about 19 years (1061-1080). He invented an improved astrolabe called *Safihah (Saphaea Arzachelis)* on which he also wrote a treatise. It was translated into Latin, Hebrew and many vernaculars.

Al-Zarqali was the first to prove explicitly the motion of the solar apogee with reference to the stars. According to his calculations it was equal to 12.04" per year (the real value being 11.8"). He edited the planetary tables called *Toledan Tables.* These tables were probably the result of the observations made in Toledo by him and by a great observer Ibn Said in collaboration with other Muslim and Jewish astronomers. They were translated into Latin and enjoyed much fame.

A famous astronomer, mathematician and poet, Umar Ibn-al-Khayyam, reformed the old Persian calendar which had been replaced by the Islamic calendar after the Muslim conquest of Persia. This reformed calendar was called *Al-Tarikh-al-Jalali* after the name of the Seljuq Sultan Malik Shah Jalal-al-Din who in 1074-75 called Umar ibn-al-Khayyam to his observatory for making this reform. Many interpretations have been given to it. Each interpretation is accurate to a certain degree, but at any rate Umar's calendar was probably more accurate than the Gregorian (Christian) calendar. Three interpretations, the second of which seems to be the most accurate, are being quoted here along with the authority giving the interpretation and the resulting error.

1. Al-Shirazi's interpretation: 17 intercalary days in 70 years; error, 1 day in about 1540 years.
2. Ulugh Beg's interpretation: 15 intercalary days in 62 years; error, 1 day in about 3770 years.
3. Modern interpretation: 8 intercalary days in 33 years: error, 1 day in about 5,000 years.

(in the Gregorian calendar there is an error of 1 day in 3330 years).

The greatest astronomer of the 12th century, who also belonged to Spain, was Abu Muhammad Jabir Ibn Aflah. He was born or lived in Seville. He vigorously criticised the Ptolemaic theory of planets, and wrote a book on astronomy entitled *Islah-al-Majisti* (the correction of the *Almagest).* He was of the view that the lower planets (Mercury and Venus), at least, must have visible parallaxes. Venus may happen to be exactly on the line joining the sun and the earth. The most important part of his book is the introduction on trigonometry. The book was soon translated into Latin and Hebrew. Jabir Ibn Aflah is said to be the inventor of the astronomical instrument called turquet (*torquetum)* which contains two graduated circles in two perpendicular planes. The same invention has also been ascribed to two other persons, namely, Frances of Leige (11th century) and Nasir-al-Din Tusi (13th century). The turquet was introduced into the Latin West by Regionomentus. It gained great popularity in the 15th and 17th centuries.

Another astronomer of the time was Abul Qasim Hibat Allah Ibn Hussain-al-Badi-al-Asturlabi. He was also a physician, mathematician, poet and literature. He was the greatest expert of his time in the knowledge and construction of astrolabes; hence his nickname Al-Asturlabi. In 1120-30 astronomical observations were made under his direction, and astronomical tables were compiled. The observations were carried out in the palace of the Seljuq Sultan of Iran, Mughith-al-Din Mahmud (1117-1131). The tables were dedicated to the Sultan, and were called after him the Mahmudic tables. Al-Asturlabi was very much praised by Muslim biographers. He died in Baghdad in 1139-40.

In the 13th century there flourished in the East a great scholar of Persian origin, named Abu Jafar Muhammad ibn Muhammad ibn-al-Hasan, Nasir-al-Din-al-Tusi-al-Muhaqqiq, (the researcher). He was born in Tus (Khurasan) in 1201, and died in Baghdad in 1274. He was a philosopher, mathematician, astronomer and physician. He was one of the greatest Muslim mathematicians and scientists. He wrote both in Arabic and Persian. It is said that he knew Greek as well. He joined the Mongol service, and was later made administrator of the *Waqf* revenues.

While he was administrator he resided at Maragha in Asia Minor (1259-1274). Here he made astronomical observations in an observatory established by the Mongol ruler Hulaqu Khan II after he had defeated the last Abbasi Caliph, Al-Mutasim, in 1258. A library was attached to it. It is said to have contained 4,00,000 volumes which the Mongol armies had collected in Syria, Mesopotamia and Persia. Nasir-al-Din was the first director of this observatory. He was succeeded by two of his sons.

Nasir-al-Din was well acquainted with the knowledge of the Greeks. He wrote about 64 works on many subjects. Here we shall consider only some of his astronomical and astrological works. The most important astronomical work of Nasir-al-Din is the *Tadhkirah fi Ilm-al-Hayah* (The description of astronomy) which is a condensed summary of astronomy. To explain it many commentaries and super-commentaries have been written. The work enjoyed much popularity. It consists of four chapters. The second chapter, beside other things, contains interesting criticism of the Ptolemy's *Almagest* in which he showed a great ingenuity.

The criticism chiefly concerns the anomalies of the moon, and the motion in the latitude of the planets (particularly Mercury and Venus); also the proposition of a new system to replace the complicated Ptolemaic machinery of deferents and epicycles. His new and forceful criticism of astronomy as well as of other Muslim astronomers helped Copernicus in making his reform. Nasir-al-Din wrote one treatise on the five quadrants and two treatises on astrolabe. He also wrote two treatises on calendar.

Nasir-al-Din made observations in the observatory of Maragha which was well equipped with good astronomical instruments. He prepared new astronomical tables called after the Mongol ruler, *Al-Zij-al-Ilkhani*. Nasir-al-Din asked the ruler to give him a period of 30 years to compile the tables, because it was the shortest period during which the planetary cycles were completed. But the ruler refused, and gave him only 12 years to accomplish this task. Nasir-al-Din tried and succeeded in completing the tables within this time. They were based upon new observations. But the use of the earlier ones had also been made.

The *Zij-i-Ilkhani* was originally written in Persian. It consists of four books dealing respectively with (a) Chinese, Greek, Arabic and Persian Chronology; (b) motions of the planets; (c) ephemerides and (d) astrological operations. The translation of the *Zij* was made into Arabic, and commentaries on it were written. Finally, a sort of supplement to it was compiled by Jamshed Ibn Masud-al-Kashi (d. 840/1436), the first director of Ulugh Beg's observatory in Samarqand. These tables enjoyed a great popularity in the East including China, and were continued to be used even after the compilation of new tables by Ulugh Beg in 1437.

A contemporary of Nasir-al-Din, Muayyid-al-Din-al-Urdi-al-Dimashqi also took part with him in compiling the tables. He was a Syrian astronomer, architect and engineer. He started his career as a technician in Syria. He did some hydraulic work in Damascus, and also constructed there an astronomical instrument for Al-Mansur Ibrahim (King of Hims, 1239-1245). In about 1259 he went to Maragha, and helped Nasir-al-Din in organising the observatory and compiling the tables. It seems that the instruments, remarkably precise, were constructed under his supervision in the foundry attached to the observatory.

Al-Urdi was the author of a treatise in which he also described the instruments used in the observatory of Maragha, and explained their use and construction. The instruments are as follows:

(1) Mural quadrant
(2) armillary sphere
(3) solstitial armil
(4) equinoctial armil
(5) Hipparch's diopter (alidade);
(6) instrument with two quadrants
(7) instrument with two limbs
(8) instrument to determine sines and azimuths
(9) instruments to determine sines and versed sines,
(10) the perfect instrument (a universal instrument)
(11) parallactic ruler (after Ptolemy).

Al-Urdi was also the author of two other treatises; one on the construction of a perfect sphere and another on the determination of the distance between the centre of the sun and the apogee. He compiled astronomical tables, and wrote on Ptolemaic astronomy.

In 1279 or 1289 Al-Urdi's son Muhammad made a celestial globe. It consisted of two brass hemispheres separated by the ecliptic. Its diameter was 140 mm. It had a horizon circle. Two movable half circles were attached to the zenith point by a pivot. These circles are graduated and are used to determine the declination and right ascension of any star. Forty-eight constellations, the equator and the ecliptic are inlaid with silver or gold. It is preserved in the mathematical salon of Drasden.

The Translations : The works of Muslim astronomers were later translated into Latin, Hebrew and vernaculars by the Christian and Jewish scholars, some of the technical terms including azimuth *(Al-Samt)*. Algol *(Alfol)*, Achernar. *(Akhir-al-Nahr)*, passe into the European languages. The names of many stars such as akrab, *(Aqrab)*, Algedi *(Al-Jadi*, the kid), Altair *(Al-*

tair), (the player), denab *(dhanb,* tail), Pherkad *(Farqad,* calf), Adara *(Adhrah)* aldebaran *(Al-dibran),* which are of Arabic origin, also passed into these languages. The stars being countless in number, their separate study is not possible. They were, therefore, divided into various groups, and the groups were named after the things and animals with which they resembled.

Agriculture

There was a great scarcity of water and vegetation in the desert of Arabia. The people living there needed plants to feed their animals. They wandered in search of vegetation, and went wherever they could find it. This great importance of plants resulted in their becoming an important topic of Arabic literature.

The study of plants was chiefly made from medical and agricultural points of view. The Arabs already knew about the medical use of some herbs and shrubs (*Aqaqir wal Hashaish).* At the advent of Islam when, in connection with preaching, *Jihad,* or some other purposes they came in contact with other people, they took interest not only in the names and uses of plants, but they became also interested in their cultivation. So they tried to know the matters relating to agriculture such as the methods of plantation and fertilization, the time suitable for sowing and harvesting, and the nature of the soil. They made correct observations on sexual differences between such plants as palms and hemps. The plants were classified into those that grow from cuttings, those that grow from seeds and those that grow spontaneously.

The Muslims' knowledge of applied botany and agriculture can be estimated by reading the accounts of gardens and crops cultivated in different parts of the Muslim world, particularly those in Spain. At one time Muslim Spain was proverbial in this respect. The Arabs introduced irrigation and agricultural methods there with the result that it was transformed into a garden. Cotton, rice, sugar cane, asparagus, oranges, lemons and pomegranates were some of the plants and fruits brought from outside and cultivated in Spain. Through that country the Europeans became aware of the cultivation of many plants which they did not know before. The famous gardens of Persia, Spain and Morocco, with well planned arrangements of trees, shrubs and flowers, with their tilled floors, their rivulets and fountains of water, built with an aesthetic taste, establishing harmony between architecture and vegetation throws light on their interest in agriculture, gardening and love for flowers.

Transfer of Knowledge : Since the Arabs did not know much about the art of agriculture, they turned towards other peoples including the Romans, Nabateans and Persians for learning it. They also translated their botanical works into Arabic.

There are many lexicographers, geographers, travellers and physicians who wrote on plants. One of them was Abu Said Abd-al-Malik Ibn Quraib-al-Asmai. He was a native of Basrah, and came to Baghdad during the reign of Harun-al-Rashid. Asmai was born in 739 and died in 831. He is the author of a number of works on different subjects. One of them is on plants and trees. In the preface of this book the author has provided a general discussion on plants. First of all he has mentioned various types of soils having different conditions regarding their capabilities for cultivation and vegetation. Then he has mentioned the trees, giving an account of their various stages of development. After that he has classified the plants, giving examples for each class. Finally, he has described those plants which grow in plains and deserts. He has mentioned 230 plants in all.

Another lexicographer and grammarian who wrote on plants was Ahmad Ibn Daud Ibn Wanand, nicknamed Al-Dinawari. He was also called *Al-Ashshab* (the herbalist). He was a trustworthy reporter, an expert botanist, astronomer and logician who compiled a number of works on various subjects.

In his book on plants Al-Dinawari described, after observing the plants in the places where they grew, all that he had discovered and also all that his predecessors had mentioned. He did not leave even the minute details. This book was considered to be a standard work on herbalism, medicine and lexicography at a time when no one could become a physician or herbalist unless he had thoroughly studied this book, and was examined in it.

Al-Beruni (d. 1048) made observation on plants. He discovered that flowers have 3, 4, 5, 6 or 18 petals, never 7 or 9.

A physician Masarjwaih also compiled a work on the properties of simple drugs mentioning their good and bad effects. He was a Syrian Jew who flourished during the reign of Umar Ibn Abd-al-Aziz, and translated for him and for the Caliph Marwan some Greek works into Arabic. He translated the second part of Galen's work on simple drugs, which consists of six discourses. The translation was corrected by Hunain Ibn Ishaq.

The Muslims attached more importance to the translation of Dioscorides' work than to other botanical works. The later writers based their works on it adding whatever they knew of plants and simple drugs. Dioscorides was a distinguished scientist and an authority on herbs. He was a native of Anazarbos, hence called Ainzarbi. He travelled extensively and made investigations on plants and their properties. When he reached certain conclusions about the plants, he entered them into his book illustrating them with the pictures representing the colours of plants. The book of Dioscorides consists of five discourses. Two more discourses on the animal poisons are ascried to him. Thus, the total number of discourses is seven.

The first discourse deals with sweet-smelling drugs. The second consists of the description of vegetables and animals and their fluids. The third discourse discusses the roots of plants, the thorny plants and similar topics. The fourth deals with the drugs which are cold in nature, those which are warm, and those which cause relief from poisonous effects. The fifth discourse mentions different kinds of drinks and mineral drugs.

One of the most important Muslim botanists was Abul-Mansur Rashid-al-Din Abul-Fadl Ibn Ali-al-Suri. He was the greatest authority on simple drugs, the variety of their names, their properties and uses. He was born in 1177 at the city of Sur in Syria, and was brought up there. Later, he came to Baghdad where he started the study of medicine from Sheikh Muwaffaq-al-Din Abd-al-Latif-al-Baghdadi. Al-Suri spent two years in Qudes, at the hospital of the city where he practised medicine.

Al-Suri went to the places where the plants could be found, like the hills of Lebanon and other places which were famous for one or the other plant. He used to take with him a painter having different kinds of colours and paints. He observed the plants and showed them to his painter. The painter noticed the colour and roots of the plants, the size of their leaves and branches, and made the pictures accordingly. Al-Suri showed the plants to the painter at the time of their growth, maturity and withering. The painter prepared the pictures of the plants at every stage of their development, and filled in them the colours which he observed at that time. Al-Suri included these illustrations in his book on simple drugs and plants. He collected in it the material that he found in the books of the ancients, and also mentioned the drugs which he had discovered himself and their use which he came to know. Al-Suri served Al-Malik-al-Adil Abu Bakr Ibn Ayub as a physician in 1215, and accompanied him from Quds to the Egyptian lands. After the death of Al-Malik-al-Adil, he served his son, Al-Malik-al-Muazzam Isa Ibn Abi Bakr. After the latter's death, Al-Suri served his son, Al-Malik-al-Nasir Daud Ibn-al-Malik-al-Muazzam. He was made the chief physician. Al-Suri died in 1241 in Damascus.

Another illustrious scholar and a distinguished botanist was Abu Jafar Ahmad Ibn Muhammad Ibn Ahmad Ibn Sayyid-al-Ghafiqi (d. 1165). As compared with others, he had a greater knowledge of the properties, uses and names of the simple drugs. His book on this subject is a valuable source of information. The author described briefly what Dioscorides and Galen wrote on this subject. He also mentioned what the later writers contributed to this branch of science. Thus, his book consists of the accounts of simple drugs given by those who are learned in this field.

One of the most important Muslim botanists was Abu Muhammad Abd Allah Ibn Ahmad-al-Maliqi-al-Nabati, known as Ibn-al-Baitar. He was the greatest expert of his time in identifying the plants. He conducted research on the plants, and acquired a good knowledge of the names of the plants and their species and the places where they grew. He travelled in the Roman lands (Asia Minor) and some other territories and observed the plants in the places where they grew. There he also met some botanists, and learnt from them about many plants. He also met some well-known botanists in the Maghrib and other places.

Ibn-al-Baitar was in the service of Al-Malik-al-Kamil Muhammad Ibn Abi Bakr Ibn Ayub. He was considered to be an authority on simple drugs and shrubs, and was appointed in Egypt as the chief of physicians and apothecaries. He remained in his service until his death. Then he was honoured by his son Al-Malik-al-Salih Najm-al-Din Ayub. He died in Damascus in 1048. Ibn-al-Baitar is the author of many works on simple drugs and other subjects. One of them is the *Kitab-al-Jami' fil-Adwiyyah-al-Mufradah.* This book is chiefly based on the works of his Greek and Muslim predecessors, but also contains his personal observations made in different lands. The opinions of the later scholars about mineral, animal and plant drugs have also been quoted in the book. The author gave in alphabetical order the Persian, Latin and Berber names of the simple drugs and also cleared the confusions in the names. He also mentioned their properties and uses. This book is the best Arabic work on this subject. It was written for Al-Malik-al-Salih Najm-al-Din Ayub Ibn-al-Malik-al-Kamil. It was translated into French and German.

Another famous scholar and botanist of Spain was Abul-Abbas Ahmad Ibn Muhammad Ibn Mufarraj Ibn Abi-Khatib known as Ibn-al-Rumiyah. He was a native of Seville. In 1216, he went to Egypt. He lived for two years in Egypt, Syria and Iraq where the people learnt something from him. In these lands he observed many plants which were not found in his native land. He observed the plants in the places where they grew. When he reached Alexandria the Sultan-al-Malik-al Adil Abu Bakr Ibn Ayub heard about his scholarship and his deep knowledge of plants. The Sultan called him to his court and honoured him. He stayed with him for sometime, and then returned to Spain.

Ibn-al-Rumiyah was a well-known scholar, a researcher on medicine, the author of many works and fond of collecting books. One of his writings is a commentary on Dioscorides' book dealing with simple drugs. He also wrote a travelogue at the end of his travels in the Eastern lands. It is entitled *Al-Rihlat-al-Mashriqiyyah.* It is a collection of his discussions and observations made particularly on the coasts of the Mediterranean."

The last famous writer on agriculture in Spain was Abu Zakriya Yahya Ibn Muhammad Ibn Ahmad Ibn Awwam-al-Ashbili. His valuable book is entitled *Kitab-al-Falahah.* It is based on the works of his Greek, Roman, Nabatean and Muslim predecessors, but also includes the author's personal observations. It is divided into two parts which consist of 35 chapters. Every chapter deals with some definite topics concerning agriculture.

Important Book : Another important book on agriculture was written by Sheikh Radi-al-Din-al-Quraishi. It is entitled Jami' Faraid-al-Malahah fi Jawami' *Fawaid-al-Falahah.* It consists of the following eight chapters:

1. Various kinds of soil.
2. Watering, digging of canals and wells and taking out of water.
3. Trees and their plantation.
4. Various methods of plantation.
5. Seeds and grains, their selection, sowing and cutting.
6. Various types of flavours, flowers, etc.
7. Description of the days, months, weathers, etc., suitable for cultivation.
8. Storage of grains, seeds, dry and fresh fruits, some vegetables, extracts, salts, yeasts, rose water, etc.

The first geographer and traveller who mentioned plants in his books was Ibn-al-Wadih-al-Yaqubi (d. 1794). He travelled throughout the Muslim world and composed a work entitled *Kilab-al-Buldan.*

The famous geographer Abu Abdullah Muhammad Ibn Muhammad Ibn Abdullah Ibn Idris-al-Hussaini-al-Saqali, commonly known as-al-Sharif-al-Idrisi, also wrote three works on plants and simple drugs. One of them entitled *'Kitab-al-Jami' li-Sifat Ashtat-al-Nabat'* contains the description of various useful drugs relating to trees, fruits, roots, flowers, minerals, etc. The names of drugs have been arranged in alphabetical order, and their Arabic, Persian, Greek, Syriac, Latin and Berber names have been described. The author has mentioned the use of some plants and the oils and gums extracted from them. The book consists of four parts. The first part contains the description of 369 simple drugs and the second one of 250.

The greatest botanist of the 16th century was Daud Ibn Umar-al-Nasir-al-Antaki. He was a distinguished physician as well. No other scientist compiled such a valuable work on simple drugs as he did. He made a remarkable addition to the knowledge of his predecessors regarding the simple drugs and their uses.

An important botanist of the 18th century was Abd-al-Razzaq Ibn Muhammad Ibn Hamadush Al-Jazairi. In 1717-18, he left for Mecca for the performance of Hajj. He wrote a book called 'Kashif-al-Rumuz fi *Sharh-al-Aqaqir wal-Ashab*. This book seems to be a summary of the books written on this subject by Abd-al-Razzaq's predecessors with the addition of the new substances which were used by the Europeans as drugs. He also gave their common and local names. He derived information from the works of Ibn Sina, Ibn-al-Baitar and Daud-al-Antaki. One thousand simple drugs in all have been dealt with. This was translated into French.

Bibliography

Adams, C.C. : *Islam and Modernism in Egypt,* Oxford University Press, New York, 1953.

Ahmad, Bherhan : *The Mujaddid's Conception of Tauhid,* Feroz Pub., Lahore, 1940.

Ahmad, Imtiaz : *Divorce and Remarriage among Muslims in India,* Manohar Publishers, New Delhi, 2003.

Ahmad, K. N. : *Muslim Law of Divorce,* Kitab Bhavan, New Delhi, 1988.

Ahmad, Manzuruddin : *Islamic Political System,* Kitab Bhavan, New Delhi, 1991.

Ali, Chiragh : *The Proposed Political Legal and Social Reform under Muslim Rule,* Popular Prakashan, Bombay, 1883.

Badrul, S. : *Muslim Behaviour,* Kitab Bhavan, New Delhi, 1991.

Bahedur, Kalim : *The Jamaat-i-Islami of Pakistan,* Progressive Books, Lahore, 1978.

Baksh, S. K. : *Politics in Islam,* Kitab Bhavan, New Delhi, 2003.

Bawer, Raymond : *The New Man in Soviet Social Psychology,* Oxford, New York, 1990.

Berger, M. : *Islam in Egypt Today : Social and Political Aspects of Popular Religion,* MacMillan, London, 1970.

Bernier, Francois : *Travels in the Mogul Empire*, MacMillan, London, 1916.

Bukhsh, S. K. : *Contribution to the History of Islamic Civilization*, Kitab Bhavan, New Delhi, 2000.

Charles, Howard : *The Constitutionalism*, Great Seal Books, New York, 1947.

Chave, F. : *Islamic Histroriography*, Cambridge University press, New York, 1990.

Davids, Waines : *An Introduction to Islam*, Cambridge University Press, New Delhi, 1995.

Durrani, F.K.K. : *Muhammad (PBUH) the Prophet*, Oxford, New York, 2001.

Enayat, Hamid : *Islam in the Political Process*, Cambridge University Press, Cambridge, 1993.

Engineer, Asghar Ali : *A Rational Approach to Islam*, Gyan Books Pvt. Ltd., New Delhi, 2001.

————: *Islam : Challenge in Twenty-first Century*, Gyan Books Pvt. Ltd., New Delhi, 2004.

Guillaume, A. : *The Traditions of Islam*, Khayats, Beirut, 1966.

Hassan, Ali : *Observations on the Musulmauns of India*, Macmillan & Co., London, 1832.

Helmut, Reifeld : *Islam in South Asia : Adaptation, Accommodation and Conflict*, Social Science Press, New Delhi, 1999.

Houtsma, T. : *Encyclopaedia of Islam*, Macmillan, London, 1934.

Irfan, Habib : *The Agrarian System of Mughal India*, Popular Prakashan, Bombay, 1963.

Jafar, Sharif : *Islam in India*, Oxford, New Delhi, 1972.

James, Burges : *The Muhammadan Architecture of Ahmadabad*, Bernard Quaritch, London,1900.

Jha, V. : *Indian Society: Historical Probings*, Rawat Pub., Delhi, 1974.

Joseph, and Bosworth, C.E. : *The Legacy of Islam,* Oxford University Press, New York, 1979.

Karl, Jaspers : *Man in the Modern Age,* Routledge & Kegan Paul Ltd., London, 1997.

Katharine, Scarfe : *Perception of the Islamic Word,* Cambridge University Press, New Delhi, 1992.

Lewin, Roger : *In the Age of Mankind,* Simithsonian Books, Washington, D.C., 1956.

Lewis, Richards : *Universe,* Harmony Books, New York, 1973.

Martin, Lings : *A Sufi Saint of the Twentieth Century*, Century Pub., London, 1971.

Mirza, Waheed : *The Life and Works of Amir Khusrau,* Kaveri Pub., Calcutta, 1935.

Mortimer, Edward : *Faith and Power, the Politics of Islam,* Oxford, New York, 2002.

Muhammad, Iqbal : *Six Lectures on the Reconstruction of Religious Thought in Islam,* Royal Pub., Lahore, 1930.

Nabith, A. : *The Foundations of the Articles of Faith,* Feroz Pub., Lahore, 1963.

Nasr, Seyyed H. : *An Introduction to Islamic Cosmological Doctrines,* Cambridge, 1964.

Nicholson, R.A. : *Literary History of the Arabs,* Kitab Bhavan, New Delhi, 1994.

Nusservanji, D. : *Zoroastrian Civilization,* Oxford, New York, 1922.

Oage, Charles H. : *The Society,* Macmillan & Co., London, 1959.

Padwick, C.E. : *Muslim Devotions,* MacMillan & Co., London, 1960.

Phillips, O. Hood : *Reform of the Constitution,* MacMillan & Co., London, 1970.

Pierce, R.A.: *Russia in Central Asia, 1867-1917,* University of California, Berkeley, 1960.

Qadir, Abdul, : *Criminal Law of Islam,* Kitab Bhavan, New Delhi, 1999.

Qazi A. Qadir : *The Changing World of Islam,* Royal Pub., Lahore, 1992.

Rizvi, Hasan Askari : *Islami Reassertion : a Socio Political Study,* Progressive Publishers, Lahore, 1981.

Robert, D. : *Exploring our Living Planet,* National Geographic Society, Washington, 1989.

Saukat, S. : *Human Rights in Islam,* Kitab Bhavan, New Delhi, 2001.

Sharma, Arvind : *Women in World Religion,* New York Press, New York, 1990.

Syed, M. H. : *History of Muslims in India,* Anmol Publications, New Delhi, 2003.

———— : *Islamic Terrorism : Myth or Reality,* Gyan Books, New Delhi, 2002.

Tarn, W. W. : *The Greeks in Bactria and India,* Cambridge, London, 1938.

Thomas, Arnold : *The Legacy of Islam,* Oxford University Press, New York, 2000.

Thompson, H.R. : *Sculptures and Inscriptions of Darius the Great on the Rock of Behistan,* Oxford, London, 1907.

Tritton, A.S. : *The Caliphs and their Non-Muslim Subjects,* Oxford, New York, 1930.

Tutsch, Hans E. : *Facets of Arab Nationalism,* Wayne State University Press, Detroit, 1965.

Underhill, E. : *Mysticism : a Study in the Nature and Development of Man's Spiritual Consciousness,* Oxford, New York, 1956.

Usmani, J.M. : *The Authority of Sunnah,* Kitab Bhavan, New Delhi, 1998.

Von, Edmund : *Modern Islam,* University Press, Los Angeles, 1952.

Von, Grunebaum : *Unity and Variety in Muslim World,* Oxford, New York, 2003.

Waheed, Akhtar : *Sufi Approach to the Problem of Alienation,* Wilson & Co., New Delhi, 1975.

Weiner, Myron : *Sons of the Soil : Migration and Ethnic Conflict in India,* University Press, Prineton, 1978.

Williams, Michael : *Outlines of World Military History,* Oxford, New York, 1996.

Wilson, Lambron : *Traditional Modes of Contemplation and Action,* University Press, Tehran, 1977.

Wolfson, H.A. : *Glimpses of Medieval Indian Culture,* Popular Pub., Bombay, 1959.

Yahanan, Friedmann : *Tolerance and Coercion in Islam : Interfaith Relations in the Muslims Traditions,* Cambridge, New York, 1990.

Yazbeck, Haddad : *Islamic Values in the United States,* Oxford, New York, 1997.

Zaehner, R.C. : *Hindu and Muslim Mysticism,* Oxford, London, 1960.

Zahid, Malik : *Subjects of Quran,* Kitab Bhavan, New Delhi, 1998.

Zahurul, Hasan : *Tarikb-i-Sufiya-i-Gujarat,* Jamil Academy, Ahmadabad, 1981.

Zaki, Azam : *The Ideas of Arab Nationalism,* Cornell University Press, New York,1956.

Index

C

D

E

F

G

P

Q

❑❑❑